Praise for *Teach Students How*

"If you are already convinced—or are at least willing to consider the possibility—that your students could learn more deeply and achieve more success than they are at present, this book is for you. If you are frustrated by students who seem unmotivated and disengaged, this book is for you. If you find it challenging to teach underprepared students, this book is for you. And if you care about educational equity and fairness, this book is for you.

The not-so-familiar good news is that these unmotivated or underprepared students can both survive and thrive in higher education. The message from relevant research is quite clear: What students *do* in college matters more than who they are or which institution they attend. What these underprepared students need most to do is to *learn how to learn*.

In this book, Saundra McGuire provides specific, practical, research-based strategies to teach students how to learn, focusing on the three key Ms—mindset, motivation, and metacognition.

This book offers a broad range of strategies for teachers and for students along with a wealth of examples, illustrations, and resources." —***Thomas A. Angelo***, *Clinical Professor of Educational Innovation & Research, The Division of Practice Advancement and Clinical Education and Director of Educator Development, Eshelman School of Pharmacy ,University of North Carolina—Chapel Hill*

"This book is a wonderful resource for college faculty. It provides us with practical yet powerful learning strategies and metacognition techniques that can be easily incorporated into our courses and will improve student learning. McGuire shares both research and her personal experiences, as well as her expertise in teaching all kinds of diverse students with tremendous success. This book is a welcome addition for the postsecondary teaching and learning field and should be read and utilized by all." —***Kathleen F. Gabriel***, *Associate Professor, School of Education, California State University, Chico*

"I believe the study cycle handout was particularly useful because it provided a helpful step-by-step approach for students to learn the material in a class more effectively. Moreover, it is a good way to place the accountability for student success where it belongs—on the shoulders of the students (with professors providing guidance and support for their learning)." —*Larry Gragg, Curators' Teaching Professor and Chair, Department of History and Political Science, Missouri University of Science and Technology*

"An electrifying book! McGuire demonstrates how learning strategies can improve learning, and then charges faculty to teach them, complete with the slides for doing so in your class. . . A must-read—and must-do—for every teacher who struggles with students who don't learn as much as they could or should!"—*Tara Gray, PhD, Director, The Teaching Academy, New Mexico State University*

"Teachers need to learn as much as their students. In a masterly and spirited exposition spangled with wit and exhortation and rife with pragmatic strategies, Saundra McGuire teaches teachers how to awake in their students the powers dormant in them. Be aware, and you will learn!"—*Roald Hoffmann, 1981 Nobel Laureate in Chemistry*

"Based on solid scientific theory and real classroom case studies, Dr. McGuire's workshop on metacognition provides the participants with sound pedagogical advice and an impressive array of ready-to-use, results-oriented teaching techniques for a twenty-first-century classroom. With a metacognitive approach to teaching and learning, everything comes together."—*Irina Ivliyeva, Associate Professor of Russian, Missouri University of Science and Technology*

"McGuire's specific strategies are paradigms I can adapt for my literature courses. Many of the specific exercises McGuire uses to illustrate metacognition quickly convinced my students that cognitive functions such as pattern recognition effectively guide the close reading of a text while taking time to overview a text and place it in context helps more advanced students take on the challenges of literary theory. The strategies outlined here take away the mystery, not the magic, of writing about literature."—*Helen Whall, Professor of English and Director of Comprehensive Academic Advising, College of the Holy Cross*

TEACH STUDENTS HOW TO LEARN

TEACH STUDENTS HOW TO LEARN

Strategies You Can Incorporate Into Any Course to Improve Student Metacognition, Study Skills, and Motivation

Saundra Yancy McGuire with

Stephanie McGuire

Foreword by Thomas A. Angelo

Copublished in association with

NISOD

STERLING, VIRGINIA

Published by Stylus Publishing, LLC.
22883 Quicksilver Drive
Sterling, Virginia 20166-2102

Library of Congress Cataloging-in-Publication Data
Names: McGuire, Saundra Yancy, author. | McGuire, Stephanie,
author.
Title: Teach students how to learn : strategies you can incorporate
into any course to improve student metacognition, study skills, and
motivation / Saundra Yancy McGuire with Stephanie McGuire ;
foreword by Thomas A. Angelo.
Description: First edition.
Sterling, Virginia : Stylus Publishing, LLC, [2016] |
Includes bibliographical references and index.
Identifiers: LCCN 2015016254 |
ISBN 9781620363164 (pbk. : alk. paper) |
ISBN 9781620363157 (cloth : alk. paper) |
ISBN 9781620363171 (library networkable e-edition) |
ISBN 9781620363188 (consumer e-edition)
Subjects: LCSH: Effective teaching. | Learning--Study and teaching. |
Study skills--Study and teaching. | Motivation in education.
Classification: LCC LB1025.3 .M356 2016 | DDC 371.102--dc23
LC record available at http://lccn.loc.gov/2015016254

13-digit ISBN: 978-1-62036-315-7 (cloth)
13-digit ISBN: 978-1-62036-316-4 (paperback)
13-digit ISBN: 978-1-62036-317-1 (library networkable e-edition)
13-digit ISBN: 978-1-62036-318-8 (consumer e-edition)

Printed in the United States of America

All first editions printed on acid-free paper
that meets the American National Standards Institute
Z39-48 Standard.

Bulk Purchases

Quantity discounts are available for use in workshops and for
staff development.
Call 1-800-232-0223

First Edition, 2015

10   9

To my grandmother, Effie Jane Gordon Yancy,
whose commitment to academic excellence and higher education
continues to inspire the generations who followed her.

CONTENTS

FOREWORD

This foreword is for those who have not yet heard Dr. Saundra Yancy McGuire present on improving student learning. Those who already know Dr. McGuire and her work will need no convincing of the value and usefulness of this book. For nearly two decades, Dr. McGuire has been one of American higher education's most respected and sought-after speakers and consultants on improving student learning and success. The quality and influence of her work as a teacher, mentor, science educator, and academic leader have been recognized by numerous national organizations, as well as by the president of the United States.

If you are already convinced—or are at least willing to consider the possibility—that your students could learn more deeply and achieve more success than they are at present, this book is for you. If you are frustrated by students who seem unmotivated and disengaged, this book is for you. If you find it challenging to teach underprepared students, this book is for you. And if you care about educational equity and fairness, this book is for you.

In the United States, through the lottery of birth or zip code, far too many students are victims of low expectations and poor schooling. Many of these same students enter college without the mindset, motivation, and metacognitive skills needed to learn from, take advantage of, and succeed in higher education. That's the all-too-familiar bad news.

The not-so-familiar good news is that these same students can both survive and thrive in higher education. The message from relevant research is quite clear: What students *do* in college matters more than who they are or which institution they attend. What these underprepared students need most to do is to *learn how to learn*.

In this book, Dr. McGuire provides specific, practical, research-based strategies to teach students how to learn, focusing on the three key M's—mindset, motivation, and metacognition. This book offers a broad range of strategies for teachers and for students, along with a wealth of examples, illustrations, and resources.

For those who haven't yet met Dr. McGuire, I can attest that this book well reflects her core qualities. Her passion, commitment, and generosity of spirit are manifest throughout the book, as is her deep respect for research, evidence-based practice, and the intelligence of her colleagues and students.

This book, like its author, is down-to-earth and high-minded, inviting and rigorous, hardheaded and softhearted.

I have long been convinced that virtually all teachers could benefit from Dr. McGuire's experience, expertise, creative suggestions, and infectious optimism. Now, thanks to her book, we all have the opportunity to do so. I encourage you to take it.

Thomas A. Angelo, EdD
Clinical Professor of Educational Innovation & Research
The Division of Practice Advancement and Clinical Education and
Director of Educator Development, The Academy
UNC Eshelman School of Pharmacy
University of North Carolina–Chapel Hill

ACKNOWLEDGMENTS

Writing this book has been a labor of love, and I have many individuals and groups to thank for their contributions. First and foremost, I must thank Sarah Baird, the wonderful learning strategist who introduced me to the idea that we could teach students how to become better learners, and who showed me how to do it. Her workshops were paradigm-shifting experiences for me, as she demonstrated just how to teach students effective strategies, make them believe in their ability to excel, and motivate them to change their behavior. And I thank my colleagues at the Louisiana State University (LSU) Center for Academic Success (CAS), especially Melissa Brocato, Pam Ball, Diane Mohler, Nanette Cheatham, Susan Saale, Dr. Erin Wheeler, Christy O'Neal, and Naresh Sonti for actively participating in a collaborative effort to teach students effective learning strategies. Very special thanks go to Lisa Gullett, the CAS office manager who not only developed systems to help keep track of the thousands of students who used the Center, but also kept us sane when we were juggling too many projects at once. Thanks also go to Dean Carolyn Collins and Dr. Rhonda Atkinson for establishing the LSU learning center and developing it into the outstanding unit that it was when I came to LSU in 1999.

Since 1999 I have attended many workshops and faculty development sessions that have helped to develop and shape the ideas presented in this book. The organizations that I thank for providing particularly insightful sessions and access to immensely helpful mentors are the National College Learning Center Association (NCLCA), the College Reading & Learning Association (CRLA), the Professional and Organizational Development (POD) Network, and the Southern Association of Colleges and Schools Commission on Colleges (SACSCOC). Several individuals from those organizations have been invaluable mentors to me. Chief among them was the late and inestimable Dr. Frank L. Christ. Dr. Russ Hodges, Dr. Karen Agee, and Dr. Dee Fink have also given me indispensable guidance and support.

I sincerely thank the thousands of students who used the strategies and who dispelled my initial skepticism about their effectiveness. These students had enough faith in me and my colleagues to try the approaches we were suggesting, even though they may have had their doubts about whether those changes would make a difference. And I thank them for sharing the strategies with their friends when their grades began to soar.

When I was convinced that the strategies were effective with all students, regardless of discipline or level, I began encouraging other faculty members to teach them to their students. I am indebted to Dr. Muhammad Dawood of New Mexico State University who taught his students the strategies and saw great improvement in test performance. Additionally, I am equally grateful to Dr. Elzbieta (Elizabeth) Cook of LSU and Dr. Ningfeng (Peter) Zhao of East Tennessee State University who published the impact of teaching their first-year chemistry students learning strategies in peer-reviewed journals. I am also indebted to Dave Bock for offering insight about limitations of the study designs and helping with statistical analysis. I extend thanks to Dr. Eugene Kennedy of LSU for designing the statistical analyses of numerous data sets and to Dr. Tara Gray of New Mexico State University for reading parts of the manuscript and making valuable suggestions for improvements. Dr. Evanna Gleason should also be acknowledged for the invaluable feedback and guidance she gave regarding the neurobiology of stress, memory, and learning. Lorenzo Foster has my deep appreciation for presenting learning strategies to his Advanced Placement physics students and for sharing their exam scores with me.

Sincere thanks also go to my friend Dr. Roald Hoffmann for inviting me to coauthor articles about teaching learning strategies in *Science* and the *American Scientist*. These accounts allowed me to spread the word to a much wider audience. And I extend special thanks to my friend Dr. Isiah Warner and the staff of the LSU Office of Strategic Initiatives (OSI). They incorporated the strategies into programs offered to students in OSI programs and obtained funding to provide the information to more students.

I give very special thanks to two of my best friends and colleagues, Dr. Phyllis Worthy Dawkins and Dr. Vicki Vernon Lott. After they participated in one of my workshops they encouraged me to write a book about teaching students metacognitive learning strategies. Although I didn't take their suggestion seriously at the time, they kept encouraging me until I started to envision what this book might be.

When I made the definitive decision to write this book, I immediately knew that I wanted to work with John von Knorring and Stylus Publishing, LLC. John's reputation as an outstanding editor who provides insightful guidance to authors is well known in the academy. I thank him sincerely for guiding me to craft a book that perfectly communicates the message I want to convey. I also want to thank McKenzie Baker, associate production editor, and her production team who wonderfully fine-tuned the text. Designer Kathleen Dyson also deserves heartfelt acknowledgement for her gorgeous cover art.

Words cannot adequately express my gratitude to my friend Dr. Tom Angelo, who readily accepted my request to write the foreword. His unique perspective on the ideas in this book has been shaped by his decades of work with faculty interested in improving student learning.

I also want to acknowledge and thank my wonderful family. I was blessed to be born into a family of educators. My grandmother, Mrs. Effie Jane Gordon Yancy, my parents, Mr. and Mrs. Robert (Delsie) Yancy Jr., and most of my aunts and uncles were outstanding educators who inspired their students to excel. Special thanks also go to my brothers, Robert Yancy III and Dr. Eric A. Yancy, who have both served as sounding boards for many of the ideas presented here. I extend deep appreciation to my sister, Annette L. Yancy, an academic adviser at LSU who was recognized as the 2012 National Advisor of the Year by the National Academic Advising Association. She has taught the strategies to many of her students during advising sessions, demonstrating that staff as well as faculty can teach students how to learn.

I am most grateful for the unwavering support, encouragement, guidance, and inspiration that my husband, Dr. Stephen C. McGuire, the love of my life, has provided throughout the four decades of our marriage, and—more specifically—during the process of completing this book. When we met as college freshmen he was already using metacognitive learning strategies—even before the label was coined! And I offer sincere thanks to our daughters, Dr. Carla McGuire Davis and Dr. Stephanie McGuire, and to our grandchildren, Joshua, Ruth, Daniel, and Joseph Davis. All of them have been willing subjects as I used them to test the effectiveness of many of the strategies presented here.

There are no words to adequately express my gratitude for my coauthor and daughter, Dr. Stephanie McGuire. She provided valuable insights and suggestions about the content of the book, and she created most of the text for the book. I can unequivocally state that this book would not exist were it not for her collaboration on the project. She is thankful for the assistance of Dr. Joseph Maher, who contributed ideas about quantitative analysis, and Ms. Gabriella Callender, who provided indispensable support and encouragement throughout this project.

If we have left anyone out, please accept our apologies and know that we thank you, too. Producing this book has been a community effort, and we are truly grateful for the part that everyone played in its development.

INTRODUCTION

Comeback Kids

Miriam, a freshman calculus student at Louisiana State University (LSU), made 37.5% on her first exam but 83% and 93% on the next two exams. Robert, a first-year general chemistry student at LSU, made 42% on his first exam and followed that up with three 100%s in a row. Matt, a first-year general chemistry student at the University of Utah, scored 65% and 55% on his first two exams and 95% on his third exam. I could go on. I could tell you scores of stories like this from the last 15 years of my teaching career.

Something happened to all of these students between their last failing grade and their first good grade. They learned something new.

No Miracles, Just Strategies

Recently I was talking to a colleague who had heard about these remarkable transformations. She exclaimed, "You're a miracle worker! I want to be a miracle worker, too!" I quickly told her that there was really nothing magical about the surges in students' test scores after I worked with them; hundreds of faculty and learning center professionals are getting these same results on campuses around the country. But there are tens of thousands of faculty members, like my colleague, who don't know what we're telling students to bring about these seemingly miraculous results. **I wrote this book to let everyone in on one of the best kept secrets in education: If you teach students how to learn, and give them simple, straightforward strategies to use, they can significantly increase their learning and performance.** The good news is that you will not have to change your entire course or devote an inordinate amount of time to teaching these strategies. Often, teaching students *how* to learn can be accomplished in one session, in as little as 50 minutes. In that amount of time we can provide students with information that will fundamentally change their view of what learning entails. They can be transformed, in one session, from memorizers and regurgitators to students who begin to think critically and take responsibility for their own learning. **The information is not rocket science; anyone can teach students these techniques. This book will show you how.**

Late to the Party

It might surprise you to learn that I have only recently (within the last 15 years of my 43-year teaching career) begun to understand the power of the concepts and strategies in this book. For the first 30 years, I believed that it was not my responsibility to teach students what they should have already known when they got to college. I felt that I couldn't afford to take the time to teach that information.

Furthermore, when I first encountered some of these learning strategies, at LSU's Center for Academic Success (CAS), I was skeptical. The strategies seemed too straightforward and simple to make a difference, and I didn't think students would use them. But after I began to see students who had been making Ds and Fs turn into straight-A students, I became convinced that these simple tools work miracles.

Now that I know how little time it takes to deliver this information and the power it has to transform students, I know that I can't afford *not* to take the time to teach it.

Sharing the Good News

For a decade now, I've been traveling the country talking about metacognition and learning with faculty who are frustrated that their students are not performing according to expectations. In my travels, whenever I share these tools and strategies in a presentation, faculty and administrators often ask me, "So, where's the book?" Well, here it is. Here are all the ideas that I've been developing, collecting, and sharing since I began this work. Recently, faculty around the country at other universities have begun using this approach and facilitating the same kind of dramatic successes with their students. **The verdict is in: It's not difficult to teach college students how to learn.**

Who Should Read This Book?

Because much of the book is about presenting effective learning and study strategies, you may, at times, find yourself wondering if the book is written for faculty and teaching assistants or for tutors and learning center professionals. The answer is that I've written this book for anyone who teaches. In order for faculty to teach students how to learn, they must know some of the same strategies that are used by learning support staff. The primary audience for this book is faculty—faculty who are concerned not just about presenting discipline-specific content but also about whether students are meaningfully learning concepts instead of rotely memorizing content.

In an effort to make the material easily accessible to faculty with no background in education or cognitive psychology, I have taken care not to use jargon or introduce esoteric concepts that require a degree in these areas to understand.

Just for STEM Educators? Not a Chance

Because I have spent my life teaching chemistry, most of the examples in this book come from the science, technology, engineering, and mathematics (STEM) disciplines. In fact, you may have noticed that all three "comeback kids" mentioned at the beginning of this introduction are math and science students. But rest assured that the strategies work just as well for students taking philosophy courses as they do for students taking engineering courses. I've heard tremendous feedback from science and humanities professors across the country that these strategies work for all students stretched beyond their academic comfort zone, whether by Maxwell's equations or James Joyce's *Ulysses*.

Moreover, I often present workshops to pre-college teachers who later tell me that the strategies worked wonders with their students. There are many "comeback kids" who were failing elementary, middle school, or high school courses but turned their performance around when they started implementing active and effective learning strategies.

One of the most dramatic examples I've seen involved an Advanced Placement physics class in rural south Louisiana. On the first exam, the class averaged 66.9%, and more than half the class scored below 70%. In response, their instructor spent a class session presenting effective learning strategies. The result was nothing short of phenomenal. On the second exam, the class average was 89.2%, and only 2 of the 25 students scored below 70%. Things got even better on the third exam—only 1 student scored below 70% and 16 of the 25 students made a perfect 100%. The class average was an astonishing 95.6%. Appendix I has more information about these students' incredible results, including exam scores.

In sum, the learning strategies and the psychological insights about learning presented in this book will be useful for teachers of students of all ages, including parents of young children.

What's in the Book?

Figure I.1 displays the content of each chapter, shown sequentially as you read it clockwise from 12:00.

Figure I.1 Chapter Content

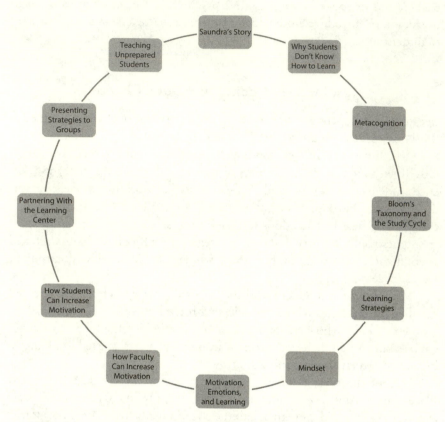

The chapters are organized so as to take you along the path I took when I learned how to teach this information to students. I first had to understand why students didn't know how to learn when they entered college (chapter 2). Some of the reasons may surprise you as much as they surprised me. In chapter 3 we'll see that teaching students about metacognition and learning strategies provides a new lens through which they can view learning activities, and we'll see how teaching Bloom's Taxonomy in conjunction with a specific study system can immediately empower students to maximize their learning (chapter 4). After that we will take a closer look at the transformative power of 10 specific metacognitive strategies, including 4 superstrategies for reading assignments and homework problems (chapter 5).

Over the years, I have been surprised to learn just how important it is for students to believe that they can improve their learning. All the learning strategies in the world cannot help students who are convinced that their situation is hopeless. Chapters 6 through 9 address these issues of attitude and motivation. In chapter 6 I discuss cognitive psychologist Carol Dweck's work on students' frame of mind, which she calls mindset. (Dweck has demonstrated that students who believe they can get smarter are more likely to make efforts to improve compared to students who believe their intelligence is innate or fixed.) I also look at four strategies to help students change their mindset. In chapter 7 I discuss the importance of a student's mindset and how to more fully appreciate the role of emotions and motivation in learning. In chapter 8 I present 21 strategies faculty can use to increase students' motivation, whereas in chapter 9 I deliver 6 strategies students can use to give a boost to their own motivation and learning.

In chapter 10 I discuss what faculty can do to partner with their campus learning center. Most institutions have a learning center with a cadre of professionals who work with students to teach not only learning strategies but also time management, test taking, stress management, and other skills that improve learning. We will see how faculty can ensure that they and their students are taking advantage of all of the support offered on campus.

Chapter 11 should be one of the most practically useful chapters in the book. In it, I take you step-by-step through the process of delivering much of the information in the rest of the book to groups of students (e.g., your classes) in as little as 50 minutes. In chapter 11 I also present research that investigates the impact of teaching learning strategies to groups. Supplements to chapter 11 include three online slide sets, a sample video lecture, and a handout summarizing the entire process (Appendix D).

Then we turn our attention toward students who arrive on campus particularly unprepared for what awaits them. Although the recommendations for unprepared students apply to all students, the six strategies presented in chapter 12 are especially helpful, and crucial, for this population of students. Because recent SAT and ACT reports indicate that less than 50% of all students entering college are academically prepared for college-level work, I trust you will find these strategies useful.

In the epilogue, I encourage you to joyfully and freely explore with your students what you've learned from the book. There is no right or wrong way to teach students how to learn, and I encourage you to pick and choose whichever strategies you feel most comfortable trying out. Even though there are more than 30 suggestions in the book (Appendix C), if you want to try only a few of them, that's awesome! I just hope you have as much fun teaching your students how to learn as I have had teaching mine.

Begin at the End . . . If You Must

I may be biased, but I believe that the very best way to encounter and digest the information in this book is to read it from beginning to end. However, if you are pressed for time, you can begin at the epilogue and use it as a departure point to explore the rest of the book. There is a suggested starter kit in the epilogue for anyone who might feel slightly overwhelmed after reading about all they can do to improve their students' learning. Alternatively, you can examine the chapter content in Figure I.1 and choose where to begin.

My Promise to You

By the time you finish this book you will

- understand why many students do not know how to learn (chapter 2);
- understand how metacognition and motivation increase students' success (chapters 3, 6, 7);
- have concrete, effective learning strategies to share with your students (chapter 5);
- have slide sets, exercises, assessments, inventories, and study tools to share with your students (chapter 11, appendices);
- have strategies for changing students' mindset and motivation (chapters 6, 8, 9);
- know how to partner with your campus learning center (chapter 10);
- know how to work with unprepared students (chapter 12);
- know where to begin (epilogue); and
- have everything you need to see positive changes in your students' performance!

Let's begin!

1

SAUNDRA'S JOURNEY

From Traditional Instructor to Academic Transformer

In 1970, I was a teaching assistant in introductory chemistry during my first year as a graduate student at Cornell University. All teaching assistants were required to attend lecture because we needed to know how the professors presented the course material. That way, we could be consistent when we held our recitation sections. The lectures I attended were brilliant marvels of efficient information delivery, but, sitting in the lecture hall, I distinctly remember thinking, "If I didn't already know this information, there's no way I would understand it from what I'm hearing and seeing here." There was so much background material in between the lines that students needed to know in order to understand the lectures, but no one was there to fill in those gaps.

At that time, in 1970, Cornell and other Ivy League institutions were trying to increase diversity on their campuses, so a fairly large number of African American students were enrolled in introductory chemistry. Many of these students had come from inner-city New York high schools. Although I knew that these students were as capable as any others at Cornell, I also knew that they were probably not prepared to do well in introductory chemistry without additional assistance. So I began to hold weekly review sessions at Cornell's Africana Studies and Research Center. Although the sessions were open to anyone enrolled in the course, most of the students who came were African American. We formed a community of scholars dedicated to making sure that everyone learned chemistry. In those sessions, I translated what they were hearing in lecture into language I knew they would understand. In addition to discussing the course material, we also talked about background information they needed to know, problem-solving approaches, and strategies for earning top grades in Cornell chemistry courses. In other words, we filled in the gaps. Many of those students who attended the review sessions I held that year and in later years went on to do very well at Cornell and beyond. Several of them are now doctors, engineers, pharmacists, or professors at prestigious institutions of higher learning. The high point of that academic year came when I received the department of chemistry's Outstanding Graduate Teaching Assistant Award.

I loved teaching and seeing the students excel, and I decided that I would pursue a teaching career rather than a career as a research chemist. So after my first semester, I decided to obtain a master's degree in science education. As fate would have it, when I changed career paths, my adviser turned out to be renowned science educator and concept-mapping guru Joseph Novak. Dr. Novak's seminal book, *Learning How to Learn* (Novak & Gowin, 1984), has a title similar to this book's. In 1970, though, I admit I found the idea of *teaching* anyone how to learn a bit nonsensical. How could you teach someone how to learn? If you tried to teach someone how to learn, and they didn't already know, then of course they wouldn't be able to learn, because they didn't know how in the first place! But now I understand that teaching students how to learn entails opening their eyes to the learning *process* and introducing them to myriad strategies they can use to increase their learning.

After I finished my master's degree in 1971, I left Cornell to join my husband, Stephen (Steve) C. McGuire, who was enrolled in the graduate program in physics at the University of Rochester, New York. While in Rochester I taught chemistry at the Educational Opportunities Center, operated by SUNY Brockport. I returned to Cornell in 1974 when Steve decided to pursue his PhD there, and I was hired as a lecturer with a joint appointment in the chemistry department and the recently established Learning Skills Center (LSC). So I was again teaching weekly review sessions and holding office hours, this time in Baker Laboratory, the chemistry building at Cornell.

In 1978, Steve completed his PhD in nuclear science at Cornell and accepted a position at the Oak Ridge National Laboratory in Oak Ridge, Tennessee. Our family, which now included our two daughters Carla and Stephanie, moved to Knoxville, where I became a visiting chemistry instructor at the University of Tennessee. I taught recitations and laboratory sessions, and I also tutored students who were not in my sections but who wanted additional help. My students liked me and did well under my tutelage. I remember one particular young lady who had a D average before she came to see me. Shortly after I started working with her, she started making As and experienced a rapid rise in confidence. In her case, she was conscientious and hardworking but didn't understand key concepts. After I explained to her what she was missing, she improved quickly and dramatically. But, as educators, you and I know that it doesn't always happen like that. Although I didn't realize it until I got to LSU over 20 years later, great explanations are only one arm of effective teaching. The other arm involves teaching students how to learn material on their own, without help. Now, I love to empower students to become their *own* tutors.

One year after I arrived in Knoxville, I began my PhD in chemical education. As part of my courseload, I took Dr. Luther Kindall's educational psychology course, which introduced me to some newly developed principles of learning in the field of cognitive psychology. The course opened my eyes to a whole new collection of ideas, but I wasn't yet ready to actively incorporate them into my teaching.

In 1983, I finished my PhD in chemical education shortly after I published my first study guide to accompany an introductory chemistry textbook written by two faculty members at Cornell. My career then took me to the department of chemistry at Alabama Agricultural and Mechanical University (Alabama A&M) in Huntsville, where I spent five years teaching general, organic, and biochemistry. I returned to Cornell in 1988 when Steve joined the faculty there. I was enthusiastically welcomed back to the LSC, this time as a lecturer in chemistry and an assistant director.

During my second stint at the LSC, a wonderful learning strategies instructor, Dr. Helene Selco, held the position of associate director of the LSC. Helene taught all of the learning strategies courses, under the umbrella title "Critical Reading and Thinking," and she presented study skills workshops with the team of talented graduate students she trained. I never knew what she was doing in those workshops, but I always sent students to her if they seemed to be having trouble learning. If after working with an "explainer" like me, and after investing significant chunks of time studying, students still could not manage to produce the results they wanted, I sent them to Helene. All I knew was that after she met with them and told them something, they came out looking happy. I didn't think I needed to know *what* she told them because I was teaching chemistry. Why would I need to know about study skills and learning strategies? In fact, when I had first heard that the LSC taught study skills, I thought to myself, "Study skills?! This is Cornell University! These kids should've learned that stuff in high school." I have since seen the error of my ways and have called Helene many times to apologize for my lack of respect and closed-mindedness. After about the eighth time I called, she said, "I *forgive* you, Saundra. Don't call me again to apologize. You've called enough times. It's okay! Let it go!"

After 11 years at Cornell, in 1999, Steve and I decided to escape the cold Ithaca winters and return to our home state of Louisiana. I left Cornell professionally satisfied; I had been promoted to senior lecturer and director of the LSC several years before, and in 1991, I had received the Clark Distinguished Teaching Award, based on the recommendation of my students and colleagues in the department of chemistry and at the LSC.

In Louisiana, Steve returned to our undergraduate alma mater, Southern University and A&M College, where he was appointed chair of the physics department. I was hired to direct the highly regarded learning center at LSU, then named the Learning Assistance Center. (I quickly renamed it the Center for Academic Success, to make it seem less like a place for remediation—which it wasn't—and to attract more students to our doors.) Even though I did not know much about learning strategies or study skills, my new directorship did not intimidate me because I knew that I would be working with another learning strategies expert like Helene Selco. Her name was Sarah Baird, and her reputation preceded her. I had heard from several people that she was "really good at this stuff," even though I had no idea what "this stuff" was. I expected to continue teaching chemistry and to send students who needed help with learning or study skills to Sarah. But two weeks before my first day on the job in August 1999, I discovered that Sarah was on maternity leave, and she was not planning to return until the following January. Additionally, I found out that *I* was expected to speak knowledgeably about learning skills and to conduct workshops and hold individual consultations with students—just like Helene did at Cornell. Still, I wasn't too alarmed because two other people had been recently hired to assist students who needed help, so I figured I could learn the strategies from them. But when the first one came to me and said she wanted to sit in on a session with me and learn my techniques, and the other confessed she had no idea what to say to a student with test anxiety, I panicked! I knew we were in big trouble.

I immediately called Sarah, who had a newborn at home. I told her that we had no clue how to teach students learning strategies and that I had heard that she was very good at it. I asked her if she would be willing to give the center four hours of her time every week, just 10% time, so that she could help us understand how to do "this stuff." She graciously agreed. The first thing I asked her to do was to give a mock individual consultation with one of her former students that we could all observe. During that session, when I saw Sarah work with the student, the flashbulbs went off. My life changed. I realized that there was a whole body of information that, if I learned it, would empower me to help my students far beyond what I could do merely by presenting step-by-step procedures for drawing Lewis structures or deriving reaction mechanisms.

Shortly after observing Sarah and her student, I started reading everything about learning strategies I could get my hands on, and I encountered the concept of *metacognition*, or thinking about thinking. When I first read the word "metacognition" in the literature, I faintly recognized it. I remembered being in our photocopy room at Cornell at the same time that a lot of Helene Selco's students had gathered around the copier. They had been talking excitedly about metacognition. I didn't know what it meant, didn't think I needed to know what it meant, and that was that. My experiences at LSU completely turned me around. I came to value metacognition as a way of helping students understand what their role in the learning process is, and now I travel the country preaching the gospel of metacognition. I find that faculty are particularly receptive to the message.

From Skeptic to Convert

When I first started sharing learning strategies and study skills with students, particularly students having trouble with subjects other than chemistry, I didn't think it would work. I thought the ideas were too straightforward, and I didn't think the students were going to follow my suggestions. Then students began to report remarkable results. "Thanks, Dr. McGuire! That stuff was so helpful. Now I'm making an A in thermodynamics, and I was flunking it before." Students on the verge of failing returned triumphant with Bs and As. I was flabbergasted. I wasn't quite sure what I'd said that had made such a dramatic difference. I hadn't explained any difficult content or translated confusing lecture jargon into more easily digestible language. So I asked each student, "Now tell me, what *exactly* did I say to you that made the difference?" I became very curious about precisely what worked for each student. Their answers formed the basis of the toolbox that I'm sharing with you in this book. As you build your own toolbox, please always ask students exactly what helped them. If your students are anything like mine, you might be surprised.

I hope it is clear at this point that, although I had always had a great degree of teaching success, my effectiveness with students skyrocketed after I started incorporating principles of metacognition into my teaching at LSU.

Physician, Heal Thyself

Let me say a little bit about why I have so much compassion for my students. Confession time: Throughout my undergraduate career, I never, ever studied until the night before an exam, yet I graduated *magna cum laude*, with a 3.5 GPA. I love to tell the following story, which illustrates my cluelessness in full Technicolor. One day, during my senior year at Southern University in Baton Rouge, I was walking down the hall with one of my favorite chemistry professors, Jack Jefferson. Dr. Jefferson asked me a question about a basic chemical reaction, and I breezily replied that I had no idea how to answer his question, feeling absolutely no shame about my ignorance. At that time, I had no learning goals. My shiny GPA was all I thought I needed.

Another story: After graduation, I headed to Cornell to pursue my graduate degree in chemistry, and I knew that when I arrived, I would have to take placement exams in general, organic, analytical, and physical chemistry. So I arrived in Ithaca a week early and set myself on a crash memorization course. I passed all my exams and was given a full load of graduate courses. I don't know why it didn't occur to me that if I passed the placement exams, the subsequent courses I took would require mastery of all the content I'd just tried to force-feed my brain! I continued my practice of cramming the night before an exam, and began to make B minuses in my courses, unheard of for an A student like me. I decided to visit one of my professors, Mel Goldstein, to discuss my grades. Dr. Goldstein gave weekly homework assignments but made them optional. Of course, I never tried to do them until the night before the test. But at that point, I had nowhere near enough time to figure out the problems, so I would give up and go back to rote memorization. During our chat in his office, Dr. Goldstein told me that he was surprised I was maintaining a B minus average without doing any of the homework. Then he asked me why I never did it. The question caught me by surprise, so I lied and said that I did the homework but didn't turn it in because it was optional. (I'm pretty sure he knew I wasn't telling the truth.) It had never occurred to me that doing nonrequired homework would help me learn the material and improve my performance on tests! Instead of seeing the relationship between effort and performance, I began to think, "If I can't make As in these courses by doing what I've always done to make As, chemistry must not be what I was meant to do."

Although I was at Cornell on a full Danforth Foundation fellowship, I was still required to teach because Cornell views teaching as crucial to its graduate students' intellectual and professional development. That requirement turned out to be my saving grace. I was given one section of introductory chemistry as a teaching assistant, and I instantly fell in love with teaching. I had never taught before, but very quickly I saw that I was effective. My success with students was addictive because I loved seeing that "aha!" moment on their faces. They would come to me in a fog of confusion, convinced that chemistry would be impossible to learn. But when I helped them understand the logic of the discipline, introduced them to a systematic way to approach the material, and expressed confidence in their intellectual abilities, they suddenly began to understand and instantly became motivated to spend time mastering the material themselves. I found, and still find, student transformation intoxicating. And I am convinced that every educator and learner can personally experience it.

In sum, because I found teaching so exciting, I decided to pursue a master's degree in chemical education and have never looked back. I'm happy to report that, thanks to the learning strategies I acquired along the way, I never earned a grade lower than A in any of my chemistry or education courses for the rest of my graduate career. And today, I know exactly what I would say to myself in 1970 to earn all As in my Cornell graduate chemistry courses!

The State of Learning in Our Nation

Even though learning centers like the LSC at Cornell and the CAS at LSU have existed for decades, I have observed in my 43 years of teaching that the learning strategies taught there still have not reached the mainstream. There are techniques and strategies that have been used successfully for at least half a century, but my experience tells me that many educators and students still do not know about them.

Since 2001, I have traveled the country, speaking to faculty, students, and administrators about how to use learning strategies to radically transform student success. Typically, at the beginning of my presentation, I ask faculty to raise their hands if they are very familiar with the learning center on their campus. Ninety-five times out of 100, I see only a smattering of hands. *There is a disconnect between faculty and learning strategies that is harming our students.*

It may be unsurprising that there is at present a chasm between most faculty and their campus learning centers given that learning centers and the learning strategies literature are only about 50 years old, according to a chronology published on the resources portal Learning Support Centers in Higher Education (LSCHE) (2014). LSCHE is the leading website for information about learning strategies and learning centers, founded by the late Dr. Frank L. Christ, venerated learning expert and founder of the modern learning center movement. The chronology tells us the following story:

Although the first known publication of a how-to-study manual appeared in 1640 for a student at St. John's College at the University of Cambridge, research did not begin to be published in specialized journals until the late 1950s and 1960s. In fact, the first time the phrase "learning center" appeared in print was in 1963. Not until 1975 did a major book on learning centers appear, and 1976 saw the publication of the first doctoral dissertation on the subject (LSCHE, 2014). Since then the field has grown and moved into the online environment, but dissemination of our message has not yet reached a tipping point.

Good News

The good news is that anyone can undergo the same transformation that I did. I freely admit that I was clueless. If I changed, you can too. You can learn the strategies that will help bright but unprepared students. The more we can spread awareness of these strategies, the happier and more successful our students and our faculty will be. There are no drawbacks to shouting this message from all of our respective mountaintops.

WHY DON'T OUR STUDENTS ALREADY KNOW HOW TO LEARN?

"What did most of your teachers in high school do the class period before the test?"
"They gave us a review."
"What did they do during the review?"
"They told us what questions were going to be on the test and gave us the answers."

This chapter investigates why so many students on our college campuses do not know how to learn. I begin by presenting a case for why we should be at least as focused on student learning as we are on our teaching. Then, we look at some statistics suggesting that students find out in high school that they can make top grades without expending much effort. Next, we look at what actually happens in high school to enable students' lackadaisical habits. Finally, we consider implications for how instructors should regard students, given that they arrive in our classrooms and lecture halls without the skills they need to succeed, and how we can address their needs.

Why Focus on Learning Instead of Teaching?

Before we examine why many students do not already know how to learn, let's take a moment to discuss why this book focuses on facilitating student learning rather than on strengthening teaching skills. Faculty development workshops typically deliver wonderful teaching strategies, and there are a number of outstanding books that address this topic. But by focusing almost exclusively on teaching and ignoring how we can help students figure out *their* role in the learning process, we are leaving out half the equation.

I used to think that if faculty teaching improved, student learning had to follow suit. But now it seems to me that even if we are the best teachers on the planet, as long as students do not come to our classrooms prepared to learn efficiently and independently, we will never see the kinds of learning gains that are possible. Conversely, if students are actively engaged in the learning process, they will be able to learn even in circumstances where the teaching is mediocre. Thus, I have come to believe that student learning should be our top priority.

So, Why Don't They Know How to Learn?

Why must our job include teaching students how to learn? Consider some interesting statistics. The Higher Education Research Institute (HERI) published a study in 2013 that revealed that 58.6% of incoming freshmen at a broad range of institutions reported spending *fewer than six hours per week* doing homework in 12th grade (Eagan, Lozano, Hurtado, & Case, 2013, p. 35), but 96.8% of survey participants said that they graduated from high school with an A or B average (Eagan et al., p. 19). These statistics demonstrate that for many students, doing the concentrated, joyful work of real learning has not been a prerequisite for good grades.

Presumably because of their grades, these students are also extremely confident; 72.1% of them believe their academic ability is above average or in the highest 10% among people their age (Eagan et al., 2013, p. 39). So, our students are not only accustomed to successfully breezing through school, but also have no idea that horizons of learning and success exist beyond those they have already encountered.

Note that the numbers in 2013 are no anomaly. Similar statistics were reported by HERI in previous years. Whether your students who do not know how to learn are in high school, college, or graduate or professional school, the same situation probably applies to them. Whatever their previous level of schooling, it did not require them to learn (Figure 2.1).[1]

Figure 2.1 Why Students Do Not Know How to Learn

- They did not *need* to learn in order to make As and Bs in high school.
- They believe they are in at least the top half of students their age, unaware that they can become smarter.

Note. Data from the Higher Education Research Institute (HERI) support the idea that students do not know how to learn because they are overconfident and academically successful without much effort (Eagan, Lozano, Hurtado, & Case, 2013).

Why Don't Many Students Need to Study in High School?

Whenever I speak to undergraduate student groups, I ask them, "What did most of your teachers in high school do the day before they gave a test?" The students usually respond, "Review." When I ask what their teachers did during the review, very often the students reply that their teachers *gave them the answers to the test questions.*

Early in my career as a speaker, I was shocked to hear these answers, and as I shared them with my faculty workshop participants, I was even more stunned that 10%–20% of those participants were not at all surprised. When I asked the faculty, "How did you know?" they responded, "I have kids in high school," or "I used to teach high school." Back then, I wondered why teachers would take such ineffective measures, but I came to see that these teachers genuinely think that they are preparing their students. They believe that if they take the time to present accurate information, the students will learn and recall it whenever necessary—for example, on the high-stakes tests given to elementary, middle, and high school students in many states.

Because teachers know their jobs are on the line if their students do not perform well on these high-stakes tests, they are subtly and perniciously motivated to use their classroom tests as an opportunity to try to fill their students' minds with accurate information. If these teachers knew more about how learning really works, they might make a different choice. But often, teaching standards and prescribed teaching methods do not allow them the creativity and flexibility to engage their students in meaningful learning and critical thinking activities. These concerns are particularly acute for teachers with large groups of at-risk students.

Here's a story that illustrates another reason many high school students do not learn how to learn. One of my freshman general chemistry students, concerned about her poor performance on the first exam, blamed her high school chemistry class. She believed she was unprepared for college chemistry because her high school teacher had been one of the school's sports coaches, and, according to her, he liked to tell stories during class rather than teach. It has become common to assign coaches to science classes in schools where there is a shortage of trained science teachers because coaches' training and education require more science courses—kinesiology, for example—than do the training and education of other teachers in the same school. I have great respect for the generous people who spend their time and energy teaching subjects they have not been explicitly trained to teach, and many of them do a commendable job, but we can all agree it is not the ideal state of affairs. This particular student told her teacher that she experienced crippling science test anxiety, so he informed her that she could bake a batch of cookies for the class on each test day, in lieu of taking the test. I asked this student about her final course grade, expecting her to say that she made a B or C. To my surprise she responded, "Oh, I made an A."

Even though this story is not typical, I hear stories like it often enough to know that it is also no outlier.

Okay, So High School Was Easy. Why Don't Students Heed Our Warnings About What Will Be Required of Them in College?

One struggling math major from rural Louisiana on a full scholarship at LSU explained, "People told me that college was going to require a lot more of my time and effort, but I didn't believe them because I had heard it before. They said that high school was going to be a lot more difficult than middle school, but it wasn't. And when I went to middle school, they had told me it was going to be much harder than elementary school. But I didn't find that at all." So this young man, along with the other 72.1% who judge themselves to be above average compared to their peers (Eagan et al., 2013, p. 39), very reasonably did not imagine that the typical warnings about a college work-load applied to him.

We often tell students that they need to change their habits and do some-thing different now that they're going to college, but imagine if someone said to you, "When you go to another planet next month, you've got to breathe differently." That would mean about as much to you as our warnings mean to students. Thankfully, we have a way to help our students understand how to breathe differently—how to engage in deep, satisfying learning.

Changing the Way We View Our Students: Good Scientists, Not Slackers

I used to think that if students frequently missed class, and, when they did come, put their heads down and looked bored and disinterested, they were not really interested in learning. At that time in my life, I also thought that there were some students who were very smart, smart enough to do engineer-ing or premed or philosophy, and then there were some students who just weren't that smart. I thought of them as "slow" learners. After these "slow" students flunked an organic chemistry test, I just *knew* that they had been put on the planet to do something other than be a doctor, chemical engineer, or molecular biology professor. I glibly wrote those students off and concen-trated on the students who seemed to be interested in learning.

Of course, now I no longer believe that disengaged students are lost causes. Over time, I began to realize that many of those students who looked bored in class or failed my tests did not suffer from a lack of motivation or smarts. On the contrary, they were just being good scientists! Scientists collect data, interpret those data, and make predictions based on them. These students were doing the same thing. They had made As in high school by following a particular course of action. So they logically chose that same course of action in college. The data they had collected in high school indicated that they didn't really need to go to class or study.

What Works?

Once I realized that these students couldn't have known that they needed to work hard in order to earn good grades, I started treating them differently. I stopped writing off students who seemed "lazy" and "unmotivated." Instead, I started talking with them about the learning process and the strategies they could use to improve their learning. My students started using those strategies and began to see immediate—and in some cases remarkable—results.

Another story: At Cornell, before my conversion to believing in the potential of every student, I ran a bridge program for at-risk incoming freshmen, called the Prefreshman Summer Program (PSP). Many of these students had gone to inner-city high schools in New York, and we spent six weeks preparing them for the rigors of life at Cornell. As chemistry department faculty, I was also part of a team that taught a general chemistry course that enrolled 1,100 students every year. At the end of each year, a single student out of 1,100 received the A. W. Laubengayer Prize, a reward for earning the top scores in the course. One year, the recipient of the Laubengayer Prize was one of my students from the PSP. In chatting with him after the awards ceremony, I said, "I know you took Dr. Selco's study skills course last summer in the PSP. Did you find it helpful?" I fully expected him to say, "It was okay, but I kind of knew all that stuff anyway." Instead, he said, "I think it's the single most important course I will take during my entire four years at Cornell." Now that got my attention. It was my first glimpse of the power of teaching students how to learn.

We Can Empower Our Students

We can help students identify and close the gap between their current behavior and the effective, productive behavior that will result in the grades they want.

We can turn our students into deep, expert learners. Let's find out how.

Note

1. Whenever I speak to groups of students at graduate, medical, dental, pharmacy, law, and business schools, I ask them whether they primarily engaged in rote learning or deep conceptual understanding as undergraduates (see pp. 36–38 in chapter 4). The vast majority respond that rote learning sufficed to earn grades good enough for acceptance into graduate or professional schools. We can infer that those grades were mostly As and Bs.

3

METACOGNITION

What It Is and How It Helps Students Become Independent Learners

"I have tried the suggestions you gave . . . and it was like magic, seriously."
—Matt J., junior in the microbiology department at Weber State University, personal communication, September 15, 2014

In this chapter, we investigate the overarching principle that enables students to stop failing their classes and start acing them: metacognition. We also get our first taste of how learning strategies can dramatically improve performance.

First, we learn what metacognition is and how it helped two students increase their exam scores by at least 30 points. Second, I ask you to do a brief exercise that demonstrates the huge difference that learning strategies can make. Third, we discuss why those strategies make such an impact and enable students to take charge of their own learning.

Throughout this book, I purposely blur the distinctions among metacognition, learning strategies, and study skills because I am most interested in students' successful application of those tools working in concert. Moreover, there is precedent for blurring those lines (Peirce, 2003). Our compass during this journey points only to student success. It is our true north.

A Tale of Two Students

Figure 3.1 shows the dramatic improvement of two students after learning about metacognition and implementing metacognitive strategies. Some

Figure 3.1 A Tale of Two Students

> Exam scores showing rapid and dramatic progress of two
> LSU students after they learned metacognitive strategies
>
> **Travis**, third-year psychology student
> 47, 52, **82, 86**
>
> **Dana**, first-year physics student
> 80, 54, **91, 97, 90** (final exam)

Note. Figure shows the exam scores of two of my students at LSU before (plain text) and after (boldface text) being exposed to metacognitive strategies. Travis received a B in introductory psychology, and Dana received an A in general physics.

faculty in my workshops have believed that these students are fictional, but I assure you they are as real as you and I. Have I got your attention?

Before we learn more about Travis and Dana, let's investigate what metacognition means.

What Is Metacognition?

Metacognition, a term coined by John H. Flavell (1976), is *thinking about your own thinking.*[1] I always say to students, "It's like you have a big brain outside of your brain looking at what your brain is doing." Aspects of Flavell's definition of *metacognition* appear in Figure 3.2.

When students employ metacognition, they become consciously aware of themselves as problem solvers, which enables them to actively seek solutions to any problems they may encounter, rather than relying on others to tell them what to do or to answer their questions. As they make the transition from being passive learners to proactive learners, students gain the ability to monitor, plan, and control their mental processing. In other words, instead of staggering through a maze, using instinct alone to look for cheese, they become aware that they need to plot a course and search systematically for cheese, keeping track of what works and what doesn't. Metacognition also gives students the ability to accurately judge how deeply they have learned something, whether they have only a superficial understanding or the ability to widely apply their knowledge. For example, they might begin to ask themselves, "Am I understanding this material, or just memorizing it?" When students use metacognition, they become tremendously empowered as learners because they begin to be able to teach themselves.

Figure 3.2 Metacognition

> The ability to
>
> - think about one's own thinking;
> - be consciously aware of oneself as a problem solver;
> - monitor, plan, and control one's mental processing; and
> - accurately judge one's level of learning.

Note. Figure shows four aspects of John Flavell's (1976) definition of *metacognition*.

Metacognition, Schmetacognition. Students Just Need to Work Harder

How do we know our students need metacognition, that they aren't already aware of themselves as problem solvers and are simply not working hard enough? I wonder whether the following scenario is as familiar to you as it is to me: A student excitedly turns in an exam, essay, or research paper, beaming with pride, telling you they just *know* they've done well. Then when you sit down to grade their work, you begin to mark most of the problems wrong or cover the essay with red ink. And you wonder: *How on earth could they have thought they did well?* Similarly, when I ask faculty during workshops what grade their students believe they're on their way to making at the beginning of their courses, I hear a chorus of "A!"

And when are our students typically divested of their fanciful notions? Usually, a splash of cold water comes after their first test. Some students start to understand they are in trouble *while* they're taking the exam, whereas others think that everything is hunky-dory until they get the exam back with D or F at the top.

When their work is returned to them with a much lower grade than expected, most students cannot process the cognitive dissonance. If our courses are telling these students that they're not the smart, competent individuals they believed themselves to be, what do they do? Their normal psychological self-defense mechanisms activate. They begin withdrawing psychologically; they might sit further back in the classroom or lecture hall; worse, they might start missing class. Then their performance on the next test is worse than their performance on the first. The downward spiral continues until they've flunked the course or barely passed it.

Clearly, students like these are not able to accurately judge their own learning. And the discouragement of thwarted expectations *prevents* them from working harder. Moreover, even if they are able to rally and work harder, doing more of what they already know how to do is not likely to help. They need to learn a different way. When students learn about metacognition and implement metacognitive strategies, their performance turns around. Let's see how well metacognition worked for Travis and Dana.

Travis, Psychology Student

Travis was a junior I started working with only the night before his third introductory psychology exam. He had made scores of 47 and 52 on the first two exams, and we spoke for about 30 minutes via telephone because Travis's schedule didn't allow time for us to meet in person. Travis called me after his test was returned to say he had made an 82! I was quite surprised because I had thought he would score in the low to mid-70s. I kept my surprise to myself and said, "That's fantastic, Travis! Okay, if you make higher than a"—racking my brain for a stretch score that would probably be just out of reach for him—"than an 85 on the next test, I will take you to lunch." Mind you, at that point in my journey with metacognition, I did not expect Travis to score higher than 85. In fact, I thought that his 82 was a fluke and that statistical regression would kick in for the next exam. These days, I know that when students use metacognition, the sky is the limit. Wouldn't you know, Travis called me back about three weeks later and said, "Dr. McGuire, I made an 86 on that test!" This alleged 86 was self-reported, so I said, "Let me look at my calendar, and I'll get back to you with a lunch date." I immediately called the professor, and she confirmed Travis's excellent performance. I started looking forward to lunch because I wanted to find out exactly how Travis had done so well. During our meal, I asked Travis, "What are you doing to earn these fabulous grades?" And he replied, "I'm just doing that stuff you told me to do." We'll see in chapter 5 exactly which metacognitive strategies made the difference for Travis.

Dana, Physics Student

Dana was a freshman physics major who had come to LSU supported by a prestigious American Physical Society scholarship, but we met for the first time at a Change Your Major workshop. Dana was trying to get out of physics. Even though she'd wanted to be a medical physicist since the beginning of her junior year in high school, she had become demoralized after making an 80 and a 54 on her first two general physics exams. In high school, she had been a straight-A student, so when she saw 54 at the top of an exam paper, she thought, "Okay, I'm outta here."

At the Change Your Major workshop, Dana introduced herself. "Hi, my name is Dana. I was a physics major, but I'm having trouble, so I need to find something else." The counselor replied, "Oh, yeah, I understand. Physics is haaaard. We will find you something you can do."

I raised an eyebrow and chuckled to myself.

As Dana was leaving, I called her aside and asked, "Dana, do you have an hour to meet with me in my office?" She readily agreed, and I said to her, "Dana, I'm not going to try to talk you out of leaving physics, because if you really want to do something else, that's fine with me, but I want you to know that if you leave physics, it's not because you *can't* do physics. It's because you've *chosen* to do something else."

So Dana came to my office, and we talked for about an hour. She made a 91 on the next test, a 97 on the one after, and a 90 on the final exam. She received an A in her general physics course and a 4.0 that semester. Even though her next semester involved illness and two hospital stays, Dana still earned a 3.2 GPA. She graduated in 2012 with a 3.8 GPA and major in physics, and in the summer of 2014 she graduated with a master's degree in medical physics from the world-renowned University of Texas M. D. Anderson Cancer Center. Metacognition can give students back their hopes and dreams. We'll discover in chapter 5 which metacognitive strategies Dana used to make her grades soar.

Getting Students' Buy-In

If students are to become active partners in the learning process, often we must first convince them, after they've experienced abject failure, that all is not lost. I often share with new students the dramatic successes of previous students like Travis and Dana so that they can see what is possible. I say to them, "I don't care if you made a 2% on the first test. I know that you have the ability to make a 100% on the next test because your score on the first test is not any indication of how smart you are. It's a reflection of your behaviors, the way you prepared for the first test. And I can teach you a way to prepare that's going to help you ace the next test." You can have the same conversation with your students. We *can* teach our students how to succeed.

I strongly urge you to keep records of your students' "before" and "after" scores so that you have a portfolio of miracles to share with new students. I find that giving students this kind of concrete hope makes them receptive to learning about metacognitive strategies. In fact, I once began a presentation without any anecdotes about student success, and I had a surreal experience. Instead of rapt students on the edges of their seats, I faced listlessness and dismissive blank faces—not an experience I care to repeat.

I often tell students that I have lots of examples of students who turned their grades around and that I use those examples in presentations to other faculty. One student, after seeing my miracle portfolio, exclaimed, "I'm going to be in your next presentation!" I replied, "Okay, *when* you make an A, send me the score, and I will put you on a slide!" True to his word, he scored a 95 on his thermodynamics final exam, after having scored 67, 54, and 68 on the three previous exams. So I added his scores to a slide in my next presentation. Even if you don't give presentations, you can tell your students that you will use their success stories to inspire other students. That may motivate them to aspire to join the portfolio.

An Exercise for You: Count the Vowels

Now you're going to do an exercise I often do in my student and faculty workshops. Even if you've seen it before, take a moment to refamiliarize yourself with it. You'll need a few things to do this exercise:

- Timer or stopwatch (most smartphones have them, but a watch with a second hand will also work)
- A piece of paper to cover the opposing page once you turn over page 21 and start the exercise
- A pen or pencil

Once you've collected these supplies, set your timer for 45 seconds. When you press start, you're going to do three things: (a) turn page 21 over, (b) cover the opposing page with a piece of paper, and (c) count all of the vowels in the text of Figure 3.3 on page 22 until time runs out. Ready, set, go!

Turn the page for Figure 3.3.

Figure 3.3 Count the Vowels

Dollar bill	Cat lives
Dice	Bowling pins
Tricycle	Football team
Four-leaf clover	Dozen eggs
Hand	Unlucky Friday
Six-pack	Valentine's Day
Seven-Up	Quarter hour
Octopus	

After time is up, or whenever you've finished counting the vowels, immediately cover up the text and reveal the opposing page for your next instructions.

How did it go? Now close your eyes and try to recall all of the words and phrases that you just saw. List as many as you can in the blanks.

_____   _____

_____   _____

_____   _____

_____   _____

_____   _____

_____   _____

_____   _____

Now look at the original list, and write down the number of items you were able to accurately remember here: _____. Divide that number by 15, multiply by 100, and that's your score as a percentage. How did you do? C? D? F?

Typically, when I do this in workshops, the average number of correct responses is 3, or 20%, so most faculty workshop groups start out with a spectacularly failing grade. Let's call it F minus.

Now look at the list in Figure 3.3 again, reading each column from top to bottom, and see if you can figure out the underlying organizing principle. Take no more than 10–15 seconds to see if you can work it out. If after 10–15 seconds you are still unsure, turn this page, and read the top two lines on page 24.

Set your timer again for 45 seconds, and this time, study the list and try to commit all 15 phrases to memory. When time is up, turn the page and list as many items as you can remember.

The list is organized according to number. Dollar bill corresponds to the number 1, dice corresponds to 2, tricycle corresponds to 3, and so forth.

_____   _____

_____   _____

_____   _____

_____   _____

_____   _____

_____   _____

_____   _____

Again, look at the original list, and write down the number of items you were able to accurately remember here: _____. Divide that number by 15, multiply by 100, and that's your new score as a percentage. How did you do this time? A? B? C?

Typically, in workshops, the average number of correct responses for this part of the exercise is 12, or 80%, so most faculty groups improve dramatically, from F minus to B. Just as we can go from an average of 20% to an average of 80%, so can our students. In fact, when I do this exercise in student workshops, student participants typically make the same type of dramatic increase that faculty participants do. If you try this exercise with your students, which I recommend, you will likely see the same, or better, results.

Count the Vowels: What Made the Difference? Part One

Obviously, between our first and second attempts to recall the list, we had not become any smarter. So what made the difference? Two things. Before you read further, try to figure out the two differences that made better performance possible.

First, we were aware of our goal. We knew that we needed to memorize the list instead of count the vowels. How does that pertain to our work with students? Faculty will often give assignments such as, "Read chapter 1." Many students unknowingly interpret that assignment as, "My eyes should fall over every other word in chapter 1 while I'm texting and engaging in social media and talking to friends."

When I was in college and my professors gave me problem sets, I genuinely believed that my objective was to turn in correct solutions for all of the problems. Not until I began teaching did I realize that my college professors were actually more interested in how I solved the problems than in my final answers. They wanted me to understand the *concepts* relevant to each problem and to be able to apply those concepts to new contexts. Just as I totally missed that important point, our students are also missing it.

A brief, related word about practice tests: When professors give practice tests, students often think their goal should be to answer those specific questions. So they spend time memorizing specific information or problem-solving procedures required only for questions on the practice test. Well-intentioned faculty members often give the practice tests without the answers, explaining to students that they should come talk to the professor if they have questions. To their credit, these faculty are sincerely trying to prevent students from sidestepping meaningful learning. Unfortunately, though, the students usually just take the practice tests to the campus learning center or tutorial center and ask the professionals there to tell them the answers or show them exactly how to do the problems.

The take-home message here is that students are very creative in their innocent and often unknowing attempts to avoid learning, so we must be very specific about what we want students to do. We must give them precise goals for the tasks that we assign. This teaching strategy is discussed further in chapters 5 and 8.

What was the second difference between our two attempts to remember the phrases in the Count the Vowels exercise? We had a very good system for learning the information. Notice the two aspects of that statement: we have not only a system—a way to recognize how the information was organized—but also a *very good* system. What made it very good? We related the information to something very familiar to us—in this case, numbers.

Familiarity Breeds Active Learning

It is a basic learning principle that whenever the brain is trying to absorb something new, it tries to relate new information to something it already

knows (Gregory & Parry, 2006). If we do not take the time to discover what our students already know and help them relate what they are learning to their prior knowledge, then they cannot learn in the most efficient ways.

At Cornell, I was what you might call a "Heinz 57 Varieties" chemistry instructor. I could explain any concept 57 different ways; I was very patient, always saying to my students, "Let me know if you don't understand this explanation, and I will say it a different way." I was convinced that I could figure out some way to explain it that would ensure student understanding.

I now know it is absolutely not about what we say to our students; it's about what they hear. But we don't know what they are hearing unless they're doing the talking. We don't have to make connections for them; in fact it is much better if we don't. We can just throw a concept out there, like a ball, and ask, "What does this remind you of that you've encountered in your everyday life?" When students hit the ball back, they come up with the most wonderful examples and ideas that give them not only an efficient path to learning and mastery, but also *the most efficient path for them*.

When students hit the ball back, they are engaging in active learning. Learning experts and researchers have discovered in the past 30–40 years that active learning is much more lasting than passive learning (Bransford, Brown, & Cocking, 2000; Zull, 2002). I had heard the terms *active learning* and *passive learning* at Cornell, but I figured it was education jargon. I did not understand the implications for my teaching. Now I know that active learning involves encouraging students to take on a teaching role themselves so that teachers and students become equal partners in the learning process.

I remember one very conscientious chemistry student who was having a lot of trouble. Jonathan came to me on the verge of failing general chemistry. He was studying states of matter (solid, liquid, gas), and he explained that he was having trouble distinguishing liquids from gases. I was very surprised that something so basic could stymie a student who had managed to get into college. But instead of launching into one of my 57 explanations, I asked Jonathan why he was having trouble. He asked, "Aren't *all* gases liquid?" Again, I refrained from firing off an explanation about interparticle distances and instead asked him to explain his assertion. He replied that every type of gas that he'd ever pumped into his car was liquid! Makes sense, right?

This very capable student was unable to process any information presented to him about gases until this very basic misconception was cleared up. From then on, it was smooth sailing, and Jonathan saw his grades rise.

It took me a while to realize the importance of listening to students and engaging them as partners because I didn't trust the process. It takes some faith to throw the ball, not knowing whether students will hit it back. But they do. Every time. And the more they hit the ball back, instead of just

catching whatever we throw at them, the faster they advance in the game of learning.

Count the Vowels: What Made the Difference? Part Two

Another way to articulate what made the difference between our first and second attempt to count the vowels is that we had metacognitive learning strategies the second time around. Of course, for the purpose of the exercise, I intentionally misled you at first and then revealed your true task. But students can use metacognition to reveal to *themselves* the true purpose of their academic assignments and discover the learning objectives their homework has been designed to facilitate. Using metacognition to investigate why homework has been assigned is a learning strategy. Similarly, identifying ways to organize new information by relating that new information to old ideas constitutes a learning strategy. My definition of a *learning strategy* is anything that helps the learner engage with, process, remember, or apply information. Experience has taught me that when students use strategies, they excel. Strategies made the difference for us in Count the Vowels, and they can make a huge difference for our students.

Whiners to Winners

When students learn about metacognition, gain learning strategies, and become active learners, it empowers them tremendously because they begin to understand that thinking and learning are processes that *they* can control.

My colleagues (Zhao, Wardeska, McGuire, & Cook, 2014) asked a group of students who had not learned about metacognition to give reasons for their lackluster performance on their first exam in a chemistry course. Take a look at their answers:

> I studied but blanked out during [the] exam. I thought I knew it but I didn't. It made perfect sense on [the] board [during lecturing], but not when I did it [in the exam]. I couldn't figure out why I didn't know it. (p. 51)

> There were not examples of problems like the ones on the test. I have never seen these problems before. [There were] a few problems [that] we never introduced in class. (p. 51)

> You [the instructor] went through materials fast in lecture, and people answered [questions] quickly [so] I didn't follow. (p. 51)

Their performance is the professor's fault, their classmates' fault, or their brain's fault.

Now take a look at some student observations about performance in the course after learning about metacognition and metacognitive learning strategies. Again, these responses are taken from Zhao et al. (2014).

> I have continued to look at the effective learning strategies you introduced to the class last week. I have been going to group tutoring sessions (offered from the learning center on campus) and they helped tremendously. (p. 53)

> I have taken a new approach to studying by using some of your suggestions and it does seem to be helping. By previewing the chapter before lecture and studying the notes online, I better understand the material as you go over it. (p. 53)

> Thank you for setting aside our class time for this, because I feel that it was really informative and helpful. I identified a few problems with my own study methods, and have since made some changes as you suggested. (p. 53)

The language in these responses focuses on actions the students themselves are taking to improve their performance. Learning about metacognition has helped them to stop seeing themselves as victims and to take responsibility.

Bloom's Taxonomy as an Introduction to Metacognition

So how do we teach students about metacognition? I have found that introducing Bloom's Taxonomy is an extremely efficient and effective way to help students take metacognitive control of their own learning. Chapter 4 presents a particular method for introducing Bloom's Taxonomy that I have been developing and refining since 2001. I hope you will try it with your students.

Note

1. "'Metacognition' refers to one's knowledge concerning one's own cognitive processes and products or anything related to them, e.g., the learning-relevant properties of information or data" (Flavell, 1976, p. 232).

4

THE POWER OF TEACHING BLOOM'S TAXONOMY AND THE STUDY CYCLE TO STUDENTS

"I have increased my bio exam grade from a 76% to a 91.5% using your system. Ever since I started using the study cycle, my grades have significantly improved. I have honestly gained a sense of hope and confidence."
—Josiah F., first year premed student at Xavier University of New Orleans, personal communication to Algernon Kelley, October 17, 2011

In this chapter, we explore the power of teaching Bloom's Taxonomy to students. I begin by explaining why it's so crucial to teach Bloom's. Then we will walk through a four-step formula for introducing Bloom's to students, a method I have found very effective. After a thorough discussion of how to teach Bloom's with maximum impact, we will explore how to help students reach the taxonomy's higher levels by teaching them about the study cycle and intense study sessions.

Instructors can introduce Bloom's Taxonomy, the study cycle, and learning strategies (chapter 5) in one 50-minute learning strategies session given just after the first exam of the semester is returned (see chapter 11). Although the session could just as easily be given at the beginning of a course, I have found that delivering this information to students has much more impact once students plainly see from the results of their first test or quiz that their own study strategies are not working.

Without further ado, let's begin.

Bloom's Taxonomy—Not Just for Teachers

Whenever I give a faculty workshop, I ask the participants, "How many of you are familiar with Bloom's Taxonomy?" and a sea of hands appear. Then I ask, "How many of you *teach* Bloom's Taxonomy to students?" and the sea becomes a desert.

I get it. When I learned Bloom's as a graduate student in chemical education, I thought of it as a framework primarily for instructors, useful for deciding where to pitch our teaching and how to design our assessments. Before I got to LSU, I never taught Bloom's to my students. But when I arrived at the Center for Academic Success, the learning strategies experts there were teaching Bloom's to students with great success. I have found that it very effectively enables students to understand what faculty mean by "higher-order thinking skills." Teaching Bloom's is the first step in helping students acknowledge, "Ah. There is a transition I have to make."

When students understand the different levels in Bloom's, they can immediately see the difference between the kind of work required of them in high school and the work they need to do in college. I've seen knowledge of Bloom's transform many, many failing students into successful ones.

Teaching Bloom's Taxonomy: A Four-Step Winning Formula

When I teach Bloom's Taxonomy to students, either in an individual consultation or to a group, I follow a four-step procedure that I have been developing and refining since 2001 (Figure 4.1). I find that this process leads students through several epiphanies, which leave them optimally motivated to use the strategies (see chapter 5) when they leave my presence. Just as the

Figure 4.1 Teaching Bloom's Taxonomy: A Four-Step Process

1. **Ask: What's the difference between studying and learning?**

2. **Ask: Would you study harder to make an A on a test or teach the material to the class?**

3. **Present: Bloom's Taxonomy**
   Explain each level of the hierarchy and then apply Bloom's to an example like Goldilocks and the Three Bears.

4. **Ask: At what level of Bloom's have you been operating? At what level do you need to be operating now?**

success stories of other students (see chapter 3) prepare them for this four-step process, so this process prepares them to receive the strategies.

Steps one and two involve reflection questions. First I ask, "What is the difference between studying and learning?" after which I ask, "For which task would you work harder: to make an A on a test or to teach the material to the class?" Step three is a presentation and explanation of Bloom's, and step four asks students to assess where they currently are in the hierarchy and where they need to be.

Studying Versus Learning

I begin the process outlined in Figure 4.1 by asking students to articulate the difference between studying and learning. Here are some answers I've heard over the years:

- Studying is memorizing information for the exam; learning is when I understand it and can apply it.

- Studying is short-term; learning is long-term.

- Studying is like being force-fed a plate of gruel; learning is like being set in front of a gourmet table where you get to choose the delicacies you want to eat.

- Studying is what I do the night before the test to make an A; learning is what I do if I know I'm going to have to use that material later on. (My dear colleague from LSU, Pam Ball, often jokes to students, "That way of studying is like renting the information for the test and falling behind on your payments. Right after the test, the information is repossessed!" [Ball, personal communication, October 23, 2001])

A first-year dental school student described the difference this way: "Studying is focusing on the 'whats,' but learning is focusing on the 'hows,' 'whys,' and 'what ifs.'" I am particularly fond of this last response. The student who gave it went on to elaborate, "I find that when I focus on the 'whats,' if I forget them I can't recreate the information. But when I focus on the 'hows,' 'whys,' and 'what ifs,' even if I forget the 'whats,' I can recreate them."

I often hear from high school students that "Studying is when I go over what I've already learned." The first time I encountered this idea, I couldn't make sense of it. So I asked, "When did you learn what you are going to study?" The students responded, "In class." It took a few seconds, but then the lightbulb went on. I realized for the first time that some students believe they are actually *learning* information in class and only need to "go over it" in order to do well on exams. Suddenly I understood why so many students wait until the night or two before the test to begin studying. They genuinely believe they have already learned the material in class! Steps three and four will lead those students to a more accurate understanding of the learning process.

After hearing students articulate the difference between studying and learning, I ask them, "Up to this point, have you been operating more in *study* mode or in *learn* mode?" The practically unanimous response is "study mode." In fact, before I pose the question, most don't realize there is another mode available to them. I explain to them that they are not alone, that most students begin in "study mode," and that I'm going to show them how to switch to "learn mode" and stay there.

I love asking students to articulate the difference between studying and learning and sharing others' answers with them. Those differences demonstrate to them that they have personally experienced different levels of learning, which paves the way for them to intuitively accept Bloom's.

Learning It Well Enough to Teach It

After asking students to explain the difference between studying and learning, I ask them, "For which of the following tasks would you work harder: to make an A on a test or to teach the material to the class?" You can guess their answer. When I ask them why they would work harder to teach the material, they say:

> Well, I have to really know it if I have to teach it!

> If I'm going to teach it, I have to think of questions I might be asked and make sure I can answer them. I don't want to look stupid in front of the class.

> I want to make sure everybody understands and is prepared for the test, so I need to figure out how to explain the information in more than one way.

When I am in front of a group of students, rather than in an individual consultation, I ask the question like this: "What if I told you that three weeks from now, we will have finished chapters 4 through 6, and there will be an exam. You're faced with one of two tasks, and I want to know which one would make you expend more effort. Task one is: you need to make an A on that exam. Task two is: the day before the exam, we're going to have a review of all that material, and you're going to teach that review session for chapters 4, 5, and 6 to the entire class. Again, the question is: for which one of those tasks would you work harder?" I give the students several seconds to think about it and ask for a show of hands for who would work harder to make an A and who would work harder to teach the material. The vast majority indicate they would make more effort to teach the material (see also chapter 11).

Whether with individuals or groups, I then ask, "Until now, have you been in *make-an-A* mode or in *teach-the-material* mode?" Virtually everyone admits to being in the first mode. Then I explain that they don't need to be an instructor or have their own class to be in "teach-the-material" mode. I tell them, in a joking way, that if they have empty chairs in their room, or stuffed animals, or imaginary friends, that's all they need. Additionally, they can work with friends or teach the material to family members.

Then we discuss why explaining the information to someone else (real or imagined) works so well. I begin by asking students whether they've ever found themselves explaining something they thought they totally understood only to discover, in the midst of the explanation, that they were still confused about some part of it. Most of the heads in the room nod in recognition. Then I ask them to tell me, if they hadn't been explaining the information to someone, when they would have realized they didn't completely understand the material. They respond, in unison, "On the test!" Immediately they see that they need to get out of "make-an-A" mode and into "teach-the-material" mode. In fact, this difference forms the basis of one of the most important learning strategies presented in chapter 5.

Students also report that preparing to teach the material works so well as a learning strategy because they anticipate the questions they might be asked. In other words, students aiming to teach the material automatically consider a topic from multiple perspectives because they are actively searching for any confusion that might arise for their "students" instead of reacting only to the biggest, most urgent gaps in their own understanding.

When I first started giving faculty workshops, I asked participants, "When did you begin to have a very deep and broad understanding of your field of expertise?" Far and away the most common answer was, "When I started to teach it." The second most common answer was "Graduate school." Why graduate school? Because that's when those men and women began to teach. They had personally experienced what the students realized after our discussion: When we must teach a body of material, we attempt to master it so that we can answer questions beyond the material we present. Teaching requires a high level of mastery, so if students aim for that level, they can't go wrong.

After steps one and two, students are ready to undertake step three, an examination of Bloom's Taxonomy.

Bloom's Taxonomy, Up Close and Personal

Although it is an oversimplification,[1] I explain Bloom's Taxonomy[2] as simply a hierarchy of learning levels. Figure 4.2 shows two versions of Bloom's: the original version (Bloom, Englehart, Furst, Hill, & Krathwohl, 1956) and an updated version created by one of the original authors, David Krathwohl, and one of Bloom's students, Lorin Anderson (Anderson et al., 2001).

The original hierarchy of levels (Figure 4.2, left image) ascends from rote memorization (Knowledge) to Comprehension, Application, Analysis, Synthesis, and finally to Evaluation. In the revised hierarchy (Figure 4.2, right image), the names of the levels have been changed to appear more active and process-oriented. Moreover, the top two levels have been reversed. The new taxonomy proceeds from remembering to understanding, applying, analyzing, evaluating, and ultimately creating.

I find it makes absolutely no difference which form of Bloom's we teach to students as long as we convey that there are differences between memorizing information, understanding something well enough to put it in our own words, and applying it so that we can answer questions we've never seen before. Bloom's is helpful for students at any level. In fact, after learning about Bloom's, most of my students say, "I wish I had known about Bloom's in high school."

Figure 4.2 Two Versions of Bloom's Taxonomy: Original and Revised

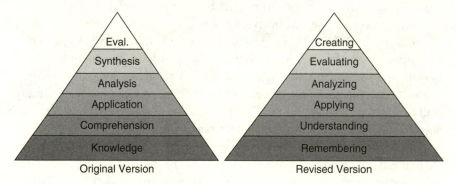

Note. Figure shows two versions of Bloom's Taxonomy: the original version published by Benjamin Bloom and colleagues (Bloom, Englehart, Furst, Hill, & Krathwohl, 1956) and the revised version by a team of his graduate students and their colleagues (Anderson et al., 2001). Adapted with permission from "Bloom's Taxonomy," by R. Overbaugh and L. Schultz, n.d., and retrieved from ww2.odu.edu/educ/roverbau/Bloom/blooms_taxonomy.htm

Bloom's in Layman's Terms

When I am working with individuals or groups of students, I try to explain Bloom's in language they will find accessible. For example, using the new hierarchy, I often explain the six levels as follows: "If you're at Remembering, then you have memorized verbatim definitions or formulas, and you could not put that information in your own words. If you're at Understanding, then you can paraphrase the material. You could explain it to your 8-year-old nephew or your 80-year-old grandmother by creating analogies and examples that apply to their lives. If you're at Applying, then you could use the information you've learned to solve problems you've never seen before. If you're at Analyzing, you can take any concept you've learned and break it down into its component concepts. So if I asked you to give me a mini-lecture on empirical formulas, you could talk to me about the historical origins of empirical formulas, how to calculate them from percent composition data or CO_2 data, and how they differ from molecular formulas. If you're at Evaluating, you can look at two different processes—proposed by others—and determine which is likelier to be correct, efficient, or desirable. If you're at Creating, you could come up with your own ideas about solving different kinds of problems or designing different processes to accomplish the same goal." Of course you do not have to follow this script, but it is available for you if you find it helpful.

Figure 4.3 shows the revised taxonomy with definitions for each level.

Figure 4.3 Bloom's Taxonomy

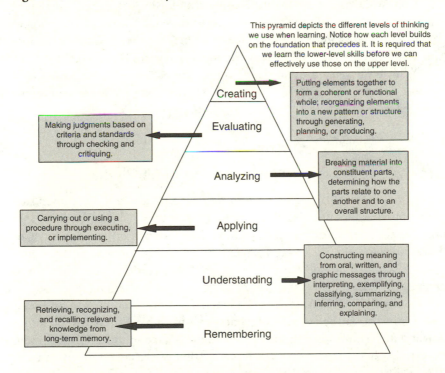

Note. This version of the revised Bloom's Taxonomy features definitions for each level. Adapted with permission from "Image of Revised Versions of Bloom's Taxonomy Featuring Definitions," by R. Overbaugh, n.d.

More Bloom's: Goldilocks and the Three Bears

Some students benefit from hearing Bloom's applied to a familiar childhood story. Using the revised hierarchy's levels, we can say that students have mastered Remembering when they can recall all of the things that Goldilocks used at the bears' home. If they can give the reason that Goldilocks preferred Baby Bear's chair, bed, or porridge, then they have mastered Understanding. Next, if they can reasonably predict what items Goldilocks would use when visiting another home, then they have reached the level of Applying. Students have mastered Analyzing if they can think critically about the context of the story and call into question particular assumptions; for example, is it plausible that bears could eat porridge out of bowls? If students can generate reasons that Goldilocks's behavior might be considered justifiable by some and unconscionable by others, then they have mastered Evaluating. Finally, students have demonstrated that they have scaled the entire hierarchy and mastered Creating if they can write their own story starring a character named Goldilocks but featuring very different themes and values—perhaps "Goldilocks and the Three Professors."

I tell students about Goldilocks only about 10% of the time, because I find that after steps one and two, students understand the simplest version of Bloom's on sight. However, many faculty report that they frequently use Figure 4.4 to explain Bloom's, particularly to entire classes (see also chapter 11).

Whichever version or versions you decide to use, when students have a solid understanding of Bloom's, it opens the door for them to become engaged, active learners.

"Aha!" Moments, Brought to You by Bloom's

After I've presented Bloom's and completed step three, we embark upon step four, applying Bloom's to students' personal academic habits. I begin by asking, "At what level do you think you had to operate in order to make As or Bs in high school?" Most say Remembering or Understanding. You might guess my follow-up question: "At what level do you think you will need to operate in order to make As in your college courses?" After taking a thoughtful moment, most say Analyzing or higher. The light goes on, and from that point forward, the darkness of vagueness and haphazard study habits cannot put it out. Just introducing students to Bloom's Taxonomy and urging them to express their learning goals in terms of Bloom's levels positively impacts their study habits and academic performance.

Figure 4.4 Bloom's Taxonomy and Goldilocks

Example
~ Bloom's Levels of Learning ~

Applied to Goldilocks and the Three Bears

Creating	Write a story about Goldilocks and the Three Fish. How would it differ from Goldilocks and the Three Bears?
Evaluating	Judge whether Goldilocks was good or bad. Defend your opinion.
Analyzing	Compare this story to reality. What events could not really happen?
Applying	Demonstrate what Goldilocks would use if she came to your house.
Understanding	Explain why Goldilocks liked Baby Bear's chair the best.
Remembering	List the items used by Goldilocks while she was in the Bears' house.

Note. Figure applies Bloom's Taxonomy to "Goldilocks and the Three Bears" in a way that may be helpful for students. Adapted from Practicing College Learning Strategies by C. Hopper, 2013.

Figure 4.5 depicts this phenomenon with two bar charts. In 2013, I taught learning strategies to a group of 250 general chemistry students, and after explaining Bloom's, I asked them the two questions in the previous paragraph. Figure 4.5 shows the distribution of their answers. You can see that these two simple questions open students' eyes to what will be required of them.

The Value of Bloom's

The day I present Bloom's Taxonomy to students is often the first day of the rest of their lives. They begin to have learning goals instead of GPA goals.

If you follow my four-step routine (Figure 4.1) with your students—(a) discuss studying versus learning, (b) distinguish "make-an-A" mode from "teach-the-material" mode, (c) introduce Bloom's Taxonomy, and (d) ask them to contrast the level of Bloom's they have occupied in the past with the level they need for future success—you will be repeatedly driving home the point that learning goals are far superior to performance goals (Grant &

Figure 4.5 Bloom's Taxonomy in High School and College

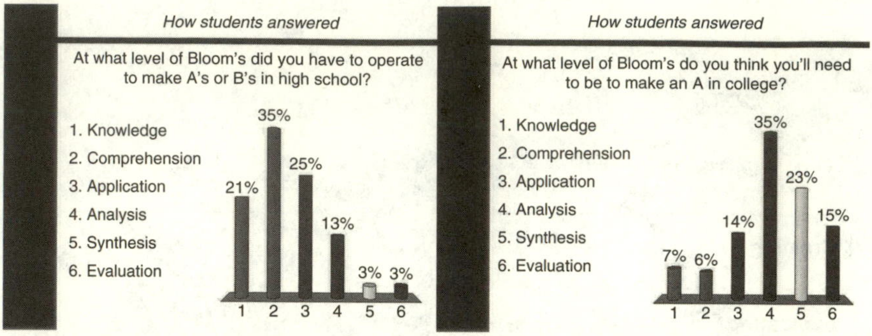

Note. Figure demonstrates that, after learning about Bloom's Taxonomy, most students recognize that college courses will require them to operate at a higher level of learning than high school classes do. The categories are based on the original version of Bloom's Taxonomy (Bloom et al., 1956).

Dweck, 2003). You will also be priming them to devour your first real chunk of practical advice: Use the study cycle with intense study sessions.

Ascending the Levels of Bloom's Taxonomy: Use the Study Cycle With Intense Study Sessions

Okay, so how do students go about pursuing deep learning goals and ascending the levels of Bloom's? They use the metacognitive strategies presented in chapter 5, all under the umbrella of the study cycle (Figure 4.6). The study cycle consists of five steps:

1. Preview
2. Attend class
3. Review
4. Intense study sessions
5. Assess

The first step, preview reading, lays the foundation for what the student will encounter in class. I often tell students, "By previewing, you're making sure that your brain sees the big picture and understands how the concepts you're about to learn fit together." Previewing will be more fully explained in chapter 5. The next step in the cycle is to go to class. We need to emphasize to students that, even though they may not have had to go to class in high school and although their professors may post lecture notes online, it is imperative that they go to class in college. College lectures are very different from high school classes, and a plethora of information will be presented in

Figure 4.6 The Study Cycle

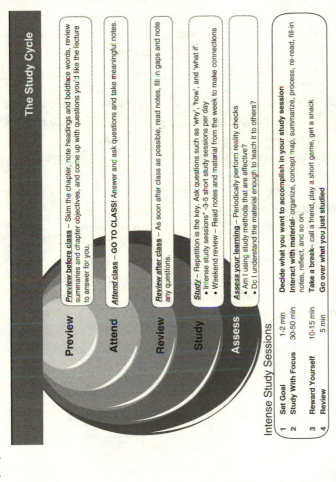

The Study Cycle

Preview *Preview before class* – Skim the chapter, note headings and boldface words, review summaries and chapter objectives, and come up with questions you'd like the lecture to answer for you.

Attend *Attend class* – GO TO CLASS! Answer and ask questions and take meaningful notes.

Review *Review after class* – As soon after class as possible, read notes, fill in gaps and note any questions.

Study *Study* – Repetition is the key. Ask questions such as 'why', 'how', and 'what if'.
• Intense study sessions* -3-5 short study sessions per day
• Weekend review – Read notes and material from the week to make connections

Assess *Assess your learning* – Periodically perform reality checks
• Am I using study methods that are effective?
• Do I understand the material enough to teach it to others?

Intense Study Sessions

1	Set Goal	1-2 min	**Decide what you want to accomplish in your study session**
2	Study With Focus	30-50 min	**Interact with material**- organize, concept map, summarize, process, re-read, fill-in notes, reflect, and so on.
3	Reward Yourself	10-15 min	Take a break– call a friend, play a short game, get a snack
4	Review	5 min	Go over what you just studied

Note. Figure presents the study cycle given to students at LSU's CAS.[3] The cycle is based on F.L. Christ's Learning Cycle (1997). © 2010 Louisiana State University, Center for Academic Success. Used with permission. © 2010 Louisiana State University, Center for Academic Success. This work is reproduced and distributed with the permission of Louisiana State University. No other use is permitted without the express prior written permission of Louisiana State University. For permission, contact cas@lsu.edu class that will not appear in the condensed, distilled lecture notes. Moreover, class time represents a golden opportunity to ask crucial questions. Only by attending class will students be able to keep pace with their courses.

As soon as possible after class, students should undertake step three and review their notes, recalling what happened in class and explaining it to themselves (a phenomenon called elaborative rehearsal), thereby enhancing the memory of what happened in class (Medina, 2008). Reviewing also helps students "determine areas of overlap between lectured material and textbook information, revisit concepts and numerical problems covered in class, and establish whether assistance will be necessary and plan accordingly" (Cook, Kennedy, & McGuire, 2013, p. 963). Sometimes, when I am discussing reviewing with a group of students, I will ask, "How many people have ever seen a movie more than once? Did you notice that the second time you saw it, you noticed things that you didn't even know were there the first time? Reviewing is like watching the movie the second time. Your brain will see things that it didn't see before."

Previewing and reviewing are powerful and efficient ways to support learning. In trying to convince individuals or groups of students to try it, I let them know how easily it can be fit into their schedules. I tell them that some students just get to class 10 minutes early and do their previewing immediately before lecture. And if there's no class following lecture, they just review for 10 minutes after lecture. Lickety-split.

During the fourth step in the cycle, students study using the framework of intense study sessions (see bottom of Figure 4.6). These sessions are effective because they enable students to break up their work into manageable chunks. Intense study sessions can be as short as 15–20 minutes (appropriate for students with attention-deficit/hyperactivity disorder) or as long as 75–90 minutes, though 50–60 minutes is a typical duration. An intense study session has four parts:

1. Set specific goals
2. Do active learning tasks
3. Take a break/Have a reward
4. Review

Students use the first few minutes of the session to set a manageable number of achievable goals. Then they engage in learning activities that have been proven to work, activities we will thoroughly explore in the next chapter. After doing the heavy lifting for 30–50 minutes, but not longer than a period for which they can maintain good focus, students should take a 10–15-minute break. The break is crucial for restoring energy and motivation, and for allowing the information they've just absorbed time to "sink in." Howard (2006) tells us that the purpose of breaks is twofold. First, newly formed neuronal connections must have time to establish themselves before the brain has to deal with new stimuli; second, if learners are too tired, they are more likely to make errors. When students come back refreshed, they should take five minutes to review what they've just studied. During this final step in the study cycle, after intense study sessions, students assess how well they have learned the material they studied by engaging in self-evaluation. They determine whether they need to tweak their learning strategies and adjust them accordingly. For example, perhaps flashcards did not quite do the trick, so a student may decide to try concept mapping in a subsequent intense study session.

You might say to your students that if they do two or three sessions during the day between classes, and another couple of sessions at night, they will have studied 4–5 hours that day without breaking a sweat. Because most of them are studying only 5 or 6 hours a *week*, the increased study time, to 20–25 hours a week, will make an enormous difference. In fact, when asked to specify what changes he'd made to turn around his academic performance, one student said, "I use that Power Hour thing." (Intense study session. Power hour. Tomato, tomahto.)

But Dr. McGuire, I Don't Have Time for This Stuff

When I first began teaching the study cycle to my students, I was pleasantly surprised that many of them followed my recommendations and saw immediate results. But I do want to acknowledge that some students will initially resist using the study cycle and implementing metacognitive learning strategies because they think it will take too much time. I assure them that previewing and reviewing each take only about 10 minutes and that they can adjust the duration of intense study sessions to suit their needs.

In chapter 10, I present time-management strategies you can introduce to your students to help them fit as many intense study sessions as they can into their busy days. And in chapter 9, I explain how to advise students whose work and family responsibilities seemingly leave them no time at all for the study cycle.

Drum Roll, Please: 10 Metacognitive Strategies

In the next chapter, we will discuss specific active learning tasks that students can use to ace their courses.

Notes

1. Many faculty have expressed to me that they do not think of Bloom's Taxonomy as a hierarchy and believe it is a mistake to represent it as a pyramid. They argue that levels do not proceed in order and instead are constantly intertwining. As support for their argument, they note that a student can create something without knowing basic foundational information. I do think that faction has a valid point. However, I like presenting Bloom's to students in hierarchy form because I want them to understand that they will likely not be able to *apply* concepts that they do not *understand* if they have not *memorized* particular facts. I like to illustrate this point with a story. Our older daughter is a professor in the allergy and immunology section of the department of pediatrics at Baylor College of Medicine. When she joined the faculty, her responsibilities included accompanying the residents on their rounds. One day, she asked a resident if it is advisable to prescribe pseudoepinephrine-based drugs like Sudafed or Actifed to pregnant women. She expected him to think critically about her question and answer accordingly. Instead, he whipped out his personal digital assistant and looked it up in the *Physicians' Desk Reference.* He correctly answered, "No," but when she asked him why, he had no clue. She explained to the residents that drugs that constrict blood vessels are never a good idea for pregnant women. My point is that many students nowadays think that they do not need to know anything because they can just look up everything on the Internet. I try to help them see that no one can solve problems using information he or she has only just read. We can solve problems and do critical thinking only with information already stored in our brains. The pyramidal form of Bloom's handily makes this point.

2. There are three domains of Bloom's: cognitive, affective, and psychomotor (Suskie, 2009). The versions of Bloom's presented here pertain to the cognitive domain only. I typically don't discuss the other domains because I find it overwhelms students. The revised taxonomy also includes a knowledge dimension, which comprises the processing levels of factual knowledge, conceptual knowledge, procedural knowledge, and metacognitive knowledge. I do not present Bloom's to students in this much detail.

3. The learning experts at the LSU CAS are constantly revising and updating their wonderful resources. A new version of the study cycle will be released soon, and interested readers should regularly visit the CAS website for its continually evolving content.

5

METACOGNITIVE LEARNING
STRATEGIES AT WORK

"Well, it's official, doing my homework problems as if they were quiz questions after studying my notes and practicing teaching the material works really well for me. Just wanted to share with you my grade on the second Chem 1421 exam: 95, A!" —Sydnie L., first-year honors chemistry student at LSU, personal communication, October 17, 2013

In this chapter, I lay out the top 10 learning strategies that I share with students. These are the strategies that make possible the dramatic results you've heard about so far (appendix F). By reading this chapter, you will get a feel for how I present the strategies in individual sessions and to groups. Chapter 11 focuses specifically on how to present the strategies to groups.

This chapter begins with a brief discussion about metacognitive strategies versus study skills and continues with my own personal introduction to the first three strategies before diving right into all 10 strategies, presented sequentially. Toward the end of the chapter, I give suggestions for how to assess the impact of an individual consultation. Finally, I underscore the importance of communicating belief and confidence in every student's ability to excel.

Study Skills Versus Metacognitive Strategies

Permit me a brief word about branding before we get to the heart of the matter. The metacognitive learning strategies presented in this book are taught all over the country in many learning centers. Some of those centers use the term *study skills* to describe the strategies. But I find that students' eyes glaze over at the mention of "study skills." Students think they don't need them or that they already know them. But when I mention "metacognitive learning strategies," I see the spark of curiosity in their eyes. In short, students hate "study skills" but love "metacognitive learning strategies" because they sound exciting and new.

Of course, in the literature, a distinction is often drawn between meta-cognition proper and study skills. But to make these strategies accessible to students, I purposely blur that distinction. Moreover, there is precedent for blurring those lines in the literature itself. Peirce (2003) writes,

> Students need to monitor their application of study strategies. Metacogni-tive awareness of their learning processes is as important as their monitor-ing of their learning of the course content. Metacognition includes goal setting, monitoring, self-assessing, and regulating during thinking and writing processes; that is, when they're studying and doing homework. An essential component of metacognition is employing study strategies to reach a goal, self-assessing one's effectiveness in reaching that goal, and then self-regulating in response to the self-assessment.

In short, we must persuade students to try these strategies. Showing them "before" and "after" scores, leading them through the four-step introduction to Bloom's Taxonomy, and using language that turns them on rather than off—these choices are all carefully calibrated to fire students up to actually go home and use the strategies. These details may seem incidental, but they are as important and substantive as the strategies themselves. I'm not saying you have to do it my way, but you must have some way of effectively convincing students of the power of the strategies so that they will actually try them.

The Heart of My Work: Metacognitive Strategies

The rest of this chapter lists and elucidates 10 metacognitive strategies, the first three of which are powerful reading strategies I have found particularly useful to teach my students:

1. Previewing
2. Preparing for active reading
3. Paraphrasing
4. Reading actively
5. Using the textbook even if it is not required
6. Going to class and taking notes by hand
7. Doing homework *without* using solved examples as a guide
8. Teaching material to a real or imagined audience
9. Working in pairs or groups
10. Creating practice exams

Keep in mind that your students do not have to undertake all of these strategies in order to see improvement in their performance. They can pick and choose what works for them, though there are some strategies that are so effective—namely, the reading strategies and homework as assessment—that everyone should use them. Finally, I want to acknowledge that you and your students may already be using powerful and effective strategies other than the 10 presented here. Plus, you can always develop additional blockbuster strategies. The sky is the limit.

My Introduction to the Reading Strategies

Remember Travis? The psychology student who flunked his first two tests (Figure 3.1)? During my first conversation with Travis, I asked him what he thought his problem was. He began to tell me about all of the reading assignments he was responsible for completing. He told me, "I do the reading, but when I get to the test I don't really remember it. I know that I've read it, but I don't remember it when it counts, so I know I'm not really getting a lot out of my reading."

Long before I met with Travis, I had heard that same refrain from so very many students: undergraduates, graduate students, business, law, medical students, you name it. I didn't really know what to tell these students. I might have given vague advice like, "Slow down when you're reading," or "Answer the questions in the text." So in 2005, when I learned about a four-week workshop on reading strategies given by the Institute of Reading Development, I decided to see if I could learn some strategies to help my students.

Incidentally, because the Institute runs this workshop all over the country, my first-grade grandson was attending that same workshop in his hometown! I often joke that when I first learned that there were graduate degrees in "college reading," I thought it was an oxymoron because I just *knew* that I had learned to read in first grade. But what I learned in that workshop I definitely had not been taught in first grade or any grade after that. And I would wager that many of your undergraduate and graduate students have not been taught effective critical reading strategies either. These strategies turned Travis's performance around (Figure 3.1), and they can do the same for your students.

What's So Hard About Reading?

What happens when you read? Well, if you're like most people, you begin reading and all is well until your mind starts to wander. But your brain doesn't immediately realize that it is no longer paying attention because your eyes are still tracking the text. Plus, if you're a subvocalizer like I am, you can hear the words as you read, even though you're thinking about something entirely unrelated. It's not until you get further down the page that you realize, "Oh, I stopped paying attention ages ago and have no idea what I'm reading."

At this point, what do you usually do? If you're like most people, you go back and reread the text from the beginning, but this time around, you concentrate harder to keep yourself from running off the rails. And you will probably get a little further, but only a little, before the same thing happens again. And then what do you do? Start over. Again. You can see where this is going.

But you can prevent this vicious cycle by engaging in particular practices before you start to read. The following three reading strategies should be taught and used in concert for the biggest impact. Think of them as one big active reading strategy with three steps.

Active Reading, Step One: Previewing

For maximally engaged reading, you must give yourself a preview of what you're about to read (**strategy #1**). We know the brain is much more efficient at learning when it has a big picture and then acquires individual details to fill in that big picture (e.g., Klingner & Vaughn, 1999). How do you give it that big picture? Look at the section headings, boldface print, italicized words, and any charts or graphs in the portion of reading you have chosen. If you are reading a novel, then read the first line of every paragraph.

To demonstrate the power of previewing to my students, I often do the following exercise with them, first devised by Bransford (1979). I explain that I am going to read a short passage and then ask the students three questions about it. I tell them that the first question will be "What specific task is this passage about?" and that I'll ask them the second and third questions after they've finished the reading. Bransford's (1979) passage follows.

> The procedure is actually quite simple. First you arrange items into different groups. Of course, one pile may be sufficient depending on how much there is to do. If you have to go somewhere else due to lack of facilities that is the next step; otherwise, you are pretty well set. It is important not to overdo things. That is, it is better to do too few things at once than too many. In the short run this may not seem important, but complications can easily arise. A mistake can be expensive as well. At first, the whole procedure will seem complicated. Soon, however, it will become just another facet of life. It is difficult to foresee any end to the necessity for this task in the immediate future, but, then, one can never tell. After the procedure is completed, one arranges

the materials into different groups again. Then they can be put into their appropriate places. Eventually they will be used once more, and the whole cycle will then have to be repeated. However, that is a part of life. (pp. 134–135)

Then, I ask the first of three questions: "What process is being described in this passage?" I have never heard a correct answer to this question during an individual consultation, and in my student and faculty workshops, occasionally two or three people out of 50 figure out the answer. I ask those people not to spoil it for everyone else.

Next I ask the second question, "Where can you go if you lack the facilities?" Usually there are blank stares and silence. Or perhaps I might hear, "Somewhere that has the facilities?"

Finally, I ask the third question, "How can a mistake be expensive?" Again, most people are confused and quiet, but a few brave souls might venture, "If you mess up," or "If it costs you time and money."

At last, I tell them what the passage is about, the equivalent of previewing and seeing "Laundry" as a boldface heading. Then I read the passage again. Please feel free to reread it right now.

Did the passage sound different to you? Were you able to engage with it more actively and derive much more meaning from its sentences? Do the questions now seem trivial rather than mystifying?

Similarly, if students have some idea of or context for what they are about to read, their brains can recognize and process much more information than if they just dive headlong into their reading.

Active Reading, Step Two: Previewing on Steroids. Come Up With Questions the Reading Can Answer

Once you've looked at the bold and italicized text as well as charts and graphs, you still need to do one more thing before you begin to read. You need to give yourself a *reason* to read. Just like no four-year-old likes hearing, "You have to," neither does your brain. So you need to come up with questions that you want the reading to answer for you (**strategy #2**). Then you've tapped into your genuine curiosity and are much more motivated to read.

Let's say I'm reading a chapter in a general chemistry textbook about acids and bases. The terms *strong acid* and *weak acid* would probably be in a distinctive font. My question might be, "What is the difference between strong acids and weak acids?" So now I've given myself motivation to read the text.

Or if I were going to read a chapter on buffer solutions, I might see "weak acids" in bold or italicized print. I might ask myself, "What do weak acids have to do with buffers? Are they different from strong acids?" When I start to read, my mind will be looking for the answers, and I will be able to stay focused longer.

One advantage of previewing is that it doesn't take a lot of time. Most faculty I've spoken to give their students reading assignments, but the students don't do them. Indeed, many students won't read before going to class, but they will preview because it takes only about 10 minutes. Previewing can prepare students for active reading or for hearing a lecture. So 10 minutes of previewing can make a big difference to students' behavior in class. If they've generated questions that they want the lecture to answer for them, then they will listen differently in class, stick with the lecturer, take notes, and ask questions. According to Cook et al. (2013), "By previewing, students become primed for pattern recognition, may experience more frequent spikes of interest in the material being taught, and even have more courage to ask questions in class because they are more comfortable with the instructor's discourse" (p. 963). By all means, assign reading, but you may find it helpful to ask students to take 10 minutes to preview the material that will be covered in lecture and generate two or three questions raised by the preview. If you collect these questions for extra credit—on a random basis so students are motivated to bring them every day—almost your entire class will come to lecture at least somewhat prepared.

When I am talking to groups of students about previewing, I will say to them, "How many of you have had the experience that you come to class and the information is going from the PowerPoint slides onto your notes without passing through your brain?" Heads all over the room nod in agreement. "That is a wasted hour. But we want you to make every hour count. If you've done the previewing, you have the skeleton you need so that during lecture you can put all the necessary meat on those bones." I have been gratified to hear in many conversations with individual students, "Wow, lecture makes so much more sense when I preview."

Active Reading, Step Three: Paraphrasing the Correct Way

Now that you've previewed the text, and you've generated interesting questions that you hope the text will answer, you're ready to begin reading. Here is the crucial instruction: When you start, read only one paragraph at a time. Just read the first paragraph. Stop. Put the information in that first paragraph in your own words.

Now move on to the second paragraph, and do the same thing, except this time, when you paraphrase, fold in the information that was in the first paragraph. Once you read the third paragraph, your paraphrase will contain all of the information from the beginning of the passage—and so on and so forth, ad infinitum (**strategy #3**). This way, you break a big task down into manageable chunks, yet the information from the chunks is integrated into a complete understanding of the topic at hand.[1]

Does that process sound like it will take a very long time? Guess what? Every single one of my students who has discussed with me their use of this method reports that it takes less time to finish their reading assignments with this system than with the one they had been using. Graduate students in particular tell me that it helps them move briskly through research papers. When I ask my students, "Why do you think it works?" they say, "I'm not rereading or having a bunch of false starts." So although they are reading more slowly, they are only moving *forward*, so the end comes much more quickly and with much deeper understanding. The tortoise and the hare. Slow and steady wins the race.

Flashcards and Maps and Outlines, Oh My!

The previous three reading strategies should often be supplemented by activities like highlighting; taking notes; jotting down questions; and creating flashcards, concept or chapter maps, and outlines (**strategy #4**). These tasks can be undertaken while reading the textbook, supplemental reading, or class notes. Chapter 9 gives some ways that students can get to know themselves as learners and choose activities most appropriate and beneficial for them.

I was surprised to learn from speaking with groups of STEM students over the years that many of them skip over example problems in their textbooks as they are actively reading. (I certainly didn't do that when I was an undergrad!) But students should always work the examples as part of their reading in order to maximize their comprehension.

Joshua, an engineering major who took general chemistry in his freshman year, learned to love active reading. This student came to me with a D average in general chemistry because he had scored 68, 50, and 50 on the first three tests. After working with me, he scored 87 on both of the next two tests and cranked out a 97 on the final exam. Joshua earned an A in the course and a 3.8 GPA that semester. When I asked him via e-mail which strategies worked for him, he responded, "I think what I did different [*sic*] was make sidenotes in each chapter, and as I progressed into the next chapter I was able to refer to these notes. I would say that in chemistry, everything builds from the previous topic." Indeed.

Textbooks, Please

We interrupt our regularly scheduled programming for a public service announcement. Please, please, please do whatever you need to do to make sure your students have access to textbooks. I hear horror stories every week about students who did not have access to books in high school, or if they did, they couldn't take the books home. Many students have even told me that their professors have given explicit, blanket permission not to buy the book. These professors tell their students that everything they need to know is in their notes.

Indulge me, and do a brief exercise. Look at Figure 5.1 at the bottom of this page and tell me the first word that comes to mind.

Did you see the word "cat"? Or perhaps "cot" or "cut"? If you know something very well, then large chunks of it can be missing or misordered, and you can still recognize it. This fact is the basis of our students' ingenious texting abbreviations or clever personalized license plates.

But what if our culture had no cats, cots, or cuts? Or what if we used different words to describe those things? Then you would look at Figure 5.1 and it would mean nothing to you. *That is the experience of students who try to use lecture notes to learn complex subjects.* After doing this exercise with students, I say to them, "The notes are the C_T version of the information. That's why the textbook has so many more pages than the lecture notes. It has charts! It has graphs! Diagrams! Supplemental problems! It's there to help you" (**strategy #5**). When we as instructors read the lecture notes, our minds fill in everything that is missing, so everything does genuinely appear to be there. If you are among those who tell your students they do not need to buy the book, I know that you are not deliberately sabotaging them and that you are just trying to save them money. But their minds are not your mind. They need the textbook.

Figure 5.1 Fill-in-the-Blank Exercise

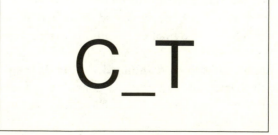

Have you ever overheard students complaining after a test that it covered material you never presented in class? But you distinctly recall having covered it in class? The phenomenon just described explains how you and your students are both correct. That material was in the notes, slides, or board work that *you* saw but not in what the students saw. You presented C_T, believing you presented CAT.

When I am trying to convince students to buy textbooks, I explain to them that their instructors' brains have all of the missing information to flesh out the lecture notes. Then I ask them, "But does your brain have all the information in organic chemistry or cell biology or philosophy or multivariable calculus to fill in the gaps?" They shake their heads no. I go on to ask, "When the professor writes the test, is he or she writing it based on what his or her brain sees in the notes or what your brain sees in the notes?" They quickly see my point.

To those who protest that textbooks are expensive, I ask, "What's more expensive, the textbook or not getting into medical school because you made a C in chemistry?" Most find the money for the textbook. To the holdouts I say, "Okay, buy the book and use it for a couple of weeks. If it isn't useful, return it to the bookstore for whatever they will give you, come back and see me and I will write you a personal check for the difference." I have never, ever had to write a check. Every single student has come back and said something to the effect of, "Wowwwww. I can't believe what a big difference the book makes! I had no idea it would be so helpful."

If our students do not have books, the four effective metacognitive strategies just presented are impossible for them to use. During my initial session with Joshua, I asked him if he had the textbook. He replied, "There is no textbook for the course." Then I asked him to show me his syllabus. Sure enough, the textbook was listed as "recommended." Because it was optional, Joshua had not even seen it on the syllabus. I convinced him to buy the textbook, and the rest is history. Without textbooks, neither Joshua nor Dana nor a host of other students would have been able to join the miracle portfolio.

I implore you to require the textbook for your course.

A Whole New World: Students May Need to Learn How to Use the Textbook

Permit me another story, if not an explicit strategy, if you would. About 10 years ago, I was working in the tutorial center at the LSU CAS, and a young woman arrived and said she was having problems arranging substances in order of increasing entropy. So I said, "Okay. Tell me what entropy is." She replied, "I don't know what it is." She had had the foresight to bring her book to the center, and it was sitting on the desk in front of her. So I said, "What if I told you that I would make you give me all of your tickets to the LSU football games left in the season if you do not give me a definition of entropy in the next five minutes. What would you do?" She said, "Well, I guess I'd just have to miss all the rest of the games."

"Noooo, no, no, no, no, you don't have to miss the rest of the games. In fact, there's something in this room that would keep you from having to give up all your tickets."

She looked around the room, scanned everything on each of the four walls, and then finally looked down on the table. It hit her:

"The book?"
"Yes!!! The book!"
"But I don't know what chapter it's in."
"How could you find out what chapter it's in?"

Fellow instructors, she had absolutely no idea. She did not know that a textbook has an index. She did not know about the table of contents either. Colleagues, there are so many students who arrive on campus having never used a textbook. So it falls to us or to the campus learning center professionals to teach students how to use the book.

You might mention on the first day of class that the textbook has an index and a table of contents, and you might at the beginning or end of each lecture mention the chapters or pages in the textbook that correspond to the material at hand. Of course, you are not required to do these things, but it could make an enormous difference for your students.

Go to Class and Take Notes by Hand

Many students underestimate the value of going to class and have not learned how to be engaged in class. Instructors should explicitly communicate their expectation that students will be in class, taking notes as full intellectual participants (**strategy #6**). Many students these days take notes on their laptop computers, tablets, or even smartphones. But recent studies show that taking notes by hand results in more learning than does taking notes with a laptop, partly because students are forced to paraphrase when they take notes by hand (Mueller & Oppenheimer, 2014). Accordingly, we should also recommend to our students that they take notes by hand. If they are afraid they will miss something important, they can record the lecture and listen to it at a later time.

Finally, we should also encourage our students who must occasionally miss class to get the notes from another reliable student rather than just downloading lecture slides or notes (Hoffmann & McGuire, 2010). A fellow student's notes will have explanations and additional material not present in the lecture notes.

Homework as Assessment

Remember Dana, the undergraduate on the verge of leaving physics who now holds a master's degree in medical physics (chapter 3)? This strategy completely transformed her performance on physics exams. In fact, most of my science students who come to me when they are earning low Cs, Ds, or Fs, and who subsequently begin to make A grades, say that doing homework without using solved examples as a guide (**strategy #7**) is the one change that turned everything around.

When introducing this strategy, I ask students, "If there were a camera recording everything you do when you sit down to do your homework, tell me exactly what it would see."

"Okay, I sit down and I open my book and then I look at the first problem."

"Have you ever looked at a problem and immediately decided to flip back in the textbook to look for an example?"

"Yes, Dr. McGuire! How did you know?"

"Because everybody is doing it. I did it myself when I was in college."

Over the years, I have learned that most students do their homework by looking at example problems in the textbook or in their class notes and trying to copy the steps laid out there in order to arrive at the correct answer. *This method is exactly the wrong way to go about doing homework problems.*

Homework and example problems in the textbook and class notes should always be treated as an opportunity for students to test themselves. They should study for the homework the way they would study for a quiz. Before looking at the homework questions or problems they should actively read the relevant part of the textbook or any class notes. As they encounter example problems, they should work those problems *without referring to the given solutions.* For each problem, even if they get stuck and don't know the next step, students should do their very best to power through and arrive at an answer. Then they should *check only the final answer* and not the entire solution. If their answer is incorrect, then they can reread the text or class notes to investigate why and where they made mistakes. Much important and deep learning takes place during that investigation process. When students arrive at the correct answer, they should compare their *approach* to the textbook's or instructor's. If the approaches are different, students can ask themselves whether both approaches are valid. Why or why not? If they are both valid, does the student prefer his or her approach or the alternative approach? Why? This method provides many opportunities for reflection, metacognition, and deep learning. Additionally, sometimes someone else's method just doesn't "click" with a student's thought process. If that student looks at that method before trying his or her own, the student may become locked into that way of thinking about the problem, which will be an unnecessary burden the student carries throughout the rest of the course and perhaps beyond. Relying on others' methods restricts students' creative flexibility and mental agility.

After working the example problems in this manner, students can then turn to the homework. They should do two or three problems at a time, treating each problem like a quiz or test question, looking at answers or worked-out solutions only after having made their best attempt to solve the group of problems.

Occasionally, students will lack the intellectual confidence to try this strategy, convinced that if they do not look at complete solutions, they will be endlessly staring at a blank page. For those students, it helps to advise them to set a timer and spend at least five minutes going through the reading or class notes to see if they can figure out how to begin the problem. If after five minutes, they are still stumped, they should look only at the first step, set another five-minute timer for step two, and continue in this way until they have solved the problem. Using this method, students maximize their opportunity to solve problems independently. I like to say to students, "Practice problems, wherever they come from, are your brain's best resource for demonstrating that it can do all the problems without relying on an example as a guide."

Whenever I present this strategy to students, as soon as I explain to them that they should try to figure out where they made a mistake before looking at solutions, I ask them, "At this point in the process, do you think that mistakes are good or bad?" How do you think they reply? Most faculty in my workshops predict that students will say mistakes are bad, but all of the student groups with whom I've worked collectively answer that mistakes are good. I quickly clarify that I'm not saying it's bad if they don't make a mistake; it is wonderful if they make no mistakes! But if they do, those mistakes represent a golden opportunity (Zull, 2011). When I ask students why mistakes are good, they answer:

> You learn from your mistakes.
> You can correct your mistakes.
> You never make the same mistake twice.

You learn where your mind has a tendency to go wrong.
You won't lose points if you make a mistake now.

Do you have students who, upon receiving a graded exam, lament, "Oh, I made so many careless mistakes!"? I believe there is almost no such thing as a careless mistake. Mistakes look careless only in retrospect. These kinds of mistakes must be made, sometimes repeatedly. "So," I tell students, "you're either going to make your mistakes now, during the homework process, or . . . where?" "On the test," they correctly answer.[2] I was surprised to find that once students understand the importance of making mistakes during the homework process, they often stop using websites like cramster.com or chegg .com to complete their homework assignments. They understand that by doing homework in the correct way, they are training their brain for the task it will face during the exam: solving problems without any model or guide.

One final note. When students are moving through example problems and homework, or quizzes and tests, they should begin with simple problems and progress to more complex ones that test mastery of more than one concept. We will see in chapters 7 and 8 that early success is a powerful motivator, and early failure is a powerful discourager. So students need to give themselves opportunities for success. Often, but not always, homework or exam problems are arranged from easiest to most difficult. If the easiest homework problems are too difficult, students can search for problems in the textbook easier than the homework and start with those. Even assessing the difficulty of problems requires metacognitive activity and helps the student absorb the material more deeply. This supplemental strategy is easy to include in your syllabus or mention when you are assigning homework.

Using homework as an opportunity to assess learning is an extremely powerful strategy. Alongside the reading strategies, it is one of the most effective and transformative strategies I offer my students.

Students as Teachers

Students can also assess their understanding of material by teaching it to a friend, who may or may not be in the same course, or by pretending to teach it to an empty sofa, a pet, or a group of stuffed toys, dolls, or action figures (**strategy #8**). In trying to explain concepts in a way that others can understand, students become aware of the gaps in their understanding or of details that are not entirely clear to them. They can then attempt to clear up their confusion themselves or ask a colleague or instructor. Students usually appreciate the power of this strategy due to our previous discussion about "make-an-A" mode versus "teach-the-material" mode (chapter 4).

Come Together, Right Now

Working in pairs or groups, in addition to working alone, can be a powerful supplement to the other learning strategies (**strategy #9**). In groups, students often have the opportunity to teach (see preceding section) and learn from each other. Working in groups helps students engage in one of the major aspects of metacognition, accurately judging their own learning (Figure 3.2). Cook et al. (2013) assert that students in groups "evaluate each other's thinking [and are] more likely to be metacognitive about how they approach information" (p. 962) than when they work alone. When discussing study groups in student workshops, I sometimes ask, "Why are study groups helpful?" Students respond:

> If I say something wrong other people can correct me.
> I can hear the way other people think about the material.

Of course, the students must actually be working rather than socializing. Vygotsky (1978) and Bruner (1985) have established that in order to be effective, study groups must engage in both discussion and problem-solving activities. Here is a link to the LSU CAS Study Group Starter Kit:[3] www.cas .lsu.edu/study-groups

Play Detective: Piece Together a Mock Exam Using Homework and Quizzes as Clues

Finally, you can playfully tell your students to stop badgering you about what will be on the test and recommend that they use the following strategy instead. From the syllabus, lecture notes, homework assignments, and quizzes, they can deduce the topics and problem types that will appear on the exam. Then they can create an outline of an exam or create their own practice exam using the bank of problems in the textbook and, if applicable, supplemental optional problems provided throughout the unit by the instructor (**strategy #10**). Practice exams can also be made in groups, with each student responsible for a different topic.

There is powerful evidence demonstrating the effectiveness of testing as a way to reinforce, deepen, and enrich learning. In articles for the *New York Times*, science writer Benedict Carey (2010, 2014) shares evidence from Roediger and Karpicke (2006) and Pennebaker, Gosling, and Ferrell (2013) that illustrates the power of testing.

Roediger and Karpicke (2006) asked college students to study science passages in preparation for a later reading comprehension test. If students studied these passages in two sequential sessions, they performed well on a test given right after the study sessions, but the material did not stick. However, another group of students, who studied the passages only once and in the second session took a practice test, did well on an assessment two days later and another test a full week later. Testing is a powerful way to deepen and lengthen learning.

Pennebaker, Gosling, and Ferrell (2013) did something radical with their introductory psychology course at the University of Texas. Instead of giving a final exam, they replaced it with "a series of short quizzes that students took on their laptops at the beginning of each class" (Carey, 2014, para. 3). The professors reported that the students groused and grumbled because they had to constantly prepare for these never-ending quizzes. But compared to another set of students taking the same course, these students not only boasted better course grades than their peers but also did better "on a larger quiz that included 17 of the same questions [from both] quizzes and on the other class's midterm" (Carey, 2014, para. 5). Carey correctly notes that "The quizzes were especially beneficial for the type of students—many from low-performing high schools—who don't realize how far behind they are until it's too late" (Carey, 2014, para. 5) (see also chapter 12).

Practice testing works. If students want to ace the real exam, they should practice first.

The Strategies: A Recap

These 10 strategies make up the heart of my work and the heart of this book. Chapters 6 through 10 and chapter 12 address the issue of student motivation and happiness, and chapter 11 explains how these strategies can be introduced to groups of students at once, either small or very large. Students need not use all 10 strategies to see fast and dramatic results. I recommend they begin with the reading, classroom, and homework strategies, and add more as they continue on their metacognitive journey.

A Useful Resource

Before presenting the strategies to students, consider giving them the Learning Strategies Inventory (LSI) that appears in appendix E. Students indicate which strategies they are currently using via a true/false assessment, and the LSI predicts the grade they will earn in the course. The purpose of the LSI is not to shame students into recognizing what they are doing wrong. Its purpose is to further convince students that their performance directly correlates with their *behavior* rather than any innate fixed ability. In fact, one major purpose of everything I have shared with you is to help students attribute their results to only their actions, to help them change their mindset. In the next chapter, we will discover the power of a student's mindset.

Wrapping Up My Pitch

When I present these strategies to a student in an individual consultation, at the end of the session, I usually ask two questions to determine the likelihood that the student will begin using the strategies. First I ask, "On a scale of 1 to 10, how different are the strategies we have talked about from the ones you have been using up to this point? A response of 1 represents no difference at all; 10 is a difference as extreme as day and night." If the student reports a number between 7 and 10, I know that the student can recognize the difference between what he or she has been doing and the actions I am encouraging. (Even though *I* know that the strategies are different, the student must recognize the difference, or he or she won't do anything different.)

My second question is: "On a scale of 1 to 10, how motivated are you to start using the strategies? 1 is not at all; 10 is 'I can't wait to start them today!'" I am satisfied if a student gives a number between 8 and 10.[4] Then I reinforce the idea that students' future performance will depend only on whether they use the strategies and not at all on how "smart" they are, explicitly expressing my confidence that all students can be successful. In individual sessions, I ask the student to keep in touch via e-mail, and I give assurances that I will be available for future meetings.

From the moment I meet a student or step in front of a group of students to the end of our first session, I focus on using everything at my disposal—including carefully chosen language and nonverbal cues—to communicate my belief that all students have the power to excel. As we will learn in chapter 6, students' expectations—their mindsets—can ensure success or failure.

Notes

1. I learned about paraphrasing each paragraph—a very well-established reading technique—at the reading strategies workshop I attended. But I added the part of the strategy whereby students cumulatively paraphrase as they continue reading.

2. Online homework systems are now ubiquitous and are used by many faculty in a variety of courses. Online homework assignments aid student learning because they allow students to attempt the problem more than once or to ask to see an example if they are stumped. However, unless students understand that consulting an example before working the problem undermines their learning and test performance, they will happily consult examples to expeditiously complete the homework.

3. I often warn students against the "divide and conquer" strategy that some study groups use, in which each member of the study group is responsible for a portion of the material. The danger is that each member will learn his or her territory very well but have a significantly shallower understanding of the majority of the material.

4. When I present these strategies to groups (chapter 11) I always end by asking the students to write down one strategy that they will commit to using for the next three weeks. As you will read in chapter 11, I tell them that if they don't start using that strategy within the next 48 hours, they probably never will.

6

MINDSET MATTERS

"I'm just not good at chemistry." —Joshua, engineering major and general chemistry student at LSU, who finished the course with an A (personal communication, May 13, 2011)

This chapter is based on the work of Carol Dweck (2006), a professor of psychology at Stanford University. Her book, *Mindset*, has proved so important and the ideas within it have been so useful that they deserve their own chapter.

The chapter is organized as follows. First, we learn the meaning of the term *mindset* and examine some supporting evidence for Dweck's findings. Second, we examine why many students and faculty arrive on campus with a fixed mindset. Third, I present four strategies faculty can use to change their students' mindsets.

Fixed Intelligence or Intelligence That Can Grow?

Dweck (2006) found that people commonly hold one of two mindsets about intelligence—either it is fixed, or it can grow. Put differently, some people believe that each person is born holding a set of intellectual cards, and little can be done to augment that hand, whereas others believe that they can acquire a few aces through effort and action. You will not be surprised to hear that, although I once had a fixed mindset, the astonishing results I have seen from students have converted me to a growth mindset.

David Shenk (2010) gives several evidence-based arguments to support his assertion that "Intelligence is a process, not a thing" (p. 29). But regardless of the truth about intelligence, *beliefs* about intelligence have been repeatedly demonstrated to have an enormous effect on performance.

Mindset as Master of Your Fate

Figure 6.1, adapted from Dweck's (2006) book, contrasts the likely attitudes and actions of a person with a fixed mindset with those of someone with a growth mindset. As shown, people with a fixed mindset tend to avoid challenges, give up easily, ignore criticism, and find the success of others threatening. By contrast, people with a growth mindset embrace challenges, persevere, use effort to achieve mastery, benefit from criticism, and find motivational fuel in the success of others.

We can conclude from Dweck's work that a fixed mindset is kryptonite in any arena, including academia. Yet so many of us—both students and faculty—believe that intelligence is largely innate and fixed. These beliefs are devastating because our confidence, or lack thereof, that we can successfully perform a task greatly influences how motivated we are to even attempt that task (Ambrose, Bridges, DiPietro, Lovett, & Norman, 2010).

Three Illustrations of the Power of Mindset

Mindset (Dweck, 2006) contains references to a number of peer-reviewed published research articles supporting the findings summarized in Figure 6.1. Here I present three illustrations supporting Dweck's findings, chosen somewhat arbitrarily given the treasure trove of supporting research: (a) a study from David H. Uttal (1997) about the attitudes of Asian and American mothers and children about mathematical ability; (b) an intervention cited in a paper from Aguilar, Walton, and Wieman (2014); and (c) anecdotal evidence from a middle-school math teacher. My own miracle portfolio, from which the stories of many students are told throughout this book, also provides strong support for Dweck's findings. Your own miracle portfolio, if it does not already do so, will soon.

Of Course They're Better at Math—They're Asian

David H. Uttal (1997) asked Japanese, Taiwanese, and American mothers—using many different questions—to assess the importance of four aspects of a school child's performance: "effort, natural ability, the difficulty of the schoolwork, and luck or chance" (p. 168). American mothers rated effort as significantly less important than did Asian mothers, and they also rated innate ability as significantly more important than did Asian mothers.

Figure 6.1 Fixed and Growth Mindsets

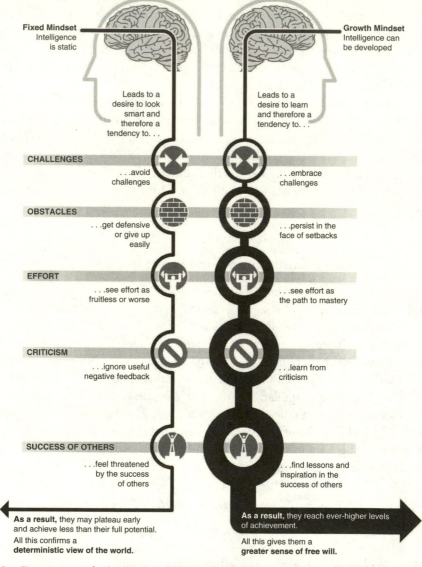

Note. Figure contrasts fixed and growth mindsets. The growth mindset is more conducive to academic success. Adapted from *Mindset: The New Psychology of Success,* by C. Dweck, 2006, p. 245. Copyright 2006 by Carol S. Dweck. Graphic by Nigel Holmes. Reproduced with permission.

Uttal argues persuasively that these differences go a long way toward explaining the differences between American and Asian students' performance on international math assessments. He relates the American mothers' emphasis on innate ability—fixed mindset—to a belief that a child's future can be accurately predicted based on early success or failure. When he asked American and Chinese mothers to say at what point it becomes possible to predict a child's high school math performance, more than a third of the American mothers but only one tenth of the Chinese mothers chose the end of elementary school rather than a later time in a child's intellectual development.

Not incidentally, the children surveyed in Uttal's study held beliefs that matched their parents'. Compared to Asian children, American children are more likely to hold a fixed mindset about mathematics achievement and believe that innate ability determines their performance.

Uttal also proposes that American parents' fixed mindsets may explain two of his other findings. First, he found American parents are satisfied with their children's mediocre performance, whereas Asian parents express much less satisfaction with their children's higher achievement. Second, American parents and children believe that Asian children are more talented in mathematics than American children.

Two additional findings complete the picture. American mothers are ambivalent about the value of homework, whereas Japanese and Taiwanese mothers are convinced that homework is important. Consistent with those findings, American fifth graders spent about 4 hours per week doing homework, whereas Japanese and Taiwanese fifth graders spent 6 to 11 hours.

Finally, Uttal cites Stevenson and Stigler's (1992) finding that mindset determines attitudes about errors. People with a fixed mindset tend to view errors as failures, whereas people with a growth mindset view errors as necessary steps in the learning process because they reveal what needs further attention. Stevenson and Stigler found that American children felt embarrassed when they made errors, whereas Japanese and Chinese children remained largely untroubled by their mistakes.

Uttal sums up his findings, saying "Perhaps more than any other school subject, mathematics requires effort, diligence, and persistence even in the face of temporary setbacks. A focus on innate ability may discourage children from doing precisely what they must do to succeed in mathematics" (1997, p. 170). I argue that this statement applies to all disciplines, not just mathematics.

I present a brief summary of Uttal's paper in my workshops because the stereotype of the talented Asian mathematician, computer engineer, or other STEM professional is so widespread in American culture. Nearly everyone has absorbed this belief to some extent, so it is an effective demonstration of the power of mindset. Mindset determines how much effort we expend and the expectations we have for ourselves, so it logically follows that it is a major factor affecting our performance.

You're Criticizing My Work Because You Think I Can Do Better, Not Because I'm a Lost Cause?

How students respond to criticism gives us further insight into the impact of mindset. When students become aware that their instructors have provided criticism in order to help them improve rather than as a judgment of their ostensibly fixed abilities, they are likelier to use that criticism constructively. Aguilar et al. (2014) cite a study by Yeager et al. (2013) wherein teachers provided feedback on student essays along with a note that read, "I have high standards but I believe you have the potential to meet them, so I am providing this critical feedback to help you meet those standards." Eighty percent of the students who received the note chose to revise their essays, whereas only 39% chose to do revisions when only feedback—that is, criticism—was provided. Aguilar et al. point out that the kind of explicit reassurance expressed in the note is very different from "vague bromides like, 'Good job, but . . .'" (p. 47).

IDK

I met a master's degree candidate in LSU's College of Human Sciences and Education, Lorena, who taught math to "gifted" middle school students. She expressed great frustration that her students were performing far, far below their potential. She had written her master's thesis on metacognitive control but was frustrated that she could not persuade her students to think productively about problems that they had not already been taught how to solve. Whenever she gave them challenging problems, they simply wrote "IDK."

Unfamiliar with this shorthand, she asked one student, "What is IDK?"

"I don't know," the student replied.

She asked another student, who gave her the same response.

"Well, if you don't know what it means, why are all of you writing it on your papers?!"

After a few more seconds of confusion, à la Abbott and Costello's famous routine "Who's on First?," one of the students told her that "IDK" is an acronym for "I don't know." With unfamiliar problems, the students just refused to try.

If we label our students as gifted, it encourages them to take on a fixed mindset, and consequently they become terrified to do anything that might contradict the idea that they are smarter than their peers. So instead of facing head-on the confusion that inevitably accompanies meaningful problem solving, they may instead throw up their hands and say, "IDK."

The Origins and Costs of a Fixed Mindset

The next sections of this chapter explore why many students and faculty hold fixed mindsets, examine some evidence both groups may use to support their fixed mindsets, and discuss the costs of holding on to a fixed mindset.

Why Do Students Have a Fixed Mindset?

When our students were in first, second, or third grade, they looked around their classrooms and saw their peers divided up into the blue group, the green group, and the yellow group. They instinctively knew what those groups stood for. Everyone knew who the "smart kids" and the "slow kids" were. Now fast-forward to tenth grade. Do you think our students saw the pecking order change at all? Of course not. The smart kids were still smart, the slow kids were still slow, and everybody still knew it.

So our students have been programmed to say things to us like, "I was just never very good at math," or, "I was always in the slow reading group." Categorizing students this way almost ensures a fixed mindset. Figure 6.1 should make clear that a fixed mindset can spell disaster, whether a student is judged as "gifted" or "slow."

Okay, But, Come On, Some Kids Are More Gifted Than Others

As I have already mentioned several times, I used to believe wholeheartedly that there are smart students and slow students. Teaching students metacognitive strategies and seeing their astonishing results have completely changed my mind: I now know that there are students who have an arsenal of strategies at their disposal and there are students who don't. It just appears that students using strategies are smart and that students without them are slow.

Now hear this: All students who are admitted to our institutions are capable of excelling. You can be certain that very successful students are using effective learning strategies. Some of them absorbed these strategies when they were two or three years old. Some students came by their strategies intuitively and instinctively; these students may not even be able to articulate them as explicit strategies. But, however it happened, these successful students arrived at school, even preschool, with strategies, or at least acquired knowledge, that the other students did not have. So it does *appear* that there really is a blue group, a yellow group, and a green group. But in reality, there are only students who have learned strategies or been given prior knowledge and students who haven't. When we teach "slow" students learning strategies, they can do as well as students in the gifted programs.

Listen, I get it. Both our daughters were in gifted programs. I used to think they were *reallllly* innately brilliant. But when I began to understand the role of metacognitive strategies, I began to rethink my assumption. I realized that they were using strategies. I had read to both of them from the time they were in the womb. Our younger daughter started reading at two and a half and went to a Montessori preschool where the teachers dedicated themselves to finding challenging reading material for her every single day. My husband started simple computer programming activities with both children when they were in elementary school. Our older daughter, without explicit prompting, frequently used the metacognitive strategy of assessing her own comprehension and mastery in order to consistently excel throughout high school. Sure, my kids are smart, but how did they get that way? They *grew* their intelligence. And so can everyone else.

Gifted programs reinforce the notion that some people are born smart and others aren't. They cement the fixed mindset. But the strategies and techniques that teachers use with gifted students should be used with *all* students after those students have been taught learning strategies.

But Really—What About Mozart? Or Einstein?

Yes, prodigies exist. I would never say that there is no such thing as a prodigy. But no student needs to be anywhere *near* a prodigy in order to earn As in the vast majority of middle and high school, college, university, and graduate and professional school courses.

Why Do Faculty Have a Fixed Mindset?

One answer might be that all faculty were once students. We observed the blue, green, and yellow groups too. And we were usually put into the blue group. In order to let go of our fixed mindset, many of us must let go of the idea that we are smarter than the average bear. That can be a tough pill to swallow.

Most of us also did very well in school. So when we have students who, for example, flunk our first two organic chemistry tests, what are we supposed to think? That those students are *smart*? Fuhgeddaboudit. Kidding aside, it should be clear from the zero-to-hero stories in this book that we should never make assumptions about students' intelligence based on their initial performance. All students can succeed and make top grades as long as they are consistently using effective strategies. Consider Adam's story.

Mindset Makes Miracles: Adam's Story

Adam enrolled in my colleague Isiah Warner's analytical chemistry course at LSU in the fall of 2005. An engineering major, Adam was due to graduate at the end of that semester, but he needed to pass Warner's class with a grade of C or higher. Unfortunately, he had scored 65, 61, and 61 on the three hourly exams given in the course. Warner told him to contact me. Adam called me on Friday with his final exam looming, scheduled for the following Wednesday. If he did not pass the course, he would not graduate.

We met Monday morning, and I introduced him to several metacognitive strategies, including concept mapping, working problems without consulting an example, and pretending to teach the concepts. Then Adam began asking me specific questions about the topics that the test would cover. I explained to him that I had no idea and that he should go speak to his teaching assistant. So Adam went straight from my office to the teaching assistant's office.

Wednesday after the exam, I got a voice mail from Adam. "Dr. McGuire! Those strategies you gave me were sooooo useful! I think the minimum I made on that test was 100!" I thought, "100?! Oh, this poor guy. If he is that deluded about his test performance, he might have scored in the 30s or 40s." So I called Warner. I said to him, "I need to know what Adam made on his final exam because he thinks he did pretty well." I didn't have the nerve to tell Isiah that he thought he made at least 100! Isiah told me, "Hmmm, I don't know what he made. I'll call the grader and find out."

Later that day, Warner called me back and said, "Saundra, the grader said he made 107, but she *knows* he cheated. She knows he cheated because he came to her office two days before the test and he didn't know anything." I quickly responded, "Well, I'm the one who sent him to her office because he had specific questions about test coverage that I couldn't answer. And it's not really true that he didn't know *anything*. Yes, it's true that he couldn't answer any questions. But he had memorized a lot of information. He just couldn't put it together to answer any questions."

Then I called Adam to find out exactly how he had pulled the rabbit out of the hat. "Adam, I need you to tell me exactly what you did to prepare for this test because they think you cheated." Adam replied, "They think I cheated? I'm so flattered they think I cheated!" Then he explained, "I changed the way I studied. I used to study for his tests the way I studied for my calculus tests. For my calculus tests, I would memorize the solutions to homework problems, and then when I saw a problem on the test, I would identify its type and carry out the steps I had memorized." But my colleague's tests couldn't be hacked that way. His tests featured only applications questions like, "You go into ACME labs and they give you a green solution and they tell you it's killing the men and not the women. What will you do to help?" Because those kinds of questions involve application of concepts, the concept mapping and other strategies I had introduced to Adam completely transformed his performance. But if he had had a fixed mindset, rather than a growth mindset, or believed that his Ds indicated inferior ability, Adam never would have been able to turn his performance around.

Once students understand that changing their behavior changes their results, they can switch from a fixed mindset to a growth mindset. Adam's case, along with the other less dramatic cases I have presented, argues strongly that we as faculty should also have a growth mindset.

Four Strategies for Changing Student Mindset

Here I offer four strategies that you can give to students to help change their mindset.

1. Inspire belief. Show students a miracle portfolio (a collection of "before" and "after" scores showing dramatic, rapid improvement). Use either your students' scores or scores from another professor's students.
2. Ask students to recall other challenges they have overcome. Share from your own experience.
3. Explain the neurobiogical basis of the growth mindset—namely, brain plasticity.
4. Help students achieve gradual, persistent growth. Do not give assignments designed to weed out weak students. Instead, give appropriate homework assignments that begin with manageable exercises and increase in difficulty.

Strategy #1: Inspire Belief.
Give Examples of Other Students Who Grew Their Intelligence

Over the past four chapters, I've told the stories of Dana, Travis, Joshua, and Adam. I've also worked with scores more students with results just as rapid and dramatic. When students learn about the success of others who were struggling just as much as or more than they are, it inspires them to believe that they can achieve more through effort.

Strategy #2: Ask Students to Recall Other Challenges
They Have Overcome. Share From Your Own Experience

Athletes and performers are particularly quick to understand the power of the strategies because they immediately see that, just as they have achieved mastery in athletics or performance through effort, they can do the same with intellectual pursuits.

To help other students make this connection, we can ask them to think of a skill that seemed impossible to them at first but became much easier over time. They can share their story with a partner, small group, or the rest of the class. Ask students to think of two examples: one where they improved significantly after only a short amount of time (less than 24 hours) due to a radical change in approach, and another for which improvement required a longer period of sustained effort (3–12 months). The first example relates to the fast-acting nature of metacognitive strategies, and the second example relates to the benefits of long-term implementation of the study cycle over multiple semesters.

Consider sharing a story from your own life to get the ball rolling. I like to tell students about my bowling. I used to be a terrible bowler. Seriously. Have you ever heard of anyone who has ever bowled a score of 0? Well, now you have. I had no idea what to do to get better. I recognized that the paths of my balls were curved, that I was a natural "hook bowler." But I considered myself in good company because I knew that most professionals were hook bowlers. After all, a good hook is more likely to result in a strike! But my ball would curve into one gutter and then into the other gutter when I over-compensated. Suffice it to say, hook bowling was not working for me. When my brother Bobby, a fantastic bowler who has rolled a perfect 300, came to town, he offered to help me with my game. We went to the lanes and got to work. After watching me bowl a few frames Bobby asked me if I used "the arrows." The arrows are marks on the lane that competent bowlers use to aim the ball; good bowlers aim the ball toward the arrows, not the pins. But I replied, "What arrows? What are you talking about? Do you mean the lane decorations?" Bobby put his head in his hands and said, "Oh, no, no, no . . ." Sure enough, once I began aiming my balls toward the arrows, my average jumped to 130. Over time, I even bowled scores of 170 and 180.

Discussing these stories gives students a personal connection to the concept of brain plasticity.

Strategy #3: Explain the Neurobiological Basis of the Growth Mindset

We know that the brain is changing all the time. These changes occur in a variety of ways (Kandel, Schwartz, Jessell, Siegelbaum, & Hudspeth, 2013). You may have learned that a synapse is the space between two neurons, or brain cells, across which communication between those two cells occurs. The brain can change via synaptic plasticity, whereby connections between particular synapses are strengthened or weakened through a number of processes. Changes also occur via synaptogenesis (creation of synapses), synaptic pruning (destruction of synapses), and neurogenesis (creation of new neurons). The brain also has the ability to functionally reorganize itself, depending on the stimuli available and the task required. For example, in the brains of deaf people, regions that usually process auditory stimuli have been shown to process visual stimuli instead (Karns, Dow, & Neville, 2012).

Explain these facts to students and help them infer that because their brains are ripe for change, they are masters of their academic fate.

Strategy #4: Help Students Achieve Gradual, Persistent Growth by Giving Appropriate Homework Assignments That Begin With Manageable Exercises and Increase in Difficulty

Consider a study inspired by Seligman and Maier's (1967) groundbreaking study of learned helplessness. Charisse L. Nixon (2007) divided her class into two groups and gave each group three anagrams to solve. The first group received an easy anagram (bat; solution, tab), a medium-difficulty anagram (lemon; solution, melon), and a tough anagram (cinerama; solution, american), in that order. The second group received two anagrams that were impossible to solve (whirl, slapstick), and a solvable tough anagram (cinerama), in that order. So the two groups received the same third anagram to solve.[1] Most students in the first group solved the third anagram but very few students in the second group solved it (Nixon, 2007). Nixon inferred that the second group suffered from learned helplessness. Even though their third anagram was solvable, their first two were impossible, leading most of the students in the second group to assume they could not solve it. On the other hand, the students in the first group, who had slowly been gaining confidence in their ability to solve anagrams, performed the task successfully.

This experiment demonstrates why a "sink or swim" approach can be so devastating to students. Even the ones who are capable of succeeding become convinced that failure is inevitable.

To convince your students that their behavior is much more important than how "smart" they are, give them assignments with appropriate gradations of difficulty to help them build their confidence.

Take-Home Message: Emphasize Action, Not Ability

Many of our students come to us with a fixed mindset. Most believe they are smart because they have always been told they are smart. When they arrive on campus and begin to make lackluster grades on tests, they think they're not smart anymore. In fact, I've heard more than one student say, "Well, maybe I was high school smart, but I'm not college smart." But we can say to them, "No, your grades are not based on how smart you are. They reflect your behavior and the actions you take. And I will teach you the strategies that will help you excel." Just hearing that inspires many students to make the effort required to succeed.

Many intellectuals roll their eyes at platitudes like "If you can see it, you can be it," or "Your attitude, not your aptitude, will determine your altitude." And I say, roll away! . . . as long as you understand that there are evidence-based scientific truths in these overused catchphrases. What you believe and what students believe both have a significant impact on their motivation and performance.

Joshua's Mindset Changed

Remember Joshua, the chemistry student who made 68, 50, and 50 on the first three tests but who scored 97 on his final exam? We've already seen an excerpt of an e-mail he wrote after he triumphed, but let's take a look at part of the first e-mail he sent, reaching out for help.

> Personally, I am not so good at chemistry and unfortunately at this point my grade for that class is reflecting exactly that. (Personal communication, April 6, 2011)

Do you see it? "I am not so good at chemistry" reflects a fixed mindset. But after the course, Joshua wrote,

> I think what I did different [*sic*] was make sidenotes in each chapter, and as I progressed into the next chapter I was able to refer to these notes. I would say that in chemistry, everything builds from the previous topic. (Personal communication, May 13, 2011)

Here, Joshua's language reflects a growth mindset. He attributes his improved performance to his behavior and the specific actions he took.

Next Up

In the next chapter we'll keep exploring the connection between learning and psychological factors—namely, motivation and emotion.

Note

1. Nixon indicated in personal communication (August 30, 2014) that she did not invent this task but discovered it in a social psychology resource.

7

CONNECTIONS BETWEEN MOTIVATION, EMOTIONS, AND LEARNING

"I'm so scared because I don't want to go home and I feel like this test just dropped my average in his class to a C. I really think I have test anxiety. It must be because I know that if I don't get a 4.0 this semester, I'll be going home." —
Marsha C., first-year graduate student on probation, now Dr. Marsha C., personal communication, May 5, 2008.

We have just seen how psychological factors can influence learning and performance. In the next three chapters, we explore these factors further. In this chapter, I lay out some basic information about motivation and emotions; in chapter 8, I give recommendations for steps that faculty can take to motivate students and make their learning pleasurable; and in chapter 9, I suggest steps that students can take to maximize their own motivation and learning.

What Is Motivation?

Ambrose, Bridges, DiPietro, Lovett, and Norman (2010) define *motivation* as "the personal investment an individual has in reaching a desired state or outcome" (p. 68). As such, "[s]tudents' motivation determines, directs, and sustains what they do to learn" (Ambrose et al., 2010, p. 5). Linda Nilson (2004) writes, "In the academy, the term 'motivating' means stimulating interest in a subject and, therefore, the desire to learn it" (p. 57).

Figure 7.1 Motivation Cycle

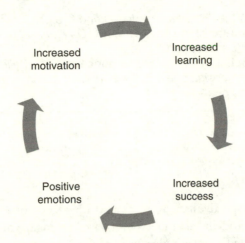

Why Is It Our Responsibility to Motivate Students? Shouldn't They Show Up on Campus Already Motivated to Learn?

As faculty, we must concern ourselves with student motivation because it so directly affects student learning. Consider Figure 7.1, a cycle involving motivation, learning, performance, and emotion. When students are motivated, they work hard to learn effectively, and as a result they perform well and feel good about themselves. To sustain this good feeling, students become motivated to continue putting in the effort to keep the cycle going.

What Influences Motivation?

Ambrose et al. (2010) define three important levers (Figure 7.2) that influence student motivation factor.

The first lever is value—what value does the student see in the goal? How important is it to the student to meet the goal? The second lever is the nature of the environment—how helpful is the learning environment? Extensive recommendations for creating a supportive environment are given in chapter 8. The third lever, one that greatly influences motivation, is belief in the ability to succeed—do students believe they are capable of executing a task? Ambrose et al. call these expectations "efficacy expectancies" (p. 80). If an individual is unsure whether performing a task will lead to a positive outcome, that person tends to be unmotivated. (How do *you* feel when you have to write a grant proposal? Or am I the only one?)

Figure 7.2 Three Levels Influencing Student Motivation

1. **Value**. *How important do I find this goal?*
2. **Nature of the environment**. *Do I feel supported or unsupported?*
3. **Belief in the ability to succeed**. *Do I believe I can design and follow a course of action to meet this goal?*

Note. Figure lists Ambrose et al.'s (2010) three important levers affecting student motivation. In order to feel motivated, students must find value in a goal, be in a supportive environment, and/or believe they can reach the goal.

From our perspective as faculty, many students do not appear to be motivated, but those students are indeed motivated to engage in many activities. They are motivated to play video games, send and read instant messages, participate in social media, party, and pursue any number of socially relevant or recreational goals. Why are they motivated to do those things? They see value in those goals, feel very supported by their peers to pursue them, and have confidence, borne of past experience, that they will be successful (Figure 7.2).

Why Must We Concern Ourselves With Students' Emotions? The Academy Is Not a Therapist's Office

Learning occurs in the brain. Emotions arise in the brain. Consequently, emotions can aid or disrupt learning. If we are interested in maximizing our students' learning, then it can't hurt to know a little something about the neurophysiology of learning and how we can positively or negatively impact our students' emotions. In short, fear and anxiety hinder motivation and learning, whereas confidence can increase motivation and learning.

A Pause for Some Neurophysiology

Although it is an oversimplification, it may be useful to think of the amygdala as the neurophysiological seat of emotion (Kandel et al., 2013). The amygdala is a structure found deep within what has come to be called the "lizard brain," the part of the brain comprising the brain stem, cerebellum, and basal ganglia.[1] Also in the lizard brain lies a structure called the hippocampus, which has been shown to play a role in forming explicit or declarative memories. These kinds of memories are consciously recallable memories pertaining to facts and knowledge rather than unconscious memories, like how to ride a bike (procedural memory) (Ullman, 2004). After rehearsal—or multiple instances of recalling particular declarative memories—the hippocampus plays a role in memory consolidation, or transporting declarative memories to other regions of the cerebral cortex. A crude way to think of it is that the hippocampus plays a role in moving information from short-term to long-term memory. When we are stressed, our adrenal glands produce a substance called cortisol. Because the hippocampus contains a large density of cortisol receptors, if there is too much cortisol around, the hippocampus can become overwhelmed and, over time, atrophy (Frodl & O'Keane, 2013). Kim, Lee, Han, and Packard (2001) produced evidence to support the idea that an amygdalar response is necessary for hippocampal impairment, and Phelps (2004) discusses at length the relationship between the amygdala and hippocampus. A coarse way to summarize the entire phenomenon is that stress, or cortisol production, can lead to short-term memory loss and impede long-term memory retrieval. In short, I may not want Freud in the classroom any more than you do, but science suggests to us that if we want our students to learn, we should do what we can to lessen their anxiety and point them toward stress-reduction practices they can undertake themselves.

The performers and athletes who visit my office instinctively know the power that anxiety or confidence can have on their artistic or athletic work, but more often than not, it hasn't occurred to them that the same principle holds for their academic performance. Explaining to students just some of the neurophysiology of anxiety and learning can open their eyes and inspire them to optimally manage their emotions, and therefore their motivation. Simple techniques like deep breathing or guided relaxation can help students decrease unhealthy levels of anxiety (see appendix B). Professionals at the campus mental health center can also teach your students these techniques.

"They Make Me Want to Tear My Hair Out!": Why Are Students So Difficult to Motivate?

Optimal learning requires a partnership between teachers and learners; similarly, behavior that increases or decreases student motivation can come from both faculty and students. Chapter 8 describes what faculty can do to increase student motivation, and chapter 9 describes how students can take matters into their own hands. In the following section, I lay out the obstacles to student success from each side of the partnership (Figures 7.3 and 7.4).

Student-Related Obstacles to High Student Motivation

These days, myriad demands compete for students' time and energy (Figure 7.3). Many students tend to work long hours and do not get enough

Figure 7.3 Student-Related Obstacles to High Student Motivation

- Students may work long hours.
- Students may have an attention-deficit disorder or related diagnoses.
- Students may be interested primarily in credentials.
- Students may feel As and Bs are their just rewards for consistent attendance.
- Students may not know how to manage their time.
- Students may have few learning skills.

Note. Figure lists reasons that today's students may be more difficult to motivate than students in the past.

rest or exercise, let alone proper nutrition. A great deal of students also lack time-management and learning skills, and an increasing proportion come to campus with diagnoses of attention deficit hyperactivity disorder or one or more learning disabilities. As a result, students often feel that they are working as hard as they can and so deserve good grades. Furthermore, many students pursue higher education primarily for credentials in order to secure better-paying, more professionally rewarding jobs. They do not yet believe that the value of earning a degree lies in fully absorbing the information presented in courses required by the degree.

Chapters 8 and 9 present several suggestions for you to share with students to address each of these obstacles.

Faculty-Related Obstacles to Student Motivation

A supportive learning environment is the second of Ambrose's three factors that influence student motivation (Figure 7.2). Figure 7.4 asserts that an unsupportive environment is the number one obstacle to student motivation that faculty have enormous power to change. In the next chapter, we investigate many ways that a student's learning environment can be helpful or harmful, but for now consider two major stumbling blocks—unclear faculty expectations and a faculty attitude that few students are likely to master very challenging course material.

When faculty's expectations of students are unclear, student motivation suffers. If a goal is unclear, students cannot effectively plan a course of action to meet that goal. In my experience, we as faculty are all over the map in terms of our expectations for students. Some of us ask our students to demonstrate very precise and accurate memorization of detailed facts; others of us look primarily for high-level mastery and creative application of concepts; and most of us fall somewhere in between those extremes. If

Figure 7.4 Faculty-Related Obstacles to Student Motivation

- The classroom environment is daunting or unsupportive.
- Faculty expectations are unclear.
- Students are paralyzed by a sink-or-swim course structure.

Note. Figure lists reasons for low student motivation that faculty have the power to change.

students are unaware of how these expectations change and shift across their course load, their performance may seem unrelated to their efforts. That disconnect can be very demotivating. Chapter 8 discusses how to be crystal clear about our expectations.

Eric Hobson (2001) studied sources of positive and negative motivation among a population of students at a college of pharmacy. He found that if faculty held the attitude that everybody in the course could learn and excel, then students were highly motivated. But if the students heard the equivalent of, "Look to your left, look to your right. Two of you are not going to be here in three weeks," then students became discouraged. The instructor's attitude, among six other factors, accounted for a full 27% of students' positive motivation and a whopping 32% of students' negative motivation (Hobson, 2001). I once knew of a professor who would tell his students on the first day of class, "I hope you've signed up for enough hours so that when you have to drop this class, you won't go under the minimum number of hours required to be a full-time student and lose your financial aid." This professor did not create a supportive learning environment or motivate most of his students to pursue success in his course. In fact, after hearing this statement on the first day of class, many students went straight to their adviser to drop the course.

Finally, recall that in chapter 6 we learned about a classroom application of Seligman and Maier's (1976) investigation of learned helplessness. When faculty give students assignments that are inappropriately challenging at the beginning of a course, students become convinced that they cannot handle even appropriate challenges. Demoralization becomes a self-fulfilling prophecy.

Sydnie's Story: The Power of Encouragement

I met Sydnie on September 23, 2013, the morning that I gave a presentation about metacognitive learning strategies to an honors-level general chemistry class at LSU. I arrived about an hour early, as I usually do, and there was Sydnie, alone in the classroom, sitting in the front row. She spotted me and brightly asked, "Are you going to teach us today?" (As you will discover in chapter 11, whenever I give presentations to classes, the students usually don't know that anyone other than the course instructor will be teaching that day. We keep it from the students so that they will not blow off class.)

"Yes!" I replied.

"What are you going to talk about?" she asked.

"I'm going to talk about learning strategies. How are you doing in this class?" I inquired.

Sydnie proudly reported, "Oh, I'm doing great! I did really well on the first exam. I made a 97.5, but I didn't think I had done that well." My attention sharpened. I knew that the test had 150 available points, so in a carefully positive tone, I said, "Oh! Well, the test had a total of 150 points, so do you know if you made 97.5 out of 150, or 97.5%?" After a sharp intake of breath, Sydnie said in a panicked tone, "I don't know. Let me check." In a flash, her laptop was open and her fingers began flying. I heard the clickety-clack of the keys as she checked the course website. All of a sudden I saw big tears begin to flow down Sydnie's cheeks. Immediately I reassured her, "No, no, don't get discouraged yet! We're going to talk about some things that will turn your chemistry grade around." Dejected, she said, "No, you don't understand. I made a D on my first calculus test too." I could see that she was beyond demoralized, so I said, "Don't worry about that either. We're going to talk about some ideas today that will help you make As on the next tests in both of those courses." Because I could see she was so distressed that she needed additional encouragement, I asked her to visit my office after class. During our meeting I didn't give her any additional learning strategies, but I did tell her that because I could see how motivated she was to use the strategies, I had complete confidence that she would ace her next tests. I let her know that I would be available if she needed any help at all. In that short meeting, I increased Sydnie's belief in herself by emphasizing that I had faith in her ability to excel, and I created a supportive learning environment. By the time she left my office she had acquired effective learning strategies as well as the motivation to use them!

Sydnie finished the semester with a 4.0 GPA (see Figure 7.5) and attributed her success to previewing, reviewing, and treating her homework assignments as assessment opportunities. She also earned a 4.0 GPA in her next semester and finished her first year in college with a perfect GPA despite having started with Ds on her first two undergraduate exams. Sydnie's grades attest to the power of encouragement, motivation, and metacognitive learning strategies to fuel the cycle depicted in Figure 7.1.

Figure 7.5 Sydnie's First-Semester Exam Scores

General chemistry: 65, **95, 90, 70, 96 (final)**
Calculus: 64, **100, 97, 96, 90, 93 (final)**

Note. Sydnie's dramatic turnaround at the beginning of her first semester demonstrates the power of encouragement, motivation, and learning strategies.

Boosting Motivation, Positive Emotions, and Learning: What Students and Faculty Can Do

The next chapter presents 21 strategies faculty can use to motivate students and increase their learning, and chapter 9 investigates students' responsibility to motivate themselves.

Note

1. The idea of a so-called triune brain (MacLean, 1990)—consisting of the reptilian complex (the so-called lizard brain), the paleomammalian complex (limbic system), and the neomammalian complex (cerebral neocortex)—is very popular, but it has its skeptics. They point out that the triune model is not supported by modern neuroanatomy. In particular, the limbic system, in MacLean's model, is supposed to be a nonreptilian part of the brain, but Bruce and Neary (1995) and Lanuza, Belekhova, Martinez-Marcos, Font, and Martinez-Garcia (1998) have presented evidence that reptiles also have a limbic system, based in part on the presence of reptilian basal ganglia.

8

WHAT FACULTY CAN DO TO BOOST MOTIVATION, POSITIVE EMOTIONS, AND LEARNING

"After I bombed the first exam in anatomy in medical school, I went to talk with the professor. He told me that he knew I could excel, but I just needed to change the way I was studying. When I found out that he believed I would succeed, and after he gave me the strategies to do so, it gave me the confidence and motivation I needed to do well in the course." —Dr. Eric Y., pediatrician, personal communication, September 13, 2011

In this chapter, I present 21 strategies that faculty can implement to boost their students' learning. The complete list appears at the end of the chapter, and the strategies are organized according to James P. Raffini's (1995) five bases of intrinsic motivation. Note that although the strategies were developed for use with pre-college students, I have applied his ideas to the undergraduate classroom and devised or adapted several strategies to address each of the five bases. Implementing only one of these strategies can make a difference for students, but please choose as many as you like. It's a buffet. Load up your plate, or choose selectively and strategically. Your students will benefit either way.

The assumption underlying all of these strategies is that you will explicitly, authentically, and regularly express your belief in your students' capabilities. I cannot underscore this point enough, partly because I know firsthand how difficult it is to grasp its importance. I had always thought students needed to bring their own motivation to a learning task in order to succeed. But I have been bowled over by the number of students who, when we first met, were completely unwilling to work, but who—as soon as I expressed support and belief in their abilities—became willing to do enormous amounts of work. I am not asking you to be a Pollyanna. In fact, research suggests that well-intentioned but badly aimed positivity or encouragement can have the opposite effect on student learning (Aguilar et al., 2014). But I am asking you to believe that your students are capable of feats of academic superheroism.

Tell Students How Their Brains Work and About Emotions and Mindset

Why not share some of the information presented in chapters 5 and 6 with your students? Tell them about plasticity, neurogenesis, and the effects of stress on the brain, and elicit from them implications for their behavior and expectations (**strategy #1**).

The following think-pair-share[1] may be a useful activity to use when implementing this strategy. Ask students, "Think of a subject/task/activity you think you are bad at. What evidence do you have that you are bad? How do you feel when someone asks you to perform this task?" Then ask, "Think of a subject/task/activity you have become very good at. What evidence do you have that you are good? What did you do to become skilled? How do you feel when someone asks you to perform this task?" After the exercise, you can help the students explicitly connect the dots between mindset, emotion, motivation, effort, and learning.

It's All In How You Say It!

Why does this strategy work? Recall my warning not to use the phrase "study skills" with students and my recommendation to instead introduce "metacognitive learning strategies." Whenever we use learning research terminology based in cognitive science to frame our recommendations, students have the experience of hearing it for the first time, and they find it fascinating. Moreover, they have an easier time seeing the difference between what we are suggesting and the study methods they are currently using. When we use more familiar words that they may have heard before, they are much more likely to go into "Charlie Brown" mode. All they hear, like Charlie, is "Wa-wa-womp-wa-womp."

Consider an analogy. We all know that if we want to become healthier, we should eat the right foods, eat appropriate portions, avoid mindless snacking on junk foods, and exercise. In fact, your eyes probably glazed over just reading that last sentence. But what if you heard, "Because you probably want to snack on chips and candy after a long, tiring day at work, try chewing a piece of gum until you can sit down to a healthy dinner." This advice is just another way of saying, "Avoid mindless snacking," but when I heard the advice for the first time, because it was framed as a specific, novel strategy, I found it much more helpful than the old, tired chestnut.

Similarly, I used to walk around in a state of perpetual dehydration without realizing it. But when I learned how much water the body needs (at least six glasses per day), and how dehydration affects the physiology of the brain, liver, and other vital organs, I became motivated to drink more water throughout the day. In both cases, in order to change my behavior I needed to hear something that (a) I didn't already know, (b) was easy for me to try, and (c) had a clear and sensible underlying rationale. We are trying to do the same for our students.

Three Strategies for Getting Started: Share Stories, Set Clear Expectations, and Encourage Big-Picture Thinking

You can create a supportive learning environment for your students by setting a clear, positive tone on the first day of class. I commonly recommend three ways to accomplish this goal.

First, share something from your personal life with students and let them see that you are human (**strategy #2**). Let them know that you like to enjoy yourself. One professor talks to her students about her love for horses on the first day of class. Because students so often think that we are omniscient automatons placed in their lives to make them feel inferior, why not share past academic struggles with them? Make it clear that you were not always the thinker and scholar that you are today and that you believe they can make a similar journey. Another professor I know shares with students that he flunked out of school his first time around and worked menial jobs before returning and succeeding with flying colors. His story lets students know that failing at a particular task does not mean you will never be successful at it. Moreover, students *want* to know that you have the same challenges that they do. Yet another professor I know courageously shares with students on the first day of class that he is always terrified when giving the first lecture to a new class. He says to his students, "I know I am going to get over my fear of lecturing because I get over it every year. And if you have any fear of what you'll be learning this semester, you'll get over it too." He tells me that his confession immediately relaxes his students and allows them to focus on learning.

Second, create your syllabus so that it makes the course structure and your expectations crystal clear (**strategy #3**).[2] Include in your course structure many opportunities for students to demonstrate competency. Recall

Eric Hobson's (2001) study where he measured the role of many factors in student motivation. He found that an instructor's attitude accounted for 27% of positive motivation and 32% of negative motivation, and that course structure accounted for 23% of positive motivation and 26% of negative motivation. In other words, if students' grades depended on only a midterm and a final exam, students were negatively motivated, but if there were many other opportunities to earn points—homework assignments, labs, quizzes—they were positively motivated. Indeed, among many factors affecting motivation, including course content, performance measures, and learning environment, Hobson found that the two most important factors were the *instructor's attitude* and the *course structure*. Together, those two factors accounted for approximately half (and sometimes more!) of a student's positive or negative motivation.

Third, tap into students' intrinsic motivation and begin building rapport among students by introducing a metacognitive get-acquainted activity on the first day of class (**strategy #4**). Arrange your students in small groups and have them answer the following three questions, the first of which was suggested by Simpson (2012):

1. What do you believe is important to understand and learn in [course name]?
2. What do you believe to be critical characteristics of successful students in [course name]?
3. How will you study and prepare for exams in [course name]?

These questions help students think about exactly what they need to do to succeed in the course, and the exercise will help you communicate your expectations to students, thereby enabling them to begin using metacognition to direct their learning.

You can make a big impact on student motivation by creating a positive atmosphere on the first day of class. Exploit every opportunity to help students independently engage with the learning process.

Raffini's Five Bases of Intrinsic Motivation

Raffini (1995), a professor of educational psychology whose research focuses on student motivation, wrote the incredibly useful text *150 Ways to Increase Intrinsic Motivation in the Classroom*. He compiled 50 research-based recommendations and 100 teacher-tested instructional strategies, which together make up his 150 suggestions. Raffini's book was written with K–12 classrooms in mind, but the strategies for high school students work very well for

Figure 8.1 Raffini's (1995) Five Bases of Intrinsic Motivation

- Autonomy
- Competence
- Belonging
- Self-esteem
- Involvement and enjoyment

Figure 8.2 Three Strategies for Enhancing Autonomy

- Allow students to choose paper, project, or discussion topics (Raffini, 1995).
- Do a weekly goal-setting exercise with your students.
- Discuss attribution with your students.

college students. I found his five bases of intrinsic motivation (Figure 8.1) so helpful as an organizing principle that I have grouped the remaining strategies under those five categories.

Essentially, the five components of intrinsic motivation mean that, if a person experiences sufficient autonomy, competence, belonging, self-esteem, and enjoyment, that person will be intrinsically motivated to carry out a task. We all want to control our own destiny, to excel at whatever we do, to be part of a group effort, to feel good about ourselves, and to take pleasure in what we do. Without any one of these things, our intrinsic motivation suffers.

Three Strategies for Enhancing Autonomy: Put the Students in the Driver's Seat

Figure 8.2 showcases three ways to give your students more control over their fate in your classroom.

First, whenever possible, let your students choose their paper, project, or discussion topics (**strategy #5**) (Raffini, 1995). In addition, you can do a weekly goal-setting exercise with them (**strategy #6**). At the beginning of the week, give them a few minutes to write down their studying and learning goals. Then, at the end of the week, give them a couple of minutes to evaluate their progress by writing a paragraph in response to the question, "How did you do this week in terms of meeting your goals for learning and studying?" Have them submit their reflections. You can choose to read them or not, but at least glance at them and give your students some course credit, perhaps bonus points, for submitting them.

Finally, explicitly discuss with students the concept of attribution (**strategy #7**). *Attribution* is a social psychology term that describes how we explain to ourselves the things we observe or experience. For example, when some students are asked why they received a low grade on an assignment or exam, they might give answers like, "It was too hard," "The things I studied weren't on the test," "The professor didn't like my topic," or "I wasn't smart enough to do better." Conversely, when these students are asked why they did well on a test or project, they might say, "I got lucky with the questions," or "The teacher gave everybody an A or a B." Whether they do well or badly, these students are attributing their results to factors they cannot control. These kinds of attributions are demotivating because the students feel subjected to the whims of fate. Another cohort of students might explain their results differently. If asked why they performed poorly, they might say, "I didn't study hard enough," "I didn't really pay attention in class," or "I was distracted by extracurricular activities the week before the due date." If asked why they performed well, these students might respond, "I worked my behind off for this test," "I used specific strategies to nail the material," or "I spent almost every afternoon in office hours or with the teaching assistant." Point out to your students that when they explain their successes or failures by blaming others or denigrating their abilities, they will be much less motivated to take action than if they account for their performance by looking at their own effort and actions. We have already discussed these ideas in chapter 3 in the student responses excerpted from Zhao et al. (2014). In that chapter, we saw that an introduction to metacognitive strategies helped students take more responsibility and become more autonomous. A discussion about attribution is also a great opportunity to introduce the importance of mindset (chapter 6).

Six Strategies for Enhancing Competence

The following six strategies will help you enhance your students' feelings of competence (Figure 8.3).

The first of these strategies recommends that you articulate your expectations clearly to students (**strategy #8**). If you assign reading to them, let them know that they should preview and use the reading strategies discussed in chapter 5. If you assign them homework, let them know you would like them to focus on the problem-solving process rather than the final answer. If you expect them to execute high-level application of concepts on your exams, then explicitly express that expectation. Moreover, assign homework that includes problems that increase incrementally in difficulty from reasonably

Figure 8.3 Six Strategies for Enhancing Competence

- Give clear expectations.
- Provide early opportunities for success.
- Test early and often.
- Use one class session to present metacognitive learning strategies.
- Do a 1–2-minute interactive activity for every 10–15 minutes of class.
- Provide targeted feedback, rubrics, and exemplars.

basic to the level they must be able to handle on your exams. We can decrease motivation if we assign homework that is not consistent with the learning goals we expect our students to meet. It is demoralizing for students to encounter a very difficult test after successfully completing relatively easy homework assignments.

Providing early opportunities for success is a second strategy to increase students' competence (**strategy #9**). Consider giving students an opportunity to earn points in the first week of class by submitting homework assignments, taking medium-difficulty quizzes, or giving an interesting class presentation on the topic of their choosing.

The third strategy— test early and often (**strategy #10**)— has proved so useful that I consider testing early virtually mandatory. But I learned to give my first test within the first 2 weeks because I recognized that students need a data point. They need to know what they've gotten themselves into. After they receive the results of their first exam, they'll be ready for the fourth of the six competence-enhancing strategies: one class session devoted to metacognitive learning strategies. Testing *often* provides students with opportunities to assess their learning frequently and to mitigate any particularly abysmal exam scores (Carey, 2014; Pennebaker et al., 2013; Roediger & Karpicke, 2006).

Testing *early* prepares students for the fourth strategy: a session about metacognitive learning strategies, Bloom's Taxonomy, and the study cycle (**strategy #11**). Chapter 11 gives detailed recommendations for how to present such a session to groups, but two guidelines are important enough to mention here. First, *present learning strategies to students only after they have received the results of their first test or quiz.* If you present a session about metacognition and learning strategies on the first day of class, most students will not listen because they won't believe that they need the information. It is better to wait until they've been bested by the first quiz or exam. Then they will be ready to change their behavior. Second, *do not let students know that you or a guest lecturer will be presenting metacognitive learning strategies.* Behave as if it will be a regular class session. Otherwise, many students will not come to class, even if they did not do well on the first exam. These students think they already know enough study skills and merely need to start studying a little sooner for the second exam than they did for the first.

A fifth strategy for enhancing competence: During class, give your students an opportunity to participate by taking a couple of minutes every 10–15 minutes to ask them a question or do an exercise like a think-pair-share (**strategy #12**). The human attention span is approximately 10 minutes (Medina, 2008), so if you lecture longer than that without an activity to reengage your students, many of them will be physiologically unable to absorb the information you present. These short breaks are perfect for asking students questions about the next topic you will introduce and for ferreting out common student misconceptions.

Consider Figure 8.4. Does the car shown in the photo have two doors or four doors?

The vehicle in Figure 8.4 is actually a car that I rented on a trip to New Mexico. Because there appeared to be no handles on the rear body panels, I assumed that it was either a two-door car or that the rear doors could be opened only from inside the vehicle. Only after about three hours did I realize that the rear door handles were in the upper right corner of the door. (If you look closely at Figure 8.4, you can see one of them.) My experience with

Figure 8.4 How Many Doors?

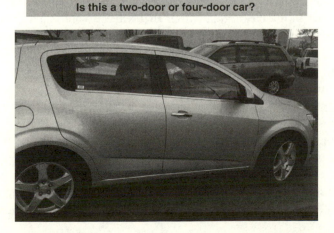

Is this a two-door or four-door car?

the car demonstrates how expectations can influence how we perceive and process new information. I expected the handles on rear doors to be in the same relative position as the handles on the front doors. These kinds of faulty expectations can affect our students' understanding of lectures. Remember Jonathan, the student who thought all gases were liquids because his car ran on liquid gas?

An undergraduate mathematics instructor once recounted to me how he taught a lesson about calculating the volume of three-dimensional rectangular solids, using a box as a prop. Throughout the entire lesson, one young woman, sitting in the front row, looked extremely confused. She came up to him after the lesson, very frustrated, and said with much consternation, "You keep talking about calculating the volume of this thing, but I don't hear a sound coming out of it." Because she believed that "volume" always meant sound amplitude, this student could not hear or digest any concepts the instructor taught during the lesson. But if the instructor had asked students to state in their own words what volume means, her misconception would have been immediately discovered and dispelled. If, every 10–15 minutes, you ask your students basic questions about the topic you will introduce, you can simultaneously reengage them and clear up any unhelpful misconceptions, so that they can absorb the material you present next.

Full disclosure: When I learned about this strategy, I did not implement it immediately because I did not believe I had the time to stop and engage students every 10–15 minutes. I had a semester's worth of chemistry to teach! I didn't have time for frivolous questions for them to ponder. I also didn't trust that my class would respond to my questions with useful information. I thought that I could explain anything better than those novices could, so why on earth would I ask them to stumble through their amateur explanations? My attitude changed when I took the plunge and started to hear from my students wonderful, clear explanations that I never would have dreamed up.

A sixth strategy to help your students gain competence is giving them targeted feedback, rubrics, and exemplars (**strategy #13**). This strategy is particularly appropriate for papers and projects. Give students very specific criticism and compliments. Let them know exactly why they received the grade they did. In addition to targeted feedback, many faculty in my workshops attest to the efficacy of rubrics,[3] which are guidelines and criteria for grading or scoring. Exemplars are also very helpful for students. If you give them examples of past papers or projects that received grades of A, C, and F, then they may be able to deduce the rubric themselves. You might even arrange students in groups of two or three to discuss and determine why each paper or project received its grade. When you had to write your first resume, cover letter, academic paper, or grant proposal, what did you want to look at first? An exemplar, I'd bet.

Three Strategies for Enhancing Belonging: We're All in This Together

I offer three strategies for encouraging a sense of belonging and relatedness among your students (Figure 8.5).

Aim to create a community of scholars where students hold each other accountable and genuinely care about each other's successes and failures. Ideally, in this community, the instructor and the students know that every student is capable of succeeding. Use the metacognitive get-acquainted activity (strategy #4), which I suggested as an activity to do with students on the first day of class, to begin to foster a sense of community.

You can extend this sense of belonging to the wider community by assigning your students authentic, real-world tasks (**strategy #14**). For example, a chemistry instructor might assign a project to explore how lead poisoning affects the local community by taking samples of paint from older houses and analyzing their lead content. A journalism instructor could ask students to cover local elections, union meetings, or other major events in the community. Students can gain a tremendous sense of usefulness and pride by working together and serving others. A third example: I myself have been surprised by the immediate and substantial increase in motivation that follows whenever I help chemistry students who are interested in entering the health professions understand how incorrect unit conversions can have fatal consequences. Students who could not be bothered to distinguish a fluid ounce from a cubic centimeter suddenly begin converting between those two units like pros.

Group learning is another great way to promote a sense of belonging among your students. Give students opportunities to work together by administering group quizzes or giving them problems to solve in small groups (**strategy #15**). When used judiciously, cooperative, team-based learning is powerful and effective[4] (Weimer, 2002).

Figure 8.5 Three Strategies for Enhancing Belonging

- Use metacognitive get-acquainted activities.
- Assign authentic, real-world projects.
- Promote cooperative (group) learning.

Figure 8.6 Four Strategies for Enhancing Self-Esteem

- Discuss mindset and emotions with students.
- Let your students know you are human; reveal your struggles in reaching your current level of mastery.
- Provide early opportunities for success.
- Do a reflection activity with students; ask them to reflect on how they have previously achieved mastery.

Four Strategies for Enhancing Self-Esteem: Help Your Students Get in Touch With Their Inner Achiever

We've already discussed many strategies that will boost students' self-esteem. When you discuss mindset and emotions (strategy #1), promote a growth mindset (strategy #2), challenge your students appropriately, and provide opportunities for early success (strategy #9), you help your students increase their sense of self-efficacy and self-worth. Here I discuss one more strategy to use in pursuit of that goal. All of the strategies to boost student self-esteem appear in Figure 8.6.

Toward the beginning of the semester, perhaps even on the first day of class, do a reflection activity with students (**strategy #16**). Ask them, "What's one thing you do very well? How did you get good at that activity?" Then ask them to reflect on the similarities between how they mastered that activity and how they can become very good at chemistry, math, philosophy, or whatever your course involves. Students who have experience as athletes or performers know that the most important thing they should do, if they want to improve, is to practice, to spend time on the activity they are trying to master. But many students do not make the connection to learning because, as we saw in chapter 1, they did not need to spend much time at all studying in high school.

Four Strategies for Enhancing Involvement and Enjoyment: Everybody Have Fun Tonight!

You can use the following four strategies throughout the semester to increase students' sense of enjoyment (Figure 8.7).

Connect to students' interests (Raffini, 1995). Find out what your students enjoy doing or what careers they are pursuing, and use examples in class that connect to those areas of interest (**strategy #17**). If you do not want to change your examples to match your students' interests, then think of how your current examples might relate to your students. Even if you connect your tried-and-true examples to only one of your students' interests, your

Figure 8.7 Four Strategies for Enhancing Involvement and Enjoyment

- Connect to students' interests (Raffini, 1995).
- Introduce "switch days," when students have the opportunity to teach and evaluate another student's teaching.
- Play learning games.
- Give students a question or task at the beginning of class that they will be required to answer or execute by the end of class.

class will still perk up and appreciate your attempt at relatedness. For example, before a discussion of sound waves, don't just refer to the students' collective interest in music; make a specific connection with the kid who always comes to class wearing his enormous headphones. (But always be kind, never sarcastic, when speaking to students.) Introducing a human element never fails.

You can also introduce "switch days," where you become the student, and your students do the teaching (**strategy #18**). At first students may find this a bit intimidating; polls show that only the fear of snakes is greater than the fear of public speaking (Doyle, 2009). But although public speaking is difficult for many people, role-playing can introduce enough fun into the mix to mitigate their fears. Furthermore, the students who are not teaching really enjoy seeing their classmates at the front of the class. A friend of mine who teaches undergraduate math in Alabama has Performance on the Spot (POTS) Days every Friday. His students know that on POTS Days, he might call on any student to come to the front of the class and explain a concept they have learned that week. My friend reports that his students really get into POTS Days and even come dressed professionally on Fridays (C. Eubanks, personal communication, August 5, 2008). As the student teacher teaches, other students also have opportunities to contribute. Knowing that the group is there to help if he or she gets stuck lessens the student teacher's anxiety and boosts confidence.

You can also give your students occasional opportunities to play learning games in class (**strategy #19**). Familiar games like *Jeopardy!* and *Who Wants to Be a Millionaire* are very well suited to some classrooms. Superteachertools.net provides free programs for teachers to set up these games in a way tailored to their course material.

Finally, consider giving students a question or task at the beginning of class that they will be required to answer or execute at the end of class (**strategy #20**). You can do this activity weekly, a few times a week, or every day. For example, you might tell students, "I'm going to ask you at the end of class to take a minute to write down in one sentence a summary of what you learned from today's lecture." You might also ask them to write down what they found most confusing or what they need clarified. Then collect the written answers at the end of class. Even if you discard them, the activity will still have helped focus students' attention during the lecture and increased their involvement. And if you have time to read the answers, you will be able to adjust your teaching accordingly. Thousands of instructors use this one-minute activity to engage students in learning (Angelo & Cross, 1993).

Bonus Strategy: Partner With Your Campus Learning Center, and Encourage Students to Go

If you work at an institution of higher education, you probably have a facility on your campus that provides the same kinds of services that are offered at the CAS at LSU. Get to know the people at your campus learning center so that when you encourage students to visit, you will know what strategies and resources the learning center professionals are encouraging your students to use (**strategy #21**). Additionally, you will learn how to better assist your students when they come to you for help with the course. Find out whether support is available from peer tutors or academic coaches so that students who have previously worked with tutors or coaches will be more motivated to visit the center. Elicit success stories from the learning experts that you can tell your students, to give them proof that the learning strategies are helpful and effective. They will sense your confidence in the center and will be more likely to go.

Some students resist visiting their campus learning center because they think it is only for students who are struggling. These students do not want to go for tutoring because, in high school, *they* were the tutors. They have a preconceived notion about who needs tutoring and who does not; consequently, it is very difficult for them to admit to themselves that they need to be on the other side of the tutoring table. So faculty must promote their campus learning centers. Your center probably has an online presence that will give you valuable information about its services and about other learning resources. See chapter 10 for extensive recommendations regarding how to partner with your campus learning center. (See also www.lsche .net.)

But I Don't Have Time to Do All That!

Neither do I! As I mentioned at the beginning of the chapter, I am not suggesting that you need to implement all 21 of these strategies. To begin with, choose one or two of the most powerful or the easiest, and continue experimenting from there. Keep track of what works best for you.

When I present strategies for faculty to use, the most common objection I hear is, "I already have too much stuff to cover. I can't afford to take the time to do extra activities." Yes, that is a position we can take. But isn't it truer that we can't afford *not* to do everything in our power to increase our students' learning? Faculty who do decide to use some of these strategies report that it takes some time at the beginning of the semester but then they end up moving faster toward the end. They absolutely do not sacrifice course content by spending time helping their students develop learning strategies.[5]

The Sweet Smell of Success

Let's hear endorsements from faculty who report that some of these strategies improved their students' performance. Here are the strategies that they say worked for them:

- Provide learning strategies information to students after the first exam, and tell them about mindset (psychology professor at Southern Crescent Technical College, personal communication, July 22, 2013)
- Increase the frequency of tests from three per semester to biweekly (mathematics professor at Miles College, personal communication, January 9, 2015)
- Have students determine their learning style and write a reflection on how they will use the information (entomology professor at LSU, personal communication, January 15, 2004)
- Present one 50-minute session on metacognition, Bloom's Taxonomy, and the study cycle (chemistry professor at East Tennessee State University, personal communication, May 22, 2012)
- Teach students how to read (chemistry professor at LSU, personal communication, July 15, 2004)
- Share a result from research about how people learn (biology professor at West Virginia University, personal communication, October 29, 2014)
- Do a short metacognition activity at the beginning of class (biology professor at West Virginia University, personal communication, October 29, 2014)

Figure 8.8 Twenty-One Strategies to Promote Optimal Learning

Enhancing Autonomy

- Allow students to choose paper, project, or discussion topics (**#5**).
- Do a weekly goal-setting exercise with your students (**#6**).
- Discuss attribution with your students (**#7**).

Enhancing Competence

- Give clear expectations, both with your syllabus and with particular assignments (**#3**, **#8**).
- Provide early opportunities for success (**#9**).
- Test early and often (**#10**).
- Use one class session to present metacognitive learning strategies (**#11**).
- Do a 1–2-minute interactive activity for every 10–15 minutes of class (**#12**).
- Provide targeted feedback, rubrics, and exemplars (**#13**).

Enhancing Belonging and Relatedness

- Use metacognitive get-acquainted activities (**#4**).
- Assign authentic, real-world projects (**#14**).
- Promote cooperative (group) learning (**#15**).

Enhancing Self-Esteem

- Discuss mindset and emotions with students (**#1**).
- Let your students know you are human; reveal your struggles in reaching your current level of mastery (**#2**).
- Provide early opportunities for success (**#9**).
- Do a reflection activity with students; ask them to reflect on how they have previously achieved mastery (**#16**).

Enhancing Involvement and Enjoyment

- Connect to students' interests (**#17**).
- Introduce "switch days," when students have the opportunity to teach and evaluate another student's teaching (**#18**).
- Play learning games (**#19**).
- Give students a question or task at the beginning of class that they will be required to answer or execute by the end of class (**#20**).

Bonus Strategy

- Partner with your campus learning center (see chapter 10) (**#21**).

Note. Figure is a comprehensive list of all of the strategies discussed in chapter 8, organized according to Raffini's (1995) five bases of intrinsic motivation.

In the next chapter, I discuss what students can do—in addition to the strategies presented in chapter 5—to enhance their motivation and learning. Figure 8.8 presents a comprehensive list of all the strategies discussed in this chapter.

Notes

1. A *think-pair-share* is an activity wherein students are asked to think about a reflection question, pair up with a partner or partners to discuss the question, and share their answers with the class.

2. There are excellent resources for creating an informative syllabus that communicates clearly what you expect from students. If your campus has a faculty development center, you can consult with someone who can help you craft one. (See www.cte.cornell.edu/teaching-ideas/designing-your-course/writing-a-syllabus.html)

3. Rubrics are guidelines and criteria for grading or scoring papers, projects, performances, or other assignments where students produce work that demonstrates their skills (Suskie, 2009). A rubric provides a list or chart that describes the criteria that will be used to evaluate and/or grade the completed assignment or project, and it provides guidelines for evaluating the criteria. Stevens and Levi's (2012) *Introduction to Rubrics* is an excellent guide for developing and using rubrics in a variety of course types. It is a great starting point for faculty who want to introduce rubrics in their courses, and the accompanying website provides useful sample rubrics and scoring guides.

4. When using cooperative learning to actively engage students, it is wise to follow certain guidelines so that students will gain maximum benefit from group work. Oakley, Felder, Brent, and Elhajj (2004) provide basic guidelines for forming effective teams for cooperative learning activities. For example, they suggest that instructors should form the teams, rather than let students choose their team members, and that the teams should have a range of ability levels. Additionally, policies and expectations should be formulated and a peer rating system implemented to ensure accountability. The authors also provide strategies for dealing with problem team members and provide answers to questions frequently asked by instructors implementing cooperative learning.

5. Michelle Withers, a biology professor at West Virginia University, offered these thoughts in response to the question, "How do you have time to teach learning strategies?":

> I think probably the real answer is that I make time. My entire first day of class is buy-in about the class format. Then I reinforce it throughout the semester by sprinkling the following into classes here and there, which doesn't eat up lots of time: (a) sharing a result from research on how people learn, or (b) doing a short learning/metacognition activity at the beginning of a class, or (c) doing occasional reflections on class activities to reinforce that I prioritize gaining a working knowledge of a concept or developing/practicing thinking and logic skills, above just knowing.
>
> Also, I've been doing active learning/reformed teaching for 10 years now so I don't wrestle with the content monster anymore. I know that I

can't cover everything (and even if I did they wouldn't remember it) so I focus on thinking skills and working understanding of fundamental concepts. That leaves me a little more time to put things like this in because I value them and realize that the class period that I took this past Tuesday, for example, to work on those top five missed exam questions will likely have a bigger impact on their learning than what I would have done that day. So, now I'll have to trim back a little on remaining topics, but they'll still be actively engaged on the fundamental concepts.

I had a really important teaching epiphany early in my career. It was very humbling, but very freeing. It actually happened at [LSU]. I was teaching intro biology to 1500 freshmen a year. My first year, when I got to protists, I basically taught the material in the book, because as a neurobiologist, I was well out of my area of specialty. It was *tons* of detailed info about the different evolutionary groups of protists (this was before I had any training in reformed pedagogies). Plus, having spent so much time on those details, I didn't hit fundamental concepts like the importance of the evolutionary transition from single-celled to multicelled organisms or from prokaryotes to eukaryotes. The next year, when I got ready to cover that topic again, I had to relearn the material. I realized that if I, the teacher, had to relearn it then my students got nothing out of it. It was incredibly humbling to know that teaching that material the way that I did had the same result on learning as not teaching it at all. That really frees a person up to focus on helping students build skills and conceptual frameworks and disciplinary habits of mind, that will then allow them to pick up any pieces of content they need for themselves when they need it. (personal communication, October 29, 2014)

9

WHAT STUDENTS CAN DO TO BOOST MOTIVATION, POSITIVE EMOTIONS, AND LEARNING

"Also as a verbal learner, I like to talk things out, meaning, usually if I can explain it to you, then I have a good understanding of the concept."
—Christopher H., psychology student at Southern Crescent Technical College, personal communication, September 22, 2014

This chapter lists six strategies that students can use to boost their own motivation and learning. In the first five strategies, we will see how students can shift their attitudes and explore how they can discover and exploit their learning style preferences. The final strategy pertains to rest, nutrition, exercise, and anxiety management, often neglected but important ingredients for student success. All of the strategies are listed in Figure 9.3. After absorbing the strategies, we will shift gears and discuss what to do about students for whom neither learning nor motivational strategies seem to work.

These Strategies Are for Students, but You Can Be the Conduit

Even though this chapter focuses on ways that students can increase their own motivation—and each strategy is directed to a student listener—I include them in a book for faculty because we can expose students to these strategies in class or during office hours.

Strategy #1: Use the Learning Strategies!

The bulk of students' efforts should go toward implementing the learning strategies presented in chapter 5. Recall the cycle depicted in Figure 7.1: Increased success leads to positive emotions, which, in turn, lead to increased motivation. In other words, academic success, brought about by implementing the learning strategies, is primary. This chapter describes how students can create a mental and emotional environment that will optimally support their learning efforts. It also discusses how students should choose among the strategies and specific study tools available to them.

Strategies #2, 3, and 4: Adopt a Growth Mindset, Monitor Self-Talk, and Attribute Results to Actions

Appendix B lists recommended books and websites for students, and Carol Dweck's (2006) book *Mindset* is near the top of the list. What about students who don't have extra time to read? They might encounter Dweck's ideas not from her book but from you or a teaching assistant, in class or during office hours. Additionally, you can recommend that they visit Dweck's website (www .mindsetonline.com) to discover more and take an online assessment of their own mindset. However it happens, students must be convinced that the most powerful influence on their grades is their behavior, not their innate intelligence or talent. Recall from chapter 8 that when students believe that success is possible, motivation increases.

Monitoring and adjusting self-talk is another great way to increase motivation. Self-talk comprises all of someone's thoughts directed toward him- or herself. For example, perhaps Bob is trying to give his car a tune-up and forgets to replace the oil cap before starting the engine. As a result, Bob makes a big mess. The thought that flies across Bob's mind might be, "Ugh! How could you have done something so colossally stupid?!" Or it might be, "Wow. I must be really tired. I remember when this happened to my good buddy Janet. We'll have a laugh about it later."

Self-talk constantly occupies students' (and everyone else's) minds. If the majority of those thoughts are negative and self-destructive, they can negatively impact students' learning efforts (Hirsch, 2001). Conversely, if their self-talk is compassionate and encouraging, it can make learning easier.

Suppose Suzanne studied very hard for her second exam in her Twentieth-Century Continental Philosophy course, but when the exam is returned to her, it is covered in red with "D" at the top. Suzanne might think, "No matter how hard I study, I'll never be good at this stuff. I must be so stupid." This response is extremely common. But a healthier, more robust response to failure is possible. As faculty, we want to encourage Suzanne to say to herself, "Wow! Well, I guess the methods and strategies I used for that test didn't work. My next assignment will be a great opportunity to try some new things that might work better." Cultivating a growth mindset and developing healthy self-talk go hand in hand.

Teach your students about self-talk and recommend that they simply pay attention to their self-talk, perhaps for a 24-hour period. During this observation period, they should not try to change anything; rather, they should just pay attention and maintain awareness. Then, once they've taken their self-talk temperature, they can begin to challenge one unhelpful thought out of 10. On hearing self-talk like, "I'll never get this stuff," the student might respond, "Never say never. I have new things I can try." Or the student might respond, "That guy David failed his first two tests and made an A on the third. Why not me?" Another response might be, "Yes, I will get this stuff if I pay attention now and keep using the strategies and putting in the time." Effective responses to negative self-talk usually embody a spirit of curiosity or gentle determination. Anything violent or punitive is probably coming from the place that produced the negative self-talk to begin with. Making self-talk more positive should not be an onerous, endless chore for students. It should happen gently and gradually so that students can maintain their new behavior.

In addition to their mindset and self-talk, students should examine how they explain their successes and failures. If I attribute my successes to plain dumb luck or Kelly's last-minute help and I attribute my failures to my inexorable stupidity, I will not be a confident, empowered learner. However, if I attribute both my successes and failures to my behavior, which I can control, then I will know what to do to maintain or increase my success and reverse my failures. Consider asking students why they did not do as well on an exam, paper, or project as they wanted to or thought they would.[1] During the ensuing discussion, encourage them to locate the answers in their behavior and attitudes, rather than external circumstances. Invite your students to metacognitively investigate their attribution theories and to consider the possibility that they hold the power to change their results by changing their behavior.

Strategy #5: Know Your Learning Style Preferences

Just like there are many different ways to teach—and goodness knows we as faculty all have our preferences—there are myriad ways to learn. We can set our students on the path to discovering optimal ways of learning by asking them to investigate their learning style preferences.

Our learning style preferences influence how we take in information from the outside world, how we process that information, how we interact with others, how motivated we are to learn a particular subject or skill, and how frustrated we may become while trying to learn that subject or skill.

I usually speak to my students about two different factors that may influence their learning style—their personality type and their sensory modality preferences.

Wait a Minute, Now. Haven't Learning Styles Been Thoroughly Debunked?

There have been recent studies that have failed to support the validity of learning styles (e.g., Pashler, McDaniel, Rohrer, & Bjork, 2008). That is part of the reason I refer to "learning style preferences" rather than "learning styles"—to communicate that no one is fixed in the way that they learn. However, although Pashler et al. (2008) describe the "lack of credible evidence" for learning styles as "striking and disturbing" (p. 117), they themselves admit that "it would be an error to conclude that all possible versions of learning styles have been tested and found wanting; many have not been tested at all" (p. 105). Richard Felder (2010), a professor of chemical engineering at North Carolina State University and codirector of the National Effective Teaching Institute, directly responds to Pashler et al. with the following:

> That study is not exactly groundbreaking. Every two years or so, some academic psychologists conduct a literature review and conclude that no research supports the use of learning styles in teaching, and journal reviewers and editors treat this conclusion as a new revelation that once and for all debunks learning styles. . . . Learning styles . . . are neither infallible guides to student behavior nor made-up constructs that have no basis in reality but simply useful descriptions of common behavior patterns. (p. 1)

Felder goes on to explain why it is not practically feasible to produce incontrovertible research supporting learning styles.

> Since the number of ways in which learning preferences may differ is unlimited, a theory that attempted to encompass most learning style dimensions would be too cumbersome to be of any practical use. A *learning styles* model specifies a small number of dimensions that collectively provide a good basis for designing effective instruction. Like all models . . . they are incomplete but potentially useful representations of reality. (p. 1)

Indeed, in my 43 years of teaching, I have seen students change their study tools according to their learning style preferences with great success. I assure you I am not alone.

But I myself did not always believe in the validity of learning style preferences. My first introduction to the idea of learning styles happened during the 1990s, when a colleague told me about a young woman in her class who declared that she needed to "be up and moving around to learn chemistry" because she was a "kinesthetic learner." I lowered my glasses, looked at my colleague with disbelief, and said, "Excuse me?" After I learned a tiny bit more about learning styles, I incorrectly concluded that I was expected, as an instructor, to know each of the individual styles of all of my students and tailor my instruction to all of those styles in every lecture! Preposterous. For years, my reaction to any talk of learning styles was, "I teach. You learn. That's the style in my classroom."

But when I got to LSU, the learning professionals at our center were using learning style preferences to great success. So I decided to give it a whirl. And what do you know? I found that my students flourished once they had greater awareness about what worked best for them.

I acknowledge that the benefit gained from knowing one's learning style might be partly due to a placebo effect, but here's the thing about placebos—they work. If a student's belief that he or she is a visual learner motivates that student to create effective concept maps, then that label is helpful. My motto is: Whatever works. The minute I hear about one example of a student whose performance was harmed by a balanced and reasonable discussion of learning styles, I will reconsider.

When you introduce learning style preferences to your students, be sure to let them know that learning style diagnostics are only an entry point and that discovering their learning style is a trial-and-error process. Therefore, they should try some study tool recommendations for *all* learning styles before settling on their choices.

Your students can find learning style diagnostics at a number of websites. One questionnaire we recommend is found at www.vark-learn.com/english/page.asp?p=questionnaire, on the VARK website of Neil Fleming, the researcher who originally introduced the sensory modalities that we teach at LSU.

At that site, Fleming suggests that there is little published evidence to support the notion of learning style preferences only because just *knowing* one's preference is not helpful. Rather, actively *using* learning strategies that match your preference(s), over time, leads to increased success. However, it is difficult to design an affordable, double-blind, controlled study for the effect of exploiting one's learning style preference(s) over time. Too many other factors are present as potential explanations for increased or decreased success whenever a student is studying and learning.

Strategy 5a: Take A Myers-Briggs Type Indicator Diagnostic

True confession time. When I first arrived on LSU's campus, I was encouraged by the learning center professionals to take the Myers-Briggs Type

Indicator (MBTI), which I understood to be a personality test. I thought to myself, "No, no, no, I don't need to do that. I'm a chemistry instructor. Molecules don't have personalities." But my colleagues were persistent, so finally I broke down and took the test. But I didn't pay too much attention to the results. For the next 2 years, all I remembered was that my results were something close to ESPN. Though I tried to keep my colleagues at bay with my trusty sense of humor, they continued to encourage me to investigate my results further. It wasn't until I started hearing about the MBTI in other venues that I said to myself, "Okay, let me see what this thing really is." As I read the implications of my results, I couldn't believe how illuminating it was. So many lightbulbs! . . . *That's* why I work better with Bill than with Bob. . . . *That's* what that look on Jane's face means after I've been talking nonstop for 10 minutes. . . . Oh, *that's* why it's a disaster whenever I ask those two people to work on a project together. . . . I immediately saw the usefulness of introducing students to the MBTI so that they could be armed with the practical knowledge I had just gained. You can direct your students to the campus career services center to find a version of the MBTI that they can take.

Katharine Cook Briggs and her daughter, Isabel Briggs Myers, developed the MBTI instrument, first published in 1962 and based on the work of Carl Jung (1921). The MBTI categorizes people according to four different personality areas. In my work, I most often talk about two of these areas: whether someone is an extravert (E) or an introvert (I) and whether someone is quick to make decisions (J) or prefers to cogitate and ruminate (P). For example, I am now E and J, although before I became an administrator, I was E and P.

Common stereotypes of extraverts and introverts portray extraverts as life-of-the-party types and introverts as shy, withdrawn, and joyless. But extraverts are simply people who draw energy from interactions with others, whereas introverts must expend energy when they spend time with others (Sellers, Dochen, & Hodges, 2005). Some extraverts might exhibit shyness, and some introverts might be the life of the party (and then retreat to a quiet place to regain their energy after the party). Here's the main difference between extraverts and introverts with implications for academia: Extraverts tend to think while they're talking, whereas introverts tend to think before they speak.

Consequently, in lecture, extraverts tend to be more participatory, raising their hands and answering questions, but introverts might be reluctant to talk about new ideas or concepts before they have had a chance to digest them. This difference can mean that as faculty, we unconsciously hold extraverts in higher regard than we do introverts. In fact, during workshops for faculty, I ask, "As instructors, who do we value more, extraverts or introverts?" The room always agrees that we prefer extraverts because they are the ones who tend to be most interactive. But introverts have a very rich thought life, and we can learn to identify them and gently coax them out of their shells. For example, we can ask for their opinions when it is obvious they have something to say but are reluctant to join the conversation. We might also announce that all students must participate, and we can avoid calling on enthusiastic students twice before everyone has had a chance to contribute. Additionally, if students know they are introverts, they can themselves take measures to compensate for their natural reluctance to speak before they fully understand.

Whether students are extraverts or introverts also bears upon their experiences with study groups, group projects, or any kind of group work. In groups, it usually happens that extraverts do most of the talking. Unchecked, the extraverts will hog all the discussion, whereas the introverts will have all sorts of wonderful ideas that they don't share because they are waiting for an opportunity to speak. Of course, because the extraverts are so chatty, that opportunity rarely or never comes. The introverts aren't talking, so the extraverts sit there thinking, "Why are these people even here? They're just like bumps on a log, not contributing anything!" Meanwhile, the introverts are thinking, "When are these people going to shut up so we can talk about the core issues underlying this project??" But if students know that any group is likely to have a mix of introverts and extraverts, one student can play referee and make sure that everybody gets a chance to speak. More importantly, though, the introverts and extraverts can learn not to judge each other so quickly and gain respect for each other's strengths. This training will also serve them well in the workplace and the wider world.

In addition to the introvert-extravert scale, I also like to explain the judging-perceiving scale. People who are categorized as judgers (Js) are not judgmental. That's not what Myers (1962) means by "judging." Rather, Js are quick to make decisions and finish tasks; they want to get it finished, get it checked off, git 'er done. Whatever they finish may not be their best work because their priority is to move on to the next thing. Conversely, people who are categorized as perceivers (Ps) constantly reflect on their work. They often wonder, "Is there something else I can do to make this better?" Ps are the people in the group who ask, "Well, what if we thought about it from this other angle or another perspective?"

Js need to realize that, in their haste to get something finished, it may not be their best work. They need to encourage themselves to take a little bit more time after they think they've finished to say, "Hmmm, is there any way I can make this better?" Ps need to understand that there is literally no end to making improvements. They need to encourage themselves to adhere to time limits, create time targets for different phases of a project, and learn to live with imperfect work. Ps and Js can learn a lot from working with each other: Js can learn how to do more thorough work, and Ps can learn how to submit work on time. As with introverts and extraverts, Js and Ps can learn to respect and understand each other, and they can bring those lessons into the rest of their lives.

Strategy 5b: Know Your Sensory Modality Preferences

Although learning styles have come under fire recently (Carey, 2010; Pashler et al., 2008), learning centers around the country still advise students to know their learning style preferences because they have witnessed firsthand how it positively impacts student learning. As I mentioned earlier in this chapter, even the naysayers concede that the lack of published evidence only means that studies meeting a high standard of proof have not been designed or carried out; it does not conclusively mean that learning style preferences are not helpful. Many learning experts believe they are.

Many learning centers use the system introduced by Fleming and Mills (1992), which introduces four modalities: visual, auditory, read/write, and kinesthetic. Together, they form the acronym VARK. Be aware that there are other learning styles models, such as the models of David Kolb (1984) or Gregorc and Butler (1984). Using an Internet search engine to investigate learning styles will yield a host of models. Learning center staff teach the VARK model because they have found it to be accessible and effective.

In addition to the four modalities in the acronym, Fleming and Mills (1992) also describe students who display a mixture of modality preferences, depending on what kind of task they are doing (VARK Type One). There are still other learners who are not satisfied until they have used *all* of their different preferred modalities (VARK Type Two). That is why it is so important that you advise students to try study tools from each of the categories, in each of the different contexts, before they decide what works for them.

The Four Modalities

Figure 9.1 describes the four modalities first introduced by Fleming and Mills (1992). When a student prefers the visual modality, that student learns best through visual representations, such as maps, pictures, symbols, charts, and graphs. For visual learners, a picture is indeed worth a thousand words. Be aware that visual learners do not benefit from just any old visual representation, such as words on a PowerPoint slide. As such, Fleming has suggested the visual modality might better be represented by the term *graphic* (www .vark-learn.com/english/page.asp?p=categories).

Figure 9.1 Fleming and Mills's (1992) VARK Learning Style Preferences

Visual
Prefers pictures, symbols, charts, graphs, and maps

Aural or Auditory
Prefers hearing lectures, reading notes out loud, and
participating in discussions

Read/Write
Prefers printed material, flashcards, notes, lists, and outlines

Kinesthetic
Prefers direct experience, experiments, fieldwork, visualizing,
or other ways of imagining

Aural or auditory learners prefer listening to lectures (live or via radio or podcast), reading their notes out loud to themselves, listening to and participating in discussions, and other ways of learning that involve listening or speaking.

Those with a read/write preference want to ingest information by looking at the printed word. These kinds of students prefer working with printed lecture notes, lists, outlines, flashcards, PowerPoint slides, text-heavy websites, and printed source material, like textbooks, papers, or essays.

Kinesthetic learners prefer direct experience. They benefit from lectures that involve demonstrations or case studies and assignments that involve solving real-world problems or doing lab work or fieldwork. Imagining themselves in situations relevant to the course material (e.g., traveling through the layers of the earth or the atmosphere) is helpful for kinesthetic learners.

Don't forget about the two types of multimodal learners. Remember, there are those who have different preferences depending on context and those who need input from all of their preferred modes. When you introduce learning style preferences to your students, be sure to explain that preferences are not hard and fast rules, nor are they limitations. Kinesthetic learners can still do very well in a class where information is delivered mostly in read/write modality because those learners can choose study tools that work for them. Notice that the learning strategies given in chapter 5 include something for all types of learners. Finally, students should not ever blindly believe the results of a questionnaire; they should decide on their preferences for specific study tools only after those tools have been proven to work for them *in a particular subject.*

Three Contexts:
What to Do in Class, While Studying, and During Exams

Table 9.1 is a great resource for students and gives recommendations for how learners of each preference should proceed in three different contexts: in class, while studying, and during exams. Across the rows, Table 9.1 is organized by modality preference; down the columns, it is organized according to setting.

The table is mostly self-explanatory, but I would like to unpack just one phrase. The recommendation to visual learners to "dump" formulas and diagrams on exams means that as soon as they receive the exam, they should write down all salient formulas and/or sketch all relevant diagrams or flow-charts that they have memorized. For more recommendations for specific study techniques organized according to learning preference, see www.vark-learn.com/english/page.asp?p=helpsheets.

Strategy #6: Rest, Nutrition, and Exercise. Good for the Body, Good for the Brain

Higher education is an environment where students are expected to push themselves past their limits. Consequently, students may save time by eating mostly fast foods, skimping on sleep, and diminishing extracurricular activity, like exercise and hobbies. But the brain is part of the body. Students should be encouraged to exercise regularly and maintain a minimum level of physical fitness—different for each student—to support their learning (Medina, 2008).

All-nighters may be necessary evils a couple of times per semester, but persistent sleep deprivation is one of the fastest ways to undermine a student's health and GPA. Some students might need only four hours a night, but some students need nine. Students should figure out the minimum amount of sleep they need and make sure to consistently get it. When students cannot get enough sleep or are feeling stressed out, simple techniques like deep breathing or guided relaxation have proven very effective in helping to decrease unhealthy levels of anxiety.

Nutrition is as important to the brain as oxygen and rest are. Doing an Internet search for "recipes for busy college students" will yield a plethora of quick and simple recipes that will keep students alert and fueled for success.

The Aim of Chapters 7 Through 9? Make Learning as Fun as Possible!

Over the course of the last three chapters, we have seen that faculty and students can work together to create an environment most conducive to student

Table 9.1 Different Learning Types in Different Contexts

Visual Learner *(prefers pictures, charts, diagrams, graphs, etc.)*		
In Class	*While Studying*	*During Exams*
• Underline important points • Highlight with different colors • Use symbols, charts, graphs	• Underline notes and text • Highlight notes and text (in color) • Summarize with images and concept maps	• Recall pictures • Draw concept map of essay • "Dump" formulas/diagrams

Aural or Auditory Learner *(prefers hearing information)*		
In Class	*While Studying*	*During Exams*
• Attend lectures, discussions and tutorials • Tape lecture for later	• Discuss material in study group • Summarize notes, then read out loud • Read onto tape, then listen back	• Listen to inner voice to recall information • Talk out question under breath

Reading/Writing Learner *(prefers reading or writing about information)*		
In Class	*While Studying*	*During Exams*
• Create lists and headings • Take complete lecture notes	• Identify key words and associate them with details • Reread notes and text and summarize them in writing • Reread and summarize old tests • Answer (in writing) the review questions	• Use key words to trigger more complete answers • At the beginning of the exam, write out important lists • Essay—write thesis, then outline

Kinesthetic Learner *(prefers moving, touching, visualizing movement, or hands-on activities to learn information)*		
In Class	*While Studying*	*During Exams*
• Use all senses in class • Participate in labs and field trips	• Trial and error is important—can learn from mistakes • Create personal examples • Use pictures to illustrate notes • Stand, move, walk • Study in an exam-like environment	• Remember examples • Stretch or move to jog memory

Note. Table gives specific recommendations for learners of each of the four preferences in three settings: in class, while studying, and during exams. This table is an adaptation of the work of LSU's CAS, in turn adapted from *College Learning and Study Skills*, by D.G. Longman and R.H. Atkinson (1996). For more recommendations, see www.vark-learn.com/english/page.asp?p=helpsheets

Figure 9.2 Six Strategies for Students to Increase Motivation

- Use the learning strategies.
- Cultivate a mindset that your intelligence can grow.
- Engage in positive, healthy self-talk.
- Attribute positive and negative results to your behavior, not external circumstances.
- Know your MBTI profile and your learning style preference(s).
- Get adequate rest, nutrition, and exercise.

success. By taking the specific steps to maximize motivation and positive emotions given in Figures 8.8 and 9.2, faculty and students can make the learning experience optimally efficient and pleasurable!

Know When to Hold 'Em and When to Fold 'Em

In this final section of the chapter, we discuss three categories of students for whom I have found introducing metacognitive and motivational strategies may not work. We explore how to respond to those students.

It's Not My Fault!

I have encountered students who, even after being introduced to metacognitive strategies, mindset, and attribution theory, still refuse to take personal responsibility for anything. You may still be able to reach these students by persistently engaging them in discussion about why they are not seeing the results they want and how others have managed to overcome equally arduous obstacles by taking responsibility for their behavior.

Workin' 9 to 5 Ain't No Way to Make a 4.0

There are students who are employed for so many hours, are taking so many credits, and have so many other responsibilities that they do not have time to use any of the strategies. For example, a student with three children who is working 40 hours a week and taking 21 credit hours has set himself up for failure. Suggest to overworked students that they should either take fewer hours or cut back on their work hours if they can. If they protest that they cannot make it work financially, explain to them how expensive it will be to fail their courses. Convince these students that it is not possible to do everything they're trying to do *and* enjoy academic success. Often it is not difficult to get these kinds of students to see a different perspective and agree to cut back.

Slow and Steady Wins the Race

For some students, there is just too big a gap between the skills required to succeed in a particular course and the skills that they currently have. For example, if students know nothing about fractions, decimals, or percentages, they will likely not succeed in general chemistry. These students should take a preparatory course and return to the more advanced course later. If students protest that it will delay their graduation, counter that failing their courses will also delay it.

The Bottom Line: Noncognitive Factors Are Crucial

In the previous three chapters, we have discussed a range of influences that can affect learning much more powerfully than any purely cognitive factors. I hope that you and your students will take the myriad suggestions presented in chapters 7 through 9 to heart so that learning and teaching are maximally pleasurable and effective for all.

Note

1. Exam wrappers, a reflection activity students can do after receiving their graded exams, ask students to think about how they prepared for the exam, determine the types and causes of the mistakes they made, and explain how they will prepare differently for the next exam (Lovett, 2013). This activity ensures that students will engage metacognitively with returned tests.

10

PARTNERING WITH YOUR CAMPUS LEARNING CENTER

"I never had problems making good grades in high school, but I really struggled with adapting to college my first semester and started off with a 1.5 GPA. I was skeptical about going to a consultation [at the CAS] but decided it was worth a try. It turns out that [the consultant] really wanted to help me do better and gave me little tips that made a big difference in my study habits. I definitely think going to CAS and having a consultation had a major impact on my getting a 3.8 this semester!" —First-year student at LSU, survey comments.

In this chapter, I discuss not only what transpires at your campus learning center but also tips and techniques in the areas of time management, test preparation, and test taking. Toward the end of the chapter I also present suggestions for how faculty can partner with their campus learning centers to optimally promote meaningful learning.

Your Campus Learning Center: Just for Struggling Students?

"Do I know what the learning center does? You mean the place I send my struggling students? Um, no, I guess I don't really know exactly what goes on there."

When I visit campuses, I often ask faculty if they are familiar with the services provided by their campus learning center. Faculty usually respond, "Oh, sure. That's where I send students who are struggling so they can get tutoring." Even though many faculty know what their campus *teaching* center has to offer—because they attend professional development events for faculty there—they are unfamiliar with the range of services provided by the *learning* center.

Although it's true that learning centers do provide tutoring for students with lackluster grades, all students could derive tremendous benefit from a visit to the learning center. Most learning centers provide so much more than tutoring. For example, the learning center at LSU works with top-notch students who want to improve their learning efficiency, graduate students who want to increase their comprehension and speed when reading research articles, and members of undergraduate honor societies who want to get a head start on acquiring advanced skills for graduate school. Learning center professionals can impact learning at both ends of the performance spectrum, and at all levels in between.

And that's just what learning centers can do for *students*. Many learning centers also work with faculty to present learning strategies to their classes and to help faculty develop approaches for delivering strategies to students themselves. With the help of learning center professionals, faculty can learn to readily serve as a resource for students who may be struggling instead of just sending them to that mysterious black box called the learning center. In other words, when you partner with the campus learning center, you will learn valuable, impactful information to share with your students, and you will feel comfortable directing most of them, not just the weaker ones, to the center in order to enhance and optimize their learning.

Okay, but What Exactly Goes On at the Learning Center?

There are more than 1,500 learning centers in the nation's colleges and universities, operating in two- and four-year colleges, major research universities, and graduate and professional schools. What exactly do these centers do?

One of their most important tasks is to provide learning strategies, like the ones presented in previous chapters, via workshops and individual consultations. But learning center professionals also teach students (and faculty) simple, supplemental tips and techniques that help to improve learning.

Before I present a smorgasbord of these suggestions, let me alert you that they will seem very simple to you, and you may doubt that such simple tactics will improve student learning. Remember, no one was more surprised than I upon seeing students follow these simple suggestions and turn their performance around literally overnight! These techniques pertain to time management, test preparation, and test taking.

As Time Goes By: Time Management Tips

Implementing effective learning strategies requires that students invest the necessary time. Because many students these days spend excessive time on unproductive activities, like social media and gaming, simple time management strategies can help them use their time optimally. Even students without an Instagram addiction often need guidance regarding time management because their high school experience has taught them that they need only 6–10 hours a week to do well in all of their classes. These students are used to loading up their schedules with extracurricular activities like sports, student government, performing opportunities, and community service. Because college classes move at a faster pace and require more intellectual independence, these students often fall behind and perform poorly on their first college tests. Then they become paralyzed, and unfortunately it's all downhill from there.

Time Management Tip 1:
Keep A Semester Calendar Showing Major Events

Many of you may have heard this illustration before: Imagine you have a big bucket, and your task is to fill it with some water, some smaller rocks, some big rocks, and some sand, not necessarily in that order. In what order would you place the items in the bucket? Many people respond that they would put in the big rocks first, followed by the smaller rocks, the sand, and the water. That makes sense, right? The biggest and most unwieldy things go first, and the most flexible, maneuverable thing goes last.

So it is with time management. Students must make sure their schedules can accommodate major projects and tasks before scheduling lower-priority obligations. But how can students know which major events and projects to prioritize? They need an overall big picture. For time management success, students should create a semester calendar that shows all 16–20 weeks of the term on one page. Think of it as Semester-at-a-Glance. (Helpful templates for semester-at-a-glance and week-at-a-glance calendars can be found at www.lsu.edu/cas by clicking on "Manage Time.") Students should then use their course syllabi to enter all major tests, quizzes, papers, projects, and social events on this calendar. Figure 10.1 shows one section of an example of such a calendar. You can see that this student has a major physics exam the Monday after a big anniversary celebration for her parents. Moreover, the celebration occurs after a week packed with projects. Accordingly she will need to start studying for that physics exam two weeks before the exam date. The semester calendar can and should be updated as more information arrives.

Time Management Tip 2:
Keep a Weekly Calendar With All Scheduled Activities

Once students have a semester calendar showing the big picture, they can use a weekly calendar to get specific and schedule their time on an hourly basis.

Figure 10.1 Section of a Semester-at-a-Glance Calendar

Week	MON	TUE	WED	THU	FRI	SAT	SUN
. . .	. . .	. . .	. . .	. . .	. . .	. . .	. . .
Week 3		Calculus quiz	Lit. presentation		Figure drawing project	Parents' 40th anniv!!!	Parents' 40th anniv!!!
Week 4	Physics exam			German exam		Billy's concert	
Week 5	Calculus exam			Lit. quiz			
Week 6		Physics quiz			German quiz	NYC!!	NYC!!
. . .	. . .	. . .	. . .	. . .	. . .	. . .	. . .

Note. For effective time management, students should keep one master calendar showing all of the weeks of the semester on one page. This figure displays a section of such a calendar, showing four weeks early in the semester, in the life of this first-year physics major.

Students should include classes, work, extracurricular activities, social time, intense study sessions, grocery shopping, laundry, and sleep time on their weekly schedule. See Figure 10.2 for an example of a weekly calendar. This student is carrying 12 credit hours, a full load. You can see that he has scheduled sufficient study time for all four of his classes without sacrificing a weekly hangout with his buddies and seven hours of sleep nightly. Of course, this schedule may be a walk in the park compared to the course loads and work schedules that some of our students contend with. No matter how heavy the load, however, organizational tools like these will promote greater success.

Time Management Tip 3: Learn to Say You Have an Appointment

Once students have filled out their weekly calendars, there may be blocks of free time. Students should learn to think of that time as booked, too. During those hours, they "have an appointment with themselves."

Consider the following scenario: Angela, a first-semester freshman in the College of Music, has just filled out her weekly calendar. Her dear friend from high school Max runs into her and says with a huge grin on his face, "Angela! What are you doing Sunday at 3:00 p.m.?" Angela looks at her schedule; there's nothing there for Sunday at 3:00 p.m., so she says, "Nothing. Why?" Max responds, "Oh, I'm dying to go look at some rare wildlife on the lake across town!" Now, Angela doesn't want to go watch ducks, but she also doesn't want to disappoint her friend, and she's already told him she's free.

Figure 10.2 Week-at-a-Glance Calendar

Hours	MON	TUE	WED	THU	FRI	SAT	SUN
7–8 a.m.	Breakfast	Gym	Breakfast	Sleep	Gym	Sleep	Sleep
8–9 a.m.	ISS French	Gym	Groceries	Breakfast	Gym	Sleep	Sleep
9–10 a.m.		Breakfast	Stat preview	ISS GM	Breakfast	ISS French	Breakfast
10–11 a.m.	Statistics		Statistics	ISS French	Statistics		
11 a.m.–12 p.m.	Stat review / Econ preview	French preview	Stat review / Econ preview	French preview	Stat review	ISS Stat	Stud. Gov't
12–1 p.m.	Lunch	French	Lunch	French	Lunch	ISS Econ	Stud. Gov't
1–2 p.m.	ISS Stat	French	ISS GM	French	ISS Econ	Lunch	Stud. Gov't
2–3 p.m.	ISS Stat	French review, ISS	ISS Econ	French review/ lunch	ISS Econ	Lunch	
3–4 p.m.	Economics	Lunch	Economics	Lunch	Economics	ISS GM	ISS Econ
4–5 p.m.	Econ review	ISS GM	Dinner	ISS GM	Dinner	Relax	ISS Stat
5–6 p.m.	Dinner	Global Marketing	Dinner	Global Marketing	Dinner	Relax	Dinner
6–7 p.m.	Dinner	Dinner	ISS French	Snack	Friends & Family	Hangout	Dinner
7–8 p.m.	ISS Econ	Dinner	ISS Stat	Soccer	Friends & Family	Hangout	Movie
8–9 p.m.	ISS GM	ISS French	ISS GM	Soccer	ISS French	Hangout	Movie
9–10 p.m.	Friends & Family	ISS Stat	Friends & Family	Dinner	ISS GM	Hangout	Movie
10–11 p.m.	Laundry	Friends & Family	Wind down	Dinner	Wind down	Hangout	Wind down
11 p.m.–12 a.m.	Wind down	Wind down	Wind down	Wind down	Wind down	Hangout	Wind down

Econ = Economics, GM = Global Marketing, ISS = Intense Study Session, Stat = Statistics

Note. Figure displays a weekly calendar for a hypothetical economics major. This student has scheduled time for his classes, extracurricular activities, errands, and friends and family, and he still comfortably has time for 26 hours of intense study sessions per week.

Unless Angela has strong boundaries, she might end up at the lake instead of studying for an important advanced theory exam or engaging in an activity she truly enjoys. Let's rewind this scenario and see how it might go after Angela learns tip 3:

> "Angela! What are you doing Sunday at 3:00 p.m.?"
> "Oh, I have an appointment. Why do you ask?"
> "Well, I wanted to go watch wildlife across town with you."
> "I'm so sorry, Max. I've got a prior obligation."

Angela has effectively protected her time, and Max is not offended. Win-win. But let's say Max had free tickets to *Phantom of the Opera* instead of an offer to ogle mallards. Angela could easily tell him that she'll reschedule her appointment. This approach enables students to protect their time and to use it in the most efficient and enjoyable ways possible.

Time Management Tip 4:
Start Homework Assignments as Soon as They Are Given

In high school, most students learn that they do not need to think about homework until the due date is approaching. But the campus learning center encourages students to begin homework as soon as it is assigned and to do it in increments each day. This way, students will have time to apply the homework strategies and engage deeply with the material.

In my individual consultations with students, there comes a time when I ask, "When do you usually begin your homework?" You will not be surprised to hear that they usually say, "I start my homework the day before it's due."

"When you start the day before, what is your main goal?" I ask.

"To get it finished," comes the predictable response.

I call that being in "git-'er-done mode." I explain to students that if they're in git-'er-done mode, they are not going to be able to make themselves approach the homework meaningfully because it does take time to apply the learning strategies. I explain to undergraduate and graduate students that they must begin their homework the day it is assigned and do the problems two or three at a time, completing about a fifth of the problems each day. If they do their homework in this way, students give themselves the time they need to discover and apply the problem-solving strategies that work best for them.

In fact, in my fall 2010 general chemistry class at LSU, I performed a survey after the first exam. When I asked the students who earned As, "What did you do?" many of them reported that they began the homework the day it was assigned and did a few problems at a time. When I asked the students who made Ds and Fs, "What do you wish you had done?" many responded that they had started the homework too late and wished they had begun it sooner.

When I'm working one-on-one or talking to groups of students, I tell them, "If you start the homework too late, you won't be able to absorb the material because your brain is saying, 'We don't have time to figure this stuff out!'" Students need to understand that they are preparing for their next exam each and every day, using homework assignments and other self-assigned tasks as tools. The semester calendar and weekly calendar help students appropriately focus their efforts. If a student looks at the calendar at the beginning of the semester and sees that her first economics exam is two to three weeks later, she can set out a study schedule for that exam, spend adequate time on homework assignments, and stay on track.

Keep in mind that small chunks of time are just as useful as big chunks where homework is concerned. Consider another lesson that we can learn from the story about filling our time bucket with large rocks, smaller rocks, sand, and water: No matter how many rocks or how much sand we've packed in, there are likely still pockets of air here and there for the water to fill. Five or 10 minutes is enough time to learn the conjugation of an important verb in a difficult tense, for example.

Time Management Tip 5:
Prioritize According to Your Needs and Wants

Once students have their semester and weekly calendars and they have learned to protect their time, the only thing left is to put first things first. Invariably we schedule more than we can actually accomplish, so the time will come when the student will have to decide: Do I go grocery shopping or do a fourth intense study session? Do I go hang out with my buddies or try to go to sleep early? The right answers to these questions are not at all obvious. Students must get to know themselves, to understand when it's better to push through and keep working and when they'd be better off blowing off steam or catching a nap. As they figure out their own needs, they will make mistakes and need to forgive themselves. Once students have time management tools, remind them that optimizing time management is a lifelong process for all of us and that every step we take has tangible future benefits.

Time Management Tips Roundup

In sum, your campus learning center probably advises students to:

- Keep a semester calendar (Figure 10.1).
- Keep a weekly calendar that includes activities (Figure 10.2).
- Commit to at least 20 to 25 hours of study time each week, utilizing intense study sessions (Figure 10.2).

- Guard precious free time with your life.
- Start homework as early as possible.
- Prioritize according to your needs and wants.

Super Exam Preparation Tips

Your campus learning center also probably advises many students how to prepare for exams. Many students think that preparing for a test means memorizing information the night before or rereading the information until their brain convinces them, "I got it!" when that's just wishful thinking. The idea that test preparation begins from day one of class is foreign to most students. Test preparation workshops provided by learning centers usually emphasize the following strategies:

- Use effective learning strategies from day one.
- Determine exactly what the test will cover, and practice teaching that information to an audience—either real or imaginary—until you can do it flawlessly.
- Determine what types of questions will be asked. Preparing for a multiple-choice test is different from preparing for an essay test. If you might have to answer an essay question about the precipitating events of World War II, practice writing that essay. If you know you could be asked to solve three different types of Fourier transform problems, spend time mastering each type.
- Organize the information by preparing charts, outlines, or a study guide.
- Set aside specific time to prepare for the test.
- Make up a practice test from information in your notes and the textbook.
- Visit websites like howtostudy.org or do an Internet search for "test preparation strategies" for many more strategies.

In the Testing Room: What to Do on Test Day

I have seen many examples of students who were well prepared for a test, but who performed poorly because they did not have or failed to utilize test-taking skills. Some of the most effective strategies that learning centers often teach are:

- Write down formulas you may need on the exam before you begin.
- Read the directions *very* carefully, listen for additional directions, and ask for clarification.

- Survey the exam and budget your time.
- Begin with the easiest questions and work your way to the harder ones. This will build confidence and bring more information to your mind.
- Expect memory blocks and recognize that the information will come back to you if you move on to other questions.
- Perform deep breathing exercises to relax; use positive self-talk.
- Remain confident that if you have prepared well, you will do well.
- Visit websites on effective test-taking strategies for more tips and tools.

What to Do After the Test Is Returned

Most students don't realize how much valuable information their returned tests contain. When students get a test back, they typically put it out of sight, especially if the grade is lower than they anticipated. But campus learning centers teach students how to analyze all of their returned tests and quizzes, reflect on what they missed and why, and develop a plan for improvement. Reflecting on what went wrong and implementing a strategy to prevent future errors guarantee improvement in any area.

Just the Tip of the Iceberg:
Your Campus Learning Center Is a Vast Resource

In addition to addressing the topics presented in this chapter, learning centers often work with students to improve their general organizational skills, manage stress, and avoid procrastination. Moreover, many learning centers employ professionals specifically devoted to helping students improve their writing. Most centers also provide tutoring and peer-led study group sessions for students. Your campus learning center probably offers a vast array of services. You can tell students it's like free money. Why not spend it?

Let's Get Together:
When Learning Centers and Teaching Centers Collaborate

In 1995 Barr and Tagg wrote a seminal article, "From Teaching to Learning: A New Paradigm for Undergraduate Education." After it appeared in the November/December issue of *Change* magazine, it set off a shockwave in higher education, and institutions began shifting their focus from a paradigm of instruction to a paradigm of learning. In other words, instead of asking, "What should we be teaching students?" institutions began to investigate and answer the two-part question, "What should our students be learning, and how do we help them learn it?" Once that shift began, learning centers were held in higher esteem. Faculty and administrators also began to give teaching centers more importance. Teaching centers are typically associated with faculty professional development rather than student learning. These are places faculty can go to learn about techniques like problem-based learning, service-learning, cooperative learning, and many other methods that have been shown to increase student learning.[1]

Teaching centers are most often housed with academic affairs units, while learning centers are often housed with student affairs units. I have often found that even faculty who are very familiar with the teaching center, having regularly attended workshops there, are woefully ignorant of the menu of services provided by the learning center. Just imagine how much more successful each center could be if they collaborated and shared expertise and offerings.

Here are a few suggestions for successful partnership between teaching and learning centers on campus.

- The campus teaching center could invite learning center professionals to give a workshop to faculty about learning strategies for students. (The campus teaching center usually offers workshops designed to improve teaching, so switching the focus to student learning could be refreshing and effective.)
- During workshops held for faculty, the instructors and tutors in the learning center could introduce faculty to the types of learning problems that they help students overcome.
- During meetings with learning center staff, faculty could help the staff understand the types of learning outcomes that their students need to achieve. For example, let's say that in a first-year history course, 60% of students are getting a D, failing, or withdrawing. The university may invite the learning center to try to help, but unless the learning center professionals know exactly what faculty want students to know, understand, and be able to do, learning center staff may not be able to help much. These workshops would solve that problem.

The list could go on and on. When faculty and learning center professionals work together, students reap significant benefits.

An Example of Collaboration: The Absent Professor Program

The LSU CAS participates in a collaboration with Career Services called the Absent Professor Program. Career Services started the program and invited the CAS to join during its second year. Here's how it works. If an instructor has to miss a class for any reason, whether an emergency, a doctor's appointment, or a scheduled trip to a professional conference, then instead of cancelling class, the professor can request that a learning center professional take over her class and spend the time teaching learning strategies. When we initiated the program, student response was extremely positive. In fact, so many students reported that they found sessions with the learning center professionals helpful that faculty began inviting us to take over their class sessions whether or not they were called away! Moreover, if faculty were present during the session, then at the end, after thanking the learning center professional, the instructor would often exclaim, "I wish I had known this when I was in college!"

For our efforts, the LSU CAS won the 2000 Bright Idea award for the Absent Professor Program from the Professional and Organizational Development Network, the national organization for faculty development professionals.

Use Your Campus Learning Center: The Professionals There Would Love to Be of Service

In this chapter, we've taken a closer look at the inner workings of your campus learning center. In addition to teaching students the powerful learning strategies we've encountered throughout this book, learning center professionals teach powerful supplemental tips and techniques, and they can serve as transformative partners in the teaching and learning process. Their chosen careers reflect a desire to serve faculty and students in our mutual quest for deep, lasting, meaningful learning. Use them as much as you can.

Note

1. *Problem-based learning*, an active learning technique that has been used in medical schools for decades, involves presenting students with authentic, real-world "fuzzy" problems that have no cookbook solutions, often before students have the information to solve the problem (Nilson, 2013, p. 48). They must look up the information, and use it and their critical thinking skills to develop solutions.

Service-learning is a "course-based, credit bearing educational experience in which students (a) participate in an organized service activity that meets identified community needs, and (b) reflect on the service activity in such a way as to gain further understanding of course content, a broader appreciation of the discipline, and an enhanced sense of civic responsibility" (Bringle & Hatcher, 1995, p. 112). Service-learning differs from community service in that the activities are directly related to course content and the students engage in reflection activities to connect the two.

Cooperative learning involves having students work together in small groups to achieve a goal (Nilson, 2004). Groups might be involved in activities like answering a question posed in class, completing a class project, or preparing a class presentation.

11

TEACHING LEARNING STRATEGIES TO GROUPS

"You did it again. Just wanted to let you know that after talking to my class . . . they listened, and I was shocked that the next exam average was a 76.39. My class's first exam average was a D!" —Catherine Situma, LSU general chemistry instructor, personal communication, July 10, 2009

In this chapter, we explore how to disseminate learning strategies to groups of students. Because relatively few students will wind up in office hours or visit the campus learning center unprompted, the strategies in this book can and should be taught to entire classes. Most students will have an opportunity to encounter them only during lecture or regular class sessions. The groups you work with might be as small as 5 or as large as 5,000.

As Many Ways as There Are Instructors

Learning center professionals have been presenting learning strategies to groups for decades. Student organizations, sports teams, sororities, fraternities, and honor societies are all potential audiences for this valuable information. In my early years as a learning center director, I never knew what happened during the sessions our learning strategists presented to groups because I never sat in on any of them! But I came around and eventually started making presentations myself. (Special shout-out to Sarah Baird, whose example taught me so much of what I know. And by extension, to Rhonda Atkinson, who taught Sarah most of what Sarah taught me.) Because so many people do it, there are countless ways to present strategies to groups. This chapter is a summary of how *I* do it, but keep in mind that you can adapt my suggestions to your unique situation. You can also observe how the learning center professionals on your campus work with groups. There's no magic formula. Trust your instincts.

What This Chapter Covers

In this chapter, I walk you, step-by-step, through a 50-minute session that introduces metacognition and learning strategies to general chemistry students. I also present studies, both published and unpublished, that demonstrate the kinds of results that follow this kind of intervention. Here is a detailed outline of the chapter.

I start by describing the differences between working with individuals and working with groups, and then I direct you to several online resources to help you create your own learning strategies session for groups. These resources include two exemplar slide sets, a template slide set, a video of a session for groups (all at styluspub.presswarehouse.com/Titles/Teach StudentsHowtoLearn.aspx), and a handout that you can find in appendix D.

After we've walked through the presentation, you will have finished about a third of the chapter. The middle third of the chapter presents published and unpublished quantitative studies that demonstrate an association between this kind of group intervention and improved student performance. If you start yawning at the mention of population sizes and standard error, feel free to skip to pages 134-150. But if you stay the course, you'll read about three preliminary studies conducted by Cook et al. (2013), Zhao et al. (2014), and Dawood (2014). Reading my summary of these studies, you will discover three slightly different approaches to delivering the intervention, and you will also see three different kinds of analyses. I present these results partly in hopes that it will inspire you to design your own studies and contribute to the literature. Once we've reviewed the quantitative results, I then present additional qualitative feedback that suggests the efficacy of the intervention.

During the final third of the chapter, I lay out my secret ingredients for success: six simple ways that you can maximize the impact of your intervention by creating exceptional rapport with students. Because I have had a lot of experience with public speaking, I consistently receive feedback that my personal style is engagingly charismatic. I also occasionally receive reports from instructors that their attempts to transform student performance via metacognition and learning strategies fall flat. As a result, some surmise that my success with students can be explained only by my personal style. This conclusion is simply not true. Even if statistics bore you, you might still want to read the middle third of the chapter just to hear about the different professors who made the intervention their own and witnessed their students' improved performance. By the end of the chapter, I hope you will be convinced that *anyone can deliver an effective intervention.*

There's a lot going on in this chapter, so I want to give you the overview one more time. To start, we'll learn about the differences between dealing with individuals versus groups; then we'll walk through a 50-minute session; then we'll review published and unpublished quantitative studies; next we'll review qualitative feedback; and finally, we'll learn the six secret ingredients for spectacular success with students.

Let's get started.

One Versus Many

What is the main difference between introducing the strategies one-on-one and delivering them to groups? When you work with students individually, you can ask them to bring in old tests or quizzes and systematically diagnose their learning troubles. For example, some students may begin studying too late; others may put in an appropriate amount of time but use that time ineffectively, methodically memorizing when they should be focusing on overarching concepts. Still, other students might believe they are focusing on concepts but lack a sufficient grasp of supporting details. But with an entire class, you can't pinpoint each student's problem. Furthermore, you cannot meet each individual's specific emotional needs. Some students need gentle encouragement, whereas others need a stronger hand. When you work with groups, you'll need to split the difference and project a generous, compassionate confidence.

Fortunately, there are a few things that we know most students are doing wrong. So even if you can't zero in on each student's needs, you can address general learning troubles, confident that at least a few things you say will apply to almost everyone in the room. For example, if a group of people has high blood pressure but you don't have access to all their medical charts, you can still advise them to minimize their sodium intake, eat moderate portions, consume lots of fruits and vegetables, take their medication, and stay particularly vigilant if high blood pressure runs in their family. The 50-minute presentation I have created hits all the major strategies that usually make the biggest difference for students.

Resources for You

When you go to the resources link mentioned at the beginning of this chapter, you will find three sets of PowerPoint slides and a demonstration video. The first slide set, named *General Presentation*, is a presentation about metacognitive learning strategies for a general student audience. It follows the structure of chapters 3 through 5 of this book.

The second slide set, named *Chemistry Presentation*, is a presentation tailored specifically for a particular course, first-semester general chemistry at LSU. *Chemistry Presentation* features slides with material specific to the science, technology, engineering, and math (STEM) field, including questions from the first exam of that course, as well as a focus on strategies particularly useful in STEM courses. This more specific slide set is the one that I will walk you through during the next part of this chapter.

The third slide set, named *Presentation Template*, is a set of slides based on *Chemistry Presentation*, included so that you can create your own set of course-specific slides. *Presentation Template* is identical to *Chemistry Presentation* except all of the course-specific or STEM-specific material has been removed and can be replaced with whatever you choose. *General Presentation* is already so general that you can adapt it to your needs as you see fit.

At the resources link, there is also a video of my presentation of a learning strategies session to a group of general chemistry students at LSU. The slides that appear during that video are similar to the slides in *Chemistry Presentation*, but be aware that there are differences. I provide the video as a supplemental resource so that you can see the session in action.

Finally, in appendix D, you will find a handout that summarizes the process I use to introduce metacognitive and learning strategies to students. The handout is called "Introducing Metacognition and Learning Strategies to Students: A Step-by-Step Guide."

The Intervention: A 50-Minute Session on Metacognition and Learning Strategies

For the next part of this chapter, I will walk you through the *Chemistry Presentation* slides, a set specifically created for general chemistry students. You can go to appendix H to view the slides as you read. Note that learning strategies presentations can be given in sessions lasting 50 minutes, 75 minutes, or even 90 minutes, a common class duration for courses that meet twice a week. During longer sessions, the additional time can be spent giving students more time to discuss the reflection questions or allowing them to share the strategies they commit to using in the future.

First Things First

There are a couple of guidelines I have learned to follow when giving presentations to students during their regular class meetings. First, I encourage you to wait until students have received the results of their first test or quiz. If you try to give the presentation sooner in the semester, students may think that they don't need to hear the information; they will be confident that they'll make an A or a B studying the way they always have. Waiting may feel like withholding lifesaving treatment until people are sick instead of giving them preventative medicine, but trust me: If students refuse to *follow* a preventative course of treatment, that treatment is worthless.

Second, do not tell students that the class session will be about learning strategies. Most students need to believe that class will proceed as normal and that there will be regular course content presented during that lecture period. Only after they arrive in class that day should students learn what will be covered. Otherwise, they might consider the lecture supplemental, and attendance may be low. During a recent summer term, I remember arriving early to set up for a presentation to a general chemistry class. Two young men noticed my arrival. When they saw me, one of them said to the other, "Oh! We got a substitute teacher today! Man, we don't have to stay in class!" He promptly went on his merry way, none the wiser. His friend stayed, was very engaged in the discussion, and came to me afterward to tell me how helpful the information had been.

Generalist or Specialist? Two Ways to Offer the Intervention

As I mentioned at the beginning of this chapter, I offer you two basic ways to deliver this 50-minute intervention. One is called *General Presentation* and is a more general version of the intervention, and the other is called *Chemistry Presentation* and is a course-specific version. They can both be found at at this book's accompanying resources website, and the slides for *Chemistry Presentation* are in appendix H. In this chapter, I will walk you through the more specific version because we have already walked through the more general version in chapters 4 and 5. In particular, *Chemistry Presentation* features course-specific or field-specific reflection questions, results, strategies, and exam questions. Both versions of the intervention are highly effective, and both feature examples of dramatic test score improvements, Bloom's Taxonomy, and the study cycle, so it is completely up to you which one you decide to use.

Remember that the slide sets are only suggestions. If you get hung up on any one aspect of a particular slide, don't worry about it. And if you don't want to use course-specific examples, feel free to use the first presentation and not the second. Make your presentation your own, and have fun delivering it to students!

Putting Meat on the Bones

Although I walk you through the presentation step-by-step, I leave out many details. To get a feel for how you can fill in the sketch presented here with important details and color, please do refer to chapter 4 (Bloom's Taxonomy and the study cycle), chapter 5 (metacognitive learning strategies), and the online resources.

Presentation Part One: Stoking the Fires of Interest and Confidence

I often begin by presenting a slide with several common career fields and asking students to indicate their career interest by a show of hands. Why? By sharing their career goals, students are primed to see how the material directly relates to their ultimate goals and desires. The second slide in *Chemistry Presentation* lists many STEM fields, but the corresponding slide in *Presentation Template* is blank, left for you to fill in.

After you've connected your students to their ultimate goals, you can begin to spark their confidence in themselves and in the power of the strategies you are about to present. Show them some individual miracles either from your own experience or from others'. Please feel free to use slide 4 from *Chemistry Presentation*, which shows the improvement of only chemistry students, or slide 3 from *General Presentation*, which shows the improvement of chemistry, physics, and psychology students.

I add two more things to the opening of my presentation that you might consider using. First, I ask students a pair of questions: "Did you think the exam was difficult?" and "Did you do less well than you wanted to?" Usually, although most of the students didn't think the exam they just took was difficult, the majority did not do as well as they wanted to. This exercise communicates to students that, to date, they have not been good judges of their own mastery. Second, I explicitly tell students that I have come to teach them these strategies after their first exam because I want them to know that it doesn't matter what their first exam score was. I know that they can still do well in the course.

Presentation Part Two: Whet Their Appetites

At this point, give students one very powerful strategy that can account for the dramatic results they've just witnessed. In my presentation, I share the homework strategy (chapter 5) because it is so effective with STEM students. Presenting one strategy up front kills two birds with one stone: students can begin to see how those dramatic results came into being *and* they can begin to imagine the types of suggestions they're going to hear for the rest of the discussion. For non-STEM students, you may want to start with the reading strategies (chapter 5).

Then continue to increase students' interest and confidence by giving examples—if you have them—of dramatic differences between students who were exposed to the material you are about to deliver and students who were not. Again, feel free to use slides 6 and 7 from *Chemistry Presentation*, which show differences in the grades of entire classes rather than individuals, if you do not yet have your own results to share.

End this part of the discussion by sharing with students what they will walk away from the session with. Make bold, realistic promises that will hook the students' interest. Slide 8 in the *Chemistry Presentation* set accomplishes these aims in my presentation. The outcomes I promise are listed here:

- You will analyze your current learning strategies for Chemistry 1421.
- You will understand exactly what changes you need to implement to make an A in the course.
- You will have concrete strategies to use during the remainder of the semester, and you will *use* them in Chem 1421 and beyond!
- You will become a more efficient learner by studying *smarter*, not necessarily *harder*.

Presentation Part Three: Beginning the Investigation

Now begin to take your students through the reflection questions laid out in chapter 4. To summarize, you will ask the students to describe the difference between studying and learning. They will likely respond by saying something like studying is memorizing whereas learning is understanding. Then you will ask, "Given an upcoming exam, would you work harder to make an A on the exam, or would you work harder if you had to hold a review session the day before the exam and teach the material to the entire class?"

Once you've put these questions to the students, you can engage them in a think-pair-share activity. Ask them to jot down their answers, discuss the answers with a partner, perhaps the person next to them in the lecture hall, and after a couple of minutes, ask for some volunteers to share their responses with the class.

After students have shared the differences between studying and learning with the class, you can also chime in with answers from other students you've worked with or with some of the answers in chapter 4, if you think that those answers will help clarify the distinction between superficial and deep learning. For the second question—would you work harder to get a good grade on an exam or to teach the material to the class?—you can gauge student response by a show of hands. Be aware that a few students may say that they would work harder to make a good grade; those students aren't wrong, but you can explain why having to teach the material engages most learners more deeply than trying to make a good grade does (chapter 4). (I always stress that there are no right or wrong answers to any reflection question.)

After you've had a lively discussion with the class about these reflections, ask them the following crucial questions: (a) "By a show of hands, how many of us have been in 'study mode' rather than 'learn mode'?" (almost all of the class will raise their hands); and (b) "By a show of hands, how many of us have been in 'make-an-A-on-the-test mode' rather than 'teach-the-material mode'?" (Again, almost all of the class will raise their hands.) At this point, you can give them the learning strategy of teaching material to other students, stuffed animals, or even empty chairs. You can also explain to them that it works because explaining information to an audience—real or imagined—will reveal holes in their understanding. If you choose to introduce this strategy here, you'll be only a third of the way through the presentation and will have already exposed the students to two of the most powerful strategies—getting the most out of homework and teaching the material.

Then explicitly tell them that they need to make sure to stay in "learn mode" and "teach-the-material mode." Next, make a promise: Tell them that if they can do that, they will do much better on their exams and learn much more broadly, deeply, and securely. By making this promise, you are giving them something to look forward to, a reward. During this part of the presentation, be sure to elicit answers and participation from students so that they can begin to make connections and engage in metacognition.

Once they have made those distinctions, ask them *why* they need to work harder and/or differently in order to do well in college courses compared to courses they've previously taken. After you have written down several of their ideas on the board, or just repeated them to the class, then unveil your own slide listing the reasons (slide 13, *Chemistry Presentation*). Note that by doing this, you will be making the case for advancing to higher levels on Bloom's Taxonomy without yet mentioning the taxonomy. You are preparing them to understand why they need to ascend Bloom's in order to succeed in the course. For very large classes, there may not be time to engage in discussion. In that case, simply present the reasons on the slide to the students, and periodically ask whether they've found those reasons to be true, gauging response by looking at the proportion of nodding heads. This slide also communicates to students that their performance is based only on the actions they take, not on other people or on circumstances out of their control.

Presentation Part Four: Get Specific

At this point, consider presenting one or more questions from the test they've just taken, questions that few people answered correctly. In my example slides from *Chemistry Presentation*, you can see I chose one question that almost no one got right and another that a quarter of test takers answered correctly. I also chose these two examples because they featured contrasting content: significant figures and reaction types.

Presentation Part Five: The Heart of the Matter

Now that students are thoroughly convinced that what you will present relates directly to them and their performance in the course, they are ready to hear all about metacognition, Bloom's Taxonomy, and the study cycle. Slides 18 through 24 in *Chemistry Presentation* cover this material, which is treated in depth in chapters 3 through 5 of this volume.

After you talk about learning strategies in a general way, consider presenting a summary of strategies specific to course content. It is perfectly fine if you blur the line between metacognitive strategies and study skills, as I have in slide 25 of *Chemistry Presentation* with a list of effective metacognitive learning strategies, shown here.

- Always solve problems without looking at an example or the solution.
- Memorize everything you're told to memorize (e.g., polyatomic ions).
- Always ask why, how, and what-if questions.
- Test understanding by giving "mini-lectures" on concepts.
- Spend time on chemistry every day.
- Use the study cycle with intense study sessions.
- Attend group study sessions or tutoring on a regular basis.
- Aim for 100% mastery, not 90%!

Let's discuss that last bullet point for a minute before moving on. It is important for students to maximize their efforts in order for them to maximize their grades, and the only way they will maximize their efforts is to aim for 100% mastery. We have all had the experience of having to learn a lot of material in a short period of time, and if any particular segment of that material seems more difficult and time-consuming to master than the rest, our natural instinct is to skip it. We reason, *how many points could it be worth?* If you ask students how many of them have ever fallen victim to that kind of reasoning, the hands will shoot up. Then ask them, "Well, does that material show up on the exam?" They will nod their heads knowingly, and you can tell them that it always appears on the exam because the instructor always wants to know who has aimed for 100%. Moreover, you can make the case that 100% mastery is worth pursuing because most classes are prerequisites for future classes, and that's not some bureaucratic horse poo. They really *will* need to remember concepts from general chemistry to do well in organic chemistry.

At this point in the discussion, you may also want to show students particular study tools that will be useful for that course. In my presentation, I present concept maps and compare and contrast exercises (slides 26–28, *Chemistry Presentation*).

Presentation Part Six: Get Inside Their Heads

Slides 29 through 32 of *Chemistry Presentation* are designed to help students reflect upon some of the issues discussed in chapters 6 through 8, those aspects of learning that depend on psychology and attitude. Simply showing students the top five reasons that previous students in the same course did not do well on a test encourages students to locate those problems in their own behavior. Similarly, showing students the top five reasons that previous students did well on the exam shows them what steps to take to achieve that same success. Notice that in both cases the reasons are 100% learner-focused. In the language of chapter 8, these slides are helping students formulate appropriate attribution theories. Again, we are tethering results to behavior.

If you do not have data from previous classes and you teach chemistry, feel free to use my slides. If you do not teach chemistry, take the opportunity at this point in the presentation to ask students to brainstorm the top five reasons they did not do well on the first exam or quiz or the top five reasons that they did do well, based on the learning strategies you have presented. You can write the reasons on the board in two columns and then ask the students to compare and contrast them.

In my presentation, slide 33 in *Chemistry Presentation* brings it home. Two e-mails from the same student before and after he began to implement learning strategies demonstrate how his frame of mind changed. He went from thinking he was "not so good at chemistry" to earning a 97% on his final exam and being able to pinpoint exactly which strategies (behaviors) ensured his success. Again, feel free to use my slides until you have your own stories to share.

Presentation Part Seven: Strategies and Resources

At this point in the discussion, I reiterate the strategies that I believe are most important for the particular course for which I am presenting (slide 34, *Chemistry Presentation*). In the case of many STEM students, the most important strategies are the homework strategies. You may choose to emphasize other strategies. The purpose here is to keep reiterating that these dramatic results can be obtained only through a behavioral change: spending the time to implement the strategies.

The next slide continues this message by explaining to students how best to seek help from others, including peer tutors, professors, teaching assistants, or study group members. They must do some individual preparation so that they have specific questions to ask and are prepared to teach the material to others. This slide sends the message that other people (like tutors) do not exist to pick up the students' slack. They are there to be equal partners in the learning process.

Finally, I present several campus and online resources that I believe the students will find helpful (slides 36–38, *Chemistry Presentation*). Please feel free to point your students to resources specific to your campus or geographical area.

Presentation Part Eight: Rubber Hits the Road!

Many people love a little competition. Raise the stakes by issuing a challenge. Present a slide showing the predicted results of the second exam (which will not yet have happened), much improved compared to the results of the first (slide 39, *Chemistry Presentation*). Plant the seed in the students' minds that, as a class, they can do better and that you are confident they *will* do better if they use the strategies you have discussed. Now show an example of a previous class that improved their performance (again feel free to use slide 40 in *Chemistry Presentation*) after learning about metacognition and learning strategies. Slide 40 shows a 7-point bump in a class's average exam grade after the intervention. Challenge the current class to do the same, making sure to communicate your confidence in them.

Let me introduce you to one group who met the challenge beautifully. The LSU Summer Scholars are incoming freshmen at LSU who, during the summer before their freshman year, take 6 credit hours, or approximately two classes. During the summer of 2014, I gave a learning strategies presentation to the Summer Scholars and challenged them to achieve an average group GPA higher than 3.554, the highest GPA achieved by any previous group of Summer Scholars. What do you know—these motivated youngsters earned an average GPA of 3.671! Having something to shoot for and a benchmark to exceed can be a powerful motivator.

Presentation Part Eight Continued: Elicit a Commitment

Slide 41 of *Chemistry Presentation* shows a crucial part of the intervention. Ask the students to write down one strategy that they will commit to using for the subsequent three weeks. You could show something like the list on slide 42 (*Chemistry Presentation*) in order to remind them of the strategies they have to choose from, or you could leave the question more open-ended for students to engage their creativity and tailor the strategies to their own needs. Then show them a warning like that on slide 43 (*Chemistry Presentation*) to inform them that there is an expiration date on trying something new: If they do not try a new strategy within the next 2 days, then they likely never will.

You might also try a great exercise I learned from Tom Angelo at the 2014 annual meeting of the Southern Association of Colleges and Schools (SACS) called a What/Why/How exercise (T. Angelo, personal communication, December 8, 2014). Of the strategies that you've presented, ask students to pick two or three that they're going to use and answer the following questions about each one: (a) What is the strategy? (b) Why do they want to try it? (c) How are they going to implement it?

However you choose to do it, definitely make time in your presentation to elicit a firm commitment from students. A concluding slide with contact information (slide 44, *Chemistry Presentation*) lets the students know that you are available for follow-up questions. If it is your own class, your students will already have your contact information and you can encourage them to visit you in office hours. Your availability can be reassuring to students, even if they never contact you.

Closing Considerations

Although a one-time 50-minute intervention does yield gains for students, there are relatively easy ways to ensure that those gains are maximized. Throughout the semester, after each exam is returned, consider asking students to write down the reasons they believe they earned the score they did and which specific strategies they need to implement in order to earn a higher score.

Continuing to remind students about the strategies throughout the remainder of the course, after the intervention, can make a huge difference. I'd like you to think about any major behavioral change you've made in your life. Were you able to sustain that change without considerable support? It's not by accident that addiction support groups meet weekly. Students have had 12 or more years of academic experience telling them that they don't need to preview or use any of the strategies. For most students to be able to break that cycle, regular reminders and reinforcements are needed. These can be as simple as asking at the beginning of a class two weeks after the intervention, "How many of you are still/actually using the study cycle?" If few hands go up, ask, "Well, when you used the study cycle, did it work?" When the nodding inevitably starts, pointedly ask why they have stopped using it. These questions will prod students to go back to the tools that have worked for them in the recent past. But try not to be sarcastic. Don't we all know what it feels like to stop doing something that works for goodness-only-knows what reasons? Hello, lapsed gym membership. No matter how effective new behaviors are, human beings still need reminders to persevere.

Published Studies Associating a 50-Minute Intervention With Improved Student Performance

Even though learning center professionals are well aware of the power of learning strategies and the impact that they have on student learning, knowledge of learning strategies is not widespread partly because most learning center professionals don't usually publish papers. Instead, they focus on helping students acquire effective learning strategies. And if they do write papers, they publish them in journals like the *Learning Assistance Review* or the *Journal of College Reading and Learning*, essentially preaching to the choir, not to the professors who should learn about the strategies and disseminate them to students.

At the urging of several colleagues, I have participated in three recent efforts to get the word out. In 2009 I coauthored a piece in *Science* (Hoffmann & McGuire, 2009) about metacognition and learning strategies with Nobel laureate in chemistry Roald Hoffmann. A longer version of that paper later appeared in *American Scientist* in 2010. I also encouraged my colleague Elzbieta (Elizabeth) Cook in the chemistry department at LSU, whose classes had shown improved test performance after my metacognition presentation, to publish some results, and we did so in the *Journal of Chemical Education*. Most recently, Ningfeng (Peter) Zhao, whom I met at a 2011 Gordon Research Conference, took me up on my invitation to the attendees there to present these learning strategies to their students. Peter decided to conduct a study with students at his institution, East Tennessee State University. Those results were published in the *Journal of College Science Teaching*. In the next several sections, I summarize the results from Cook et al. (2013) and Zhao et al. (2014).

Although many of you will find the quantitative results interesting and engaging, those of you whose eyes glaze over when you see too many numbers can feel free to skip several pages ahead to the section titled "Anecdotal Evidence for the Impact of a 50-Minute Intervention."

Positive Results, Not Proof

The studies in these sections were inspired by student performance that suggests an association between a learning strategies intervention and improved academic results. They are not double-blind, controlled, flawlessly designed studies of consistently large populations. Part of the issue is ethical. I feel it is unprincipled to share learning strategies with part of a population of students and withhold those strategies from another part. I've seen firsthand that learning strategies can make the difference in whether a student gets into medical school and realizes her dream of becoming a doctor. Part of the issue is practical. These professors, inspired by the power of the learning strategies, collected the data available to them to share with the wider community. My hope is that the results of these studies will inspire others, some with large classes, to carry out even more rigorously designed studies that will give further support to my claim that a 50-minute intervention, carried out with reminders and support throughout the semester, consistently improves the performance of student groups. Let's look at the encouraging results we already have.

Cook, Kennedy, and McGuire (2013)

The first journal article I published with colleagues regarding the efficacy of a 50-minute intervention given to large groups is based on my presentation to Elzbieta Cook's class of first-year general chemistry students at LSU. Cook, Kennedy, and McGuire (2013) describe the results of my delivering the intervention twice, once in fall 2010 and again in fall 2011. In fall 2010, Cook noticed that the final average course grade for the 428 students who had attended the strategies lecture was 81.5 (B), whereas the 167 students who had not attended ended up with a final average course grade of 72.6 (C) (Table 11.1). Although we cannot incontrovertibly say that the intervention caused this difference, the results were intriguing enough that we investigated further during fall 2011.

Table 11.1 Averages of Final Course Grades in General Chemistry I, LSU Fall 2010

	Number of students	Average of final course grades
Attendees (treatment group)	428	81.5
Nonattendees (control group)	167	72.6

Note. Table shows the means of the final course grades of two groups of students: 428 students who attended a 50-minute session on learning strategies and 167 students who did not attend. The session was given during a regular lecture period, and students were not informed beforehand that learning strategies rather than course material would be presented.

Table 11.2 Comparing Scores Before and After a 50-Minute Learning Strategies Session, General Chemistry I, LSU Fall 2011

	Exam 1 average (SD)	Mean of final course grades (SD)
Attendees (treatment group)	74.0% (19.9%) n = 467	81.6 (N/A) n = 473
Nonattendees (control group)	68.2% (17.1%) n = 175	70.4 (N/A) n = 195

Note. Table shows exam 1 scores (preintervention) and means of final course grades for two groups of students: approximately 450 students who attended a 50-minute session on learning strategies and approximately 175 students who did not attend. The standard deviations of the exam averages are shown in parentheses, and *n* is equal to the number of students. Standard deviations for final course grades were not available. As in fall 2010, students were not informed beforehand that a learning strategies specialist would be lecturing instead of their chemistry professor. Although comparing the average for a preintervention exam to final course grades is in no way definitive, it is intriguing that a 6-point gap nearly doubled to 11 points. Note that exam 1 average was one of several covariates in an ANCOVA analysis undertaken in Cook et al. (2013). See that paper for more details.

During fall 2011, we used two additional tools—apart from comparing the means of final course grades—to investigate the effect that the learning strategies lecture intervention might be having on student performance. First, we compared performance on the first exam of students who attended the intervention lecture to that of the students who did not. Second, we used an exit survey, designed by Cook, to determine which strategies students found most useful.

Table 11.2 shows the first-exam scores and standard deviations of students who received the intervention and those who did not. It also shows the means of the final course grades for the two groups. You can see that although the control group (*n* = 175) did indeed start out with lower grades than the intervention group (*n* = 467)—68.2% versus 74%—that gap widened over time, after the intervention, to 70.4% (*n* = 195) versus 81.6% (*n* = 473). (The difference in the numbers of students may be attributed to students who either missed the first exam or received special accommodations, such as additional time.) Cook et al. (2013) also used a detailed statistical analysis to quantify the effect of the intervention. Please see that paper for details.

We also asked Cook's students to complete an exit survey so that we could learn which strategies they were finding most useful. The students were not constrained in the number of strategies they could choose. Table 11.3

Table 11.3 Learning Strategies Deemed Useful by Students Enrolled in General Chemistry I at LSU, Fall 2011

Strategy	Percentage of students who deemed it useful
Review past exams	57.0
Review (as part of study cycle)	32.0
Study for exams earlier	32.0
Read textbook more	30.0
Attend supplemental instruction courses	29.0
Do homework earlier	25.0
Aim for 100% understanding	24.0
Use intense study sessions	24.0
Study more	23.0
Study in a group	18.0

Note. Table shows the results of an exit survey completed at the end of Elzbieta Cook's fall 2011 general chemistry I course. Students chose which strategies they found most useful from a list of options, and they could choose as many strategies as they wanted.

shows 10 strategies and the percentage of 477 students who found each strategy useful. Reviewing past exams tops the list at 57%. About a third of students found it useful to review in general, study cumulatively rather than cramming, use the textbook, and go to the campus learning center for additional help. About a quarter of students found it useful to do their homework earlier, challenge themselves to completely understand the material, use intense study sessions, and study more. And about a fifth of students found group study helpful. These strategies are a nice mix of metacognitive strategies and study strategies/skills, and the results suggest that presenting a broad range of strategies to students, in as little as 50 minutes, allows them to find what will work for them (Cook et al., 2013). The results also suggest that the 50-minute intervention was effective in motivating students to make major behavioral changes.

The results in Cook et al. (2013) suggest that introducing learning strategies to large groups of students has an effect on their performance. I assert that for a subset of students, these strategies have an outsized and profound effect on performance, and these are the students who will end up in your miracle portfolio. The thing is, you don't know who these students are, so we must shout the strategies from the rooftops so that those who *can* be helped, and dramatically so, *will* be helped.

Zhao et al. (2014)

Zhao et al. (2014) also examined exam data and survey data before and after an intervention, but the survey methodology is quite different from that in Cook et al. (2013). Moreover, the intervention was slightly different because Zhao gave the learning strategies lecture based on a set of PowerPoint slides similar to but not identical to *Chemistry Presentation*. Often faculty are convinced that I have some kind of special magic that they cannot reproduce, but the results from Zhao et al. and unpublished results from Dawood (2014) suggest that other people can deliver interventions that are just as effective.

Zhao delivered the intervention to a fall 2011 general chemistry I class at East Tennessee State University. Approximately 90 students participated in this part of the study. The first exam in the course was administered during the third week of the semester, and the intervention was given two class sessions later, during the fourth week. During the lecture period directly following the exam, the exams were returned, students filled out surveys, and they also gave the top three reasons (analogous to slides 30 and 31, *Chemistry Presentation*) they believed they'd done either well or poorly.

Exam averages for the entire semester are shown in Figure 11.1 and Table 11.4. Figure 11.1 compares exam averages from fall semester 2011 to averages from the two previous fall semesters, 2010 and 2009. Means are plotted with error bars of one standard error. Although the exams were not identical from year to year, questions were chosen from the same test bank from Wiley publishers, and the test creator sought to make sure the same range of subjects (e.g., stoichiometry, unit conversions) was tested in the same proportions and at the same level of difficulty. Table 11.4 shows the exam averages, standard deviations, and number of students who took each exam. In each case, attrition increased as the semester progressed, and the number of students who took exam 3 was between 83% and 90% of the original population.

During fall semesters 2009 and 2010, when no intervention was delivered, mean scores on all three exams barely break 70%, but during fall 2011, mean scores on exams 2 and 3, given after the intervention, are 76.5% and 77.5% respectively. Paired t-tests demonstrated that the difference between the fall 2011 exam 2 mean and the means for fall 2010 and 2009 are statistically significant. That result was repeated for exam 3. However, there was no statistically significant difference between the means of exam 1 across all 3 years. Because exam 1 was given before the intervention in fall 2011, it serves as a kind of control. Taken together, these results demonstrate a postintervention change.

Before going further, let's briefly take a look at some differences between Zhao's intervention and ours at LSU. He explicitly stated the goal of the

Figure 11.1 General Chemistry I Exam Averages Before and After a 50-Minute Intervention Delivered After Exam 1

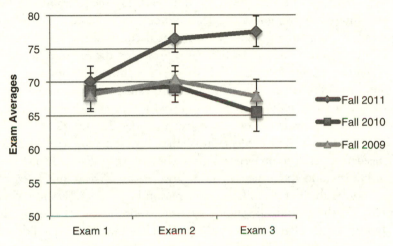

Note. Figure compares exam averages from Ningfeng Zhao's fall semester general chemistry I course over a three-year period. Averages are plotted with error bars of plus or minus one standard error. Zhao delivered a learning strategies session to his students between exams 1 and 2 of fall 2011 (diamonds). Fall 2009 and fall 2010 (triangles and circles)—semesters without any intervention—provide a historical comparison to fall 2011. According to paired t-test results, there are statistically significant differences between the means of exams 2 and 3 in fall 2011, given after the intervention, compared to exams 2 and 3 of previous years. In contrast, there is no statistically significant difference between the means of exam 1, given before the intervention, across all three years. Differences between Zhao's intervention and *Chemistry Presentation* are detailed in the text. Support for the comparability of the exams across a three-year period is also given in the text. Adapted from "Metacognition: An Effective Tool to Promote Success in College Science Learning," by N. Zhao, J.G. Wardeska, S.Y. McGuire, & E. Cook, 2014, *Journal of College Science Teaching, 43*(4), p. 52.

Table 11.4 Exam Averages, Standard Deviations, and Number of Test Takers in Figure 11.1

	Exam 1 Average (SD)	Exam 2 Average (SD)	Exam 3 Average (SD)
Fall 2011	70 (22.7) $n = 90$	76.5 (18.5) $n = 80$	77.5 (19.6) $n = 75$
Fall 2010	68.7 (25.2) $n = 91$	69.3 (21.6) $n = 88$	65.4 (25.4) $n = 78$
Fall 2009	68.1 (21.5) $n = 73$	70.2 (18.0) $n = 68$	67.8 (20.9) $n = 65$

Note. Table shows the means, standard deviations, and number of test takers for the data presented in Figure 11.1. Standard error is the standard deviation divided by the square root of *n*, and the error bars in Figure 11.1 show plus or minus one standard error.

learning-strategies session in his first slide: "The Goal: Get you an A!" and stated the path to that goal in three bullet points: (a) analyze your current learning strategies, (b) understand the difference between meaningful learning and rote memorization, and (c) introduce concrete and effective strategies (slightly paraphrased from Zhao, personal communication, August 24, 2011). In his second and third slides, Zhao presented the top three reasons for his students' As (slide 2) or Ds (slide 3), gleaned from analyzing the student responses he collected after the first exam. His fourth slide paralleled slide 13 from *Chemistry Presentation*, giving reasons why college courses are more difficult. Then he presented slides analogous to slides 21 and 22 of *Chemistry Presentation*, which show students' reasoning regarding the level of Bloom's they needed to reach to do well in high school versus college. Zhao then presented information about metacognition and constructivism in his next three slides, about a third of it similar to information in *General Presentation*. Next he presented the Bloom's Taxonomy pyramid, followed by an example using Goldilocks and the Three Bears (Figure 4.4). Then he presented a slide about the study cycle, followed by active reading strategies, chapter maps, tips about how to engage in class and how to review, and information about intense study sessions. Next he gave self-testing and homework strategies, framing these as part of the assessment part of the study cycle. His penultimate slide showed dramatic before-and-after results from LSU students and asked students to commit to strategies they would use for the rest of the semester. His final slide gave website resources for the students to investigate. So although the meat and potatoes of Zhao's presentation was very similar to mine, there were significant changes, additions, and omissions. I urge you to be just as creative. Zhao also included reminders throughout the semester to use metacognition and learning strategies.

Zhao et al. (2014) presented exam averages from the second semester, spring 2012, when Zhao gave the intervention to Wardeska's general chemistry II class. However, the follow-up to the intervention was different because Wardeska did not give reminders to students throughout the rest of the semester. Average exam scores and grades from this class appear in Zhao et al. These measures do not show as clear a difference as the fall semester measures, which might be explained by the lack of reminders throughout the spring semester to use the strategies, by the increased difficulty of material in general chemistry II, by the fact that mastery of general chemistry II depends on mastery of general chemistry I, by some combination of these factors, or by other factors. Although the spring semester scores do not demonstrate a positive effect of the intervention, the sum of the percentiles of A, B, and C grades in spring 2012 showed an increasing trend over the exams, distinguished from the overall decreasing trends of spring 2011 and spring 2010 (Zhao et al., 2014, Figure 3). This may suggest a positive impact of the application of metacognitive learning strategies. However, because of the methodological differences, I have chosen not to include a detailed discussion of the spring 2012 results here.

Intriguing Results With Small Populations

Now that we've looked at results with populations between approximately 75 and 700 students, we'll turn to some results with smaller populations, from Zhao et al. (2014) and Dawood (2014). Because n, the number of students, is very small, these results do not have statistical power (recall that standard error is standard deviation divided by the square root of n). But I present them here because, taken together, they are certainly worth consideration. They suggest that more rigorous studies involving greater numbers of students should be undertaken in search of a statistically significant effect.

Zhao et al. (2014) Continued

Zhao et al. (2014) note that during the 2011–2012 academic year, there were 11 students who received both interventions. In other words, 11 students from Zhao's first-semester general chemistry I section happened to be assigned to Wardeska's second-semester general chemistry II section. Zhao calls these students "dual participants" because they received both the fall and spring semester interventions. Zhao et al. compare the performance of the 11 dual participants to that of the 38 spring 2012 students who had not received the fall intervention, "first-time participants."

Exam averages of the dual participants compared to the first-time participants are shown in Figure 11.2 and Table 11.5. Figure 11.2 shows the average scores of each exam with error bars of one standard error. Notice the vertical distance between each square/diamond pair in Figure 11.2. Dual participants averaged 72.5%, 77.7%, 71.8%, and 78.1% on the four spring semester exams, whereas first-time participants averaged only 64.3%, 67.8%, 65.9%, and 67.4%, respectively. Students who received both interventions outperformed students who received only the later intervention, but note that this result is not statistically significant, as evidenced by overlapping error bars. The lack of statistical significance is unsurprising given the small sample size and does not rule out a correlation between the intervention and improved student performance. Figure 11.2 may suggest that participants who received the intervention during the fall semester may have been better prepared to learn the spring semester material.

Table 11.5 shows the exam averages, standard deviations, and number of students who took each exam. There was no attrition as the semester progressed.

Figure 11.2 Spring 2012 General Chemistry II Exam Averages Dual Participants Versus First-time Participants

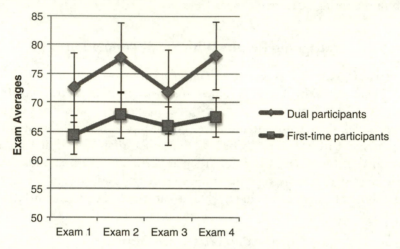

Note. Figure compares exam averages from Wardeska's spring 2012 general chemistry II course. Zhao gave the intervention to Wardeska's class after exam 1, but there were 11 students out of 49 who had taken Zhao's general chemistry I course and received the intervention the previous semester. These students received the intervention twice, so Zhao et al. (2014) refer to them as "dual participants." The 11 dual participants (diamonds) outperformed the 38 one-time participants (squares) for the entire semester. One explanation of many may be that success in general chemistry I is a prerequisite for success in general chemistry II, and so delivering the intervention in first-semester freshmen courses may be advisable. Note that the differences between the dual and first-time participants are not statistically significant (evident from the overlapping error bars of one standard error) perhaps due to small sample size; however, lack of statistical significance does not rule out a correlation between the intervention and improved student performance. Adapted from "Metacognition: An Effective Tool to Promote Success in College Science Learning," by N. Zhao, J.G. Wardeska, S.Y. McGuire, & E. Cook, 2014, *Journal of College Science Teaching, 43*(4), p. 52.

Table 11.5 Exam Averages, Standard Deviations, and Number of Test Takers in Figure 11.2

	Exam 1 Average (SD)	*Exam 2 Average (SD)*	*Exam 3 Average (SD)*	*Exam 4 Average (SD)*
Dual participants	72.5 (20.6) $n = 11$	77.7 (25.0) $n = 11$	71.8 (21.1) $n = 11$	78.1 (21.0) $n = 11$
First-time participants	64.3 (20.0) $n = 38$	67.8 (20.4) $n = 38$	65.9 (24.5) $n = 38$	67.4 (19.6) $n = 38$

Note. Table shows the means, standard deviations, and number of test takers for the data presented in Figure 11.2. Standard error is the standard deviation divided by the square root of *n*, and the error bars in Figure 11.2 show plus or minus one standard error.

Table 11.6 Zhao's Effective Learning Strategies Survey

S1	What is the level of learning you need to make As or Bs in high school? a) Remembering b) Understanding c) Applying d) Analyzing e) Evaluating f) Creating
S2	What is the level of learning you need to make As or Bs in college? a) Remembering b) Understanding c) Applying d) Analyzing e) Evaluating f) Creating
S3	I preview the lecture material before I go to class.
S4	I attend class on time.
S5	I take notes in class by hand.
S6	I review my notes and textbook after each class.
S7	I study with concentrated time and specific goals.
S8	I join study groups.
S9	I understand the lecture and classroom discussions while I am taking notes.
S10	I try to determine what confuses me.
S11	I try to work out the homework problems without looking at the example problems or my notes from class.
S12	I review the textbook, lecture notes, and homework problems and do practice testing before the exam.

Note. Table reproduces Zhao et al.'s (2014) learning strategies survey, given during the lecture period directly after exam 1, the preintervention exam, and also at the end of the course. Students rated statements S3–S12 on a scale of 1 to 4, where 1 corresponded to "almost never," 2 to "sometimes," 3 to "usually," and 4 to "always." Zhao et al. compared the results of the presurvey (given after exam 1) and the postsurvey (given at the end of the course) for both fall 2011 general chemistry I and spring 2012 general chemistry II courses.

The exam averages are intriguing, and so are the survey results. Zhao designed an Effective Learning Strategies Survey based on what he wanted his students to know about learning strategies and on his experience of what most freshmen find difficult about science courses (Zhao, personal communication, October 20, 2011). Table 11.6 shows this survey.

Zhao gave this survey to students first after exam 1 (but before the intervention) and again at the end of the course, and he thoroughly analyzed the results (Zhao et al., 2014). Seventy-eight students (out of 91) took the survey after exam 1, and 77 students (out of 90) took it at the end of the course. I would like to note just one finding in particular from the survey results (see Zhao et al., 2014, for a more detailed, informative analysis). For the first two questions, Zhao noted the percentage of students who chose each level of Bloom's Taxonomy. During the preintervention survey, when answering what level of Bloom's Taxonomy is necessary for success in college chemistry,

55.1% of students chose either level 1 or level 2. At the end of the course, only 3.9% of students chose either level 1 or level 2. The complementary result is that, preintervention, only 38.5% of students believed they needed to operate at levels 3 or 4 to do well in undergraduate chemistry, whereas 89.6% chose levels 3 or 4 at the end of the course. They got the message. It's up to students, of course, whether they use that insight to change their behavior, apply the learning strategies presented, and improve their results.

Zhao et al. (2014) provides one example of how a professor modified the intervention that I designed and sought to change students' behavior and analyze the effectiveness of the intervention. In the conclusion, the authors note several limitations of the study and what could be done to improve it. This adventurous and investigative spirit is exactly what is needed to spread the word about these tools.

A Professor Associates Exam Performance With Self-Reported Study Habits

In this section, we look at some results from Muhammad Dawood, an electrical engineering professor at New Mexico State University (NMSU). I met Dawood when he attended a faculty development workshop I presented at NMSU in October 2013. He was so inspired by the results I presented that he actually decided to deliver the intervention to his students at their very next class meeting! Dawood delivered a 60-minute presentation on metacognitive strategies to his junior-level engineering analysis class and left them with a handout of the study cycle (Figure 4.6). Because he learned of the strategies only after he had already given his first two exams, he gave the intervention after exams 1 and 2 and before exam 3. Consequently, this study is not ideal, but the results are still worth consideration (Dawood, 2014). Because Dawood wanted to quantify the power of the strategies, he designed an intriguing method of collecting and analyzing feedback about their general usefulness. This method also served as a supplemental intervention in itself.

He used three tools to investigate: First, he designed a survey based on slides 30 and 31 of *Chemistry Presentation*, which present the top five reasons that students did well or poorly, respectively, on the first exam. Dawood's survey asked students to assess which of these reasons applied to them (i.e., which study strategies they had used or failed to use). Second, he analyzed student performance—individual and aggregate—on three exams. Third, he designed a seven-question exit survey that asked students to report which specific strategies helped them and to offer suggestions for improving the intervention. In walking through his results, we look first at aggregate performance on exam 3 versus performance on exams 1 and 2. (These results are analogous to the results in Figure 11.1 but for only 1 year instead of 3 years.) Then we look at the results of Dawood's first survey and connect those results to exam performance *before* the intervention (exams 1 and 2). Next, we connect the results of the first survey to individual performance on exam 3 versus performance on exams 1 and 2. Finally, we see what we can learn and conclude from the exit survey results.

Although 18 students originally registered for Dawood's class, 2 students dropped the class, leaving 16 students who took all three exams. In reporting class averages, we will examine data from only 15 of those 16 students, a restriction I chose because only 15 students completed both surveys. With such a small population, we can draw only limited conclusions, but taken together with the other observations in this chapter and throughout the book, including appendix F, these results are certainly worth a look.

Following are the averages and standard deviations for the performance of 15 students on exams 1, 2, and 3: On exam 1, the average was 77.2% with a standard deviation of 24.6 percentage points; on exam 2, the average was 65.7% with a standard deviation of 20.8 percentage points; on exam 3, after the intervention, the class average was 80.5% with a standard deviation of 12.3 percentage points. In other words, not only did student performance improve dramatically from exam 2 to exam 3, but the consistency among students was greater. Figure 11.3 shows these results, and Table 11.7 displays raw data.

Dawood used the information on slides 30 and 31 of *Chemistry Presentation* to create an interesting instrument. He asked students to rate 10 statements on a scale of 1 to 5, where 1 represents complete disagreement and 5 represents complete agreement. The first half of the 10 statements correspond to slide 30 and describe reasons a student would not do well on an exam, and the last half of the 10 statements correspond to slide 31 and describe reasons a student would perform well. Table 11.8 shows Dawood's survey as it was presented to students, with scores from a hypothetical student.

Remember that Dawood, as part of the intervention, administered this survey after the first two exams had been given. Dawood gave each student a total score from the first five statements and a second total score from the last five statements. For example, let's say I answered 2, 4, 3, 1, 3 for the first five statements. That would give me a score of 13 for the Poor-Preparation statements. Let's say I answered 5, 3, 4, 2, 1 for the last five statements. That would give me a score of 15 for the Good-Preparation statements. After calculating scores for each of the 15 students, Dawood categorized them into groups based on whether their Poor-Preparation score or their Good-Preparation score was greater. Although Dawood called them Group 1 and Group 2, so as not to

Figure 11.3 Electrical Engineering Exam Averages Before and After a 50-Minute Intervention Delivered After Exam 2

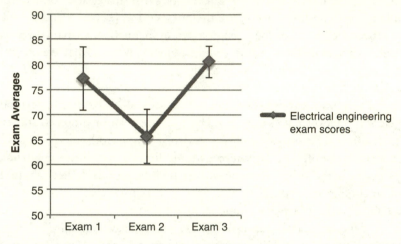

Note. Figure compares exam averages from Muhammad Dawood's fall 2013 electrical engineering course. Averages are plotted with error bars of plus or minus one standard error. Dawood delivered a learning strategies session to his students between exams 2 and 3.

Table 11.7 Exam Averages, Standard Deviations, and Number of Test Takers in Figure 11.3

Exam 1 Average (SD)	Exam 2 Average (SD)	Exam 3 Average (SD)
77.2 (24.6)	65.7 (20.8)	80.5 (12.3)
n = 15	*n* = 15	*n* = 15

Note. Table shows the means, standard deviations, and number of test takers for the data presented in Figure 11.3. Standard error is the standard deviation divided by the square root of *n*, and the error bars in Figure 11.3 show plus or minus one standard error.

shame his students, let's call these two groups the Poor-Preparation group and the Good-Preparation group for ease of discussion. Based on my hypothetical scores in Table 11.8, I would be placed in the Good-Preparation group. (You didn't really think I was going to put myself in the other group, did you?) Dawood found that seven students made up the Poor-Preparation group, six made up the Good-Preparation group, and two students had equal scores.

Immediately after tallying the survey results, Dawood then calculated average exam scores for the Poor-Preparation and Good-Preparation groups. He was quite surprised to find that the averages on the first two exams for both

Table 11.8 Dawood's Study Habits Survey With Scores From a Hypothetical Student: "Find Out Where You Belong—Group 1 or Group 2"

Group 1	Your score	Group 2	Your score
1. Didn't spend enough time on the material	2	1. Did preview-review for every class	5
2. Started the homework too late	4	2. Did a little of the homework at a time	3
3. Didn't memorize the information I needed to	3	3. Used the book and did the suggested problems	4
4. Did not use the book	1	4. Made flashcards of the information to be memorized	2
5. Assumed I understood information that I had read and reread but hadn't applied	3	5. Practiced explaining the information to others	1
Total Group 1 score	13	Total Group 2 score	15

Note. Table reproduces Dawood's study habits survey, given during his intervention. Students rated statements 1–5 on a scale of 1 to 5, where 1 corresponded to "completely disagree," 2 to "partially disagree," 3 to "neither agree nor disagree," 4 to "partially agree," and 5 to "fully agree." Students compared their "Total Group 1 score" to their "Total Group 2 score" to find out if they belonged in Group 1 (which I call the Poor-Preparation group for ease of discussion) or Group 2 (which I call the Good-Preparation group). Group 1 students were explicitly encouraged to take actions to move to Group 2. Group 2 students were encouraged to keep up the good work.

groups were so disparate: The Good-Preparation group averaged 94.5% and 80.0% (with standard deviations of 3.6 and 14.9 percentage points respectively), whereas the Poor-Preparation group averaged 58.3% and 54.2% (with standard deviations of 24.3 and 17.6 percentage points respectively) (see Figure 11.4 for these results; Table 11.9 displays raw data).

This analysis of preintervention exam scores might support a point made in chapter 5, that students who are doing well have *already* absorbed effective learning strategies, either unconsciously or consciously. It's not true that there are smart students and slow students; there are students who have (and use) effective strategies and students who do not.

As a supplemental intervention, Dawood informed the students of the group they fell into and the average exam scores (Figure 11.4 and Table 11.9) of the students in each group. He encouraged students to immediately adopt the behaviors of the students who did well (slide 31, *Chemistry Presentation*) in order to improve their performance on the third exam (see Figure 11.3). He also administered this survey a *second* time after the third exam, which was given after the intervention.

Figure 11.4 Preintervention Exam Scores From the Self-Reported Good-Preparation and Poor-Preparation Groups

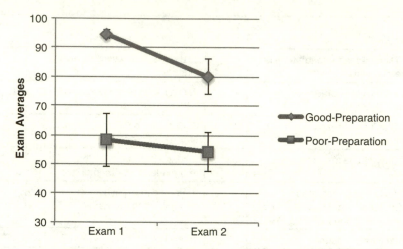

Note. Figure compares preintervention exam averages from two different groups of students. The students filled out the survey in Table 11.8, and the survey results indicated whether they had prepared well or poorly for the first two course exams. Averages are plotted with error bars of plus or minus one standard error.

Table 11.9 Exam Averages, Standard Deviations, and Number of Test Takers in Figure 11.4

	Exam 1 (preintervention) Average (SD)	Exam 2 (preintervention) Average (SD)
Good-Preparation group	94.5 (3.6) *n* = 7	80.0 (14.9) *n* = 7
Poor-Preparation group	58.3 (24.3) *n* = 6	54.2 (17.6) *n* = 6

Note. Table shows the means, standard deviations, and number of test takers for the data presented in Figure 11.4. Standard error is the standard deviation divided by the square root of *n*, and the error bars in Figure 11.4 show plus or minus one standard error.

Dawood then undertook an additional analysis of both administrations of the study habits survey. First, he observed how many students *moved* from the Poor-Preparation group to the Good-Preparation group after the intervention. Eight of his 15 students made the jump from Poor-Preparation to Good-Preparation, including all seven of the original Poor-Preparation students and one of the students who had equal scores. By the third exam only one student was poorly prepared, and that student had begun as one who had equal scores. So Dawood's observations suggest that the intervention was very effective at making students aware of their own study habits and encouraging them to make positive changes. In fact, in the seven-question exit survey, Dawood specifically asked students to assess whether being placed in one of the two groups helped them improve their habits (question #4). Nine out of 15 students said that it had, and two did not answer the question.

We can also investigate from Dawood's data whether students' efforts to better prepare themselves yielded gains. Two students' trajectories are impressive: Student #11 earned exam scores of 24, 28, and 77, and student #13 earned exam scores of 27, 44, and 90. These scores may reflect the impact of a one-hour learning strategies intervention conducted by someone other than me. Two other students' exam scores show recovery after doing badly on exam 2: Student #1 earned scores of 86, 47, and 84, and student #4 gained 30 points, with scores of 73, 33, and 66. Student #5 maintained his or her improvement from exam 1 to 2 (preintervention) with scores of 56, 82, and 80. The other two students who started out in the Poor-Preparation group and moved to the Good-Preparation group did not enjoy improved results. Their scores were 77, 62, and 65 (Student #10), and 65, 71, and 63 (Student #12). So, as I have previously conceded, learning strategies are not a panacea for all, but they can enable some students to see a dramatic turnaround (see appendix F) and allow others to see significant improvement.

Finally, we turn to Dawood's seven-question exit survey results. When asked how they changed their study habits for exam 3 compared to exams 1 and 2 (questions #1 and #2), 10 out of 15 students responded that they spent more time studying and/or doing the homework, previewed and reviewed, paraphrased class notes, read actively (underlined, highlighted, read aloud), noted areas of confusion (metacognition), consulted with the professor, began studying earlier, used examples from the textbook, started the homework as soon as it was posted, and made use of study groups. The other five students responded that they did not make many or any changes; that corresponds nicely to the fact that six students began in the Good-Preparation group. When asked whether they made use of the study cycle handout (question #3), 10 out of 15 responded that they used all or part of the handout. Interestingly, Dawood asked them when they would have preferred to receive the learning strategies information, at the beginning of the semester or after the first exam (question #5). Seven out of 15 students would have wanted it after the first exam, and 3 of 15 would have preferred it at the beginning of the semester. Four out of 15 students said they would have wanted the information between the beginning of the semester and the first exam. The remaining student commented that the lecture came at just the right time because he did worst on the second exam. Perhaps this comment suggests it might be helpful to give a difficult quiz during the first 2 weeks of the semester and present the learning strategies shortly thereafter. This approach may strike a good balance between those who need a jolting wake-up call and those who are attentive enough to benefit from the information before an important assessment.

In response to being asked whether they used the learning strategies in their other courses (question #6), 8 out of 15 students responded that they had. One student reported that he or she had made a 91 on his or her most recent test in a signals course, compared to a 77 on the previous test. Another student reported that his or her grades in a circuits course had gotten much better. Yet another student mentioned that although he or she had not used the strategies in other courses that semester, he or she planned to do so during the following semester. Question #7 in the exit survey asked students to submit any additional comments or observations.

Dawood's response to being exposed to the learning strategies is an interesting case study. He shared the strategies with his students and creatively invented instruments to investigate their impact and effectiveness. You should also feel free to be as creative as you wish, using my materials only as a template. As you think about the contribution you might make to the literature, please keep in mind that larger class sizes are more useful for persuading our statistically minded friends, and for good reason. I believe all of the evidence presented in this book presents an extremely strong case, but I am also happy to be kept on the straight and narrow by my statistician buddies. I believe that more rigorously designed studies with larger sample sizes can only help our efforts.

Anecdotal Evidence for the Impact of a 50-Minute Intervention

I'd like to share with you some feedback I received from April L. Hill, a biology professor from the University of Richmond in Virginia. After completing her introductory undergraduate biology course, which included explicit instruction in metacognition and mindset, students were asked to answer questions in an exit survey.

One question asked, "What aspects of the course contributed most to your learning?" Students were prompted with a drop-down menu with a range of options, including class lectures, in-class activities, case studies, out-of-class lectures, problem-solving sessions, authentic research experiments in lab, group study sessions, and peer tutors. An option for a free response was also included. One student wrote,

The thing that contributed most to my learning was that after I failed the first exam, the instructors said that they believed in me and that there was no reason that I could not ace the course. I just needed to adjust how I was studying. Then, they taught me how to study.

Here are some answers given in response to the question, "Please comment on how this class has changed your attitude toward this subject."

I think that prior to this class I would have been hesitant to ask for help but the teachers provided me an increased confidence in myself and asking for help.

When I first began, I had extremely low self-esteem and I wanted to quit. After working with Professor Hill and my fellow students, I began to love the class and truly make the most out of it. It was and still is challenging, but that is my favorite part.

As I truly did not like science leaving high school, the spark that the teachers have made me a lot more interested in the subject. I think that I have more confidence hearing that they believe in me.

Finally, and perhaps of most interest to us, students gave these answers in response to the question, "How has the class changed the ways you learn/study?"

When I got my first bad grade back, I freaked out. We discussed as a class study habits and what the teachers can do to help us learn. This helped me gain a new skill set. I have always had to study hard in order to understand a topic; therefore, I already had some study skills. Now I have a better set.

This course stretched my ability and has given me the tools to not just memorize and regurgitate facts on the tests, but rather to synthesize data and grasp a concept as a whole.

It has helped me see that I am more successful if I study/review material right after I am given it instead of looking back at the material a couple days later.

I have begun to prepare myself for other classes much better. I complete readings fully and I analyze them myself before I go into the classroom to discuss it.

I struggled at first to grasp the concepts because I wasn't studying the right way but as the class progressed, I found a useful method for me. This class taught me studying/learning skills I did not consider before, thus allowing me to make the most out of class time.

It may be interesting to note that these comments run the gamut; they highlight the importance of everything from noncognitive variables to study skills to metacognition to learning strategies. If we equip our students fully, they can succeed fully.

Finally, let's hear from Lynn Futral, a professor of psychology at Southern Crescent Technical College. She gives her students an assignment that requires them to study a presentation on metacognition (similar to *General Presentation*) and take learning styles diagnostics. They then write a reflection paper about how they will use this information in their learning. One of her students wrote,

> In the PowerPoint, it said, "Stay in learn mode not study mode." This was a good lesson for me because I feel as if I was studying too much and not actually learning. I also have never tried teaching the material to someone else to get a better understanding of the facts and to make sure that I have actually learned the material. This had the greatest impact on me and my study habits because it is something that I have never tried. (Futral, personal communication, November 24, 2014)

Futral is thrilled with the results, and has told me that she sees a big difference in student attitude, behavior, learning, and grades since she started doing this. At the end of the fall 2014 semester, she e-mailed me the following comment: "I have the most wonderful students this semester—engaged, prepared, participative, and positive. I owe it all to teaching them the learning strategies you presented in the workshop" (personal communication, November 24, 2014).

The Secret Ingredients

One of the reasons I wrote this book is to convince others that they can see the same dramatic results with their students as I have seen with mine and as many other educators have seen with theirs. If you have never delivered a presentation like *General Presentation* or *Chemistry Presentation* to students, it may take you a few spins around the block to feel completely comfortable and confident. But I also believe that—just as students can go from Ds to As using effective strategies—there are a few adjustments that you can make to get great results. The adjustments I describe for the rest of the chapter will help you deliver learning strategies interventions in an engaging and compelling manner. They apply to working with groups or individuals.

Secret Ingredient #1: Be Specific

Often, after I give a presentation, an exasperated instructor will approach me and insist, "But that's what I tell my students to do! They just won't do it!" Here's the conversation that usually ensues.

"Did you show them Bloom's Taxonomy?"

"No."

"Did you show them the study cycle?"

"No."

"Did you ask them any reflection questions like 'What's the difference between studying and learning?'?"

"No."

"Did you talk to them about how to get the most out of their homework?"

"No."

"Did you teach them active reading strategies?"

"No."

" . . . "

"But I told them they need to study!"

" . . . "

Secret Ingredient #2: Believe

I hope my stories have given you enough faith that you can communicate confidence in these methods. Without that confidence, you may see some results, but you are not likely to see the kinds of results that you could. Most communication is nonverbal. For example, if you have children, you know that it's pretty difficult to lie to them. If you don't believe that your students can be successful, they will probably know. And it will affect their faith in the strategies and their willingness to implement them. There's nothing magic about the strategies. Putting in the time and effort to use them will yield results. But you do need a little bit of magic to convince your students to expend that effort. That's where your confidence and belief come in.

I once met an acupuncturist who told me an interesting story about his training. Before training as an acupuncturist, he had been certified in allopathic (or traditional Western) medicine and had been an outstanding health professional. So he was very confident about his potential as an acupuncturist. Initially and unexpectedly for him, he found that his fellow acupuncture students with no medical training were much more effective at helping their patients than he was. He told me that, to his surprise, once he let go of the skepticism he had learned from Western medicine and concentrated fully on the flow of life energy (*qi*), his patients began to see results. We, too, must let go of the belief that some students are smart and some students are slow if we want to effectively teach strategies that will inspire all students to excel, no matter what their past performance has been.

Secret Ingredient #3: Take the Pressure Off

When you watch the supplemental video, you will notice that I repeatedly refer to what the brain is doing, what it wants, or its unruly behavior. It is no accident that I talk about the brain like it is an enthusiastic but sometimes unmanageable pet. Doing this accomplishes two things: First, it models metacognition for the students. I describe what the brain is doing, just as they should be learning to describe what their brains are doing and paying attention to how their minds work, including how they react to different strategies and stimuli. Second, it takes the pressure off the students and instantly improves their self-talk. Instead of, "I bombed that test because I'm stupid," they now have the option of saying to themselves, "I just didn't give my brain what it needed to perform well."

I also take the pressure off by explicitly relating to students' struggles wherever I can. For example, when I am sharing the homework strategy, I tell the students that I myself did homework the wrong way throughout my undergraduate career. Make sure students do not feel accused or guilty by helping them understand that their struggles are universal. It's a great way to ensure their buy-in.

Secret Ingredient #4: Listen Intently

Each of us loves to be listened to. When someone who believes in us listens to us, it provides safety and optimal conditions for success. You can demonstrate to audiences that you are listening to them by including interactive activities in your intervention, by paraphrasing the answers that you hear from them, and by letting their input provide variety and spontaneity to the intervention. We all love games. Listening and tailoring your response to what you hear adds an element of play that greatly facilitates learning.

Secret Ingredient #5: Use Accessible, Inclusive Language and Be Authentic

Another quality that allows us to establish rapport with students is our willingness to use unconventional, informal language. I talk about information "flying out of their heads," or about being in "git-'er-done" mode. I'm not talking down to the students, trying to use slang, or trying to be "relatable." I'm just being as comfortable and informal as possible, so that they will let their guard down and let go of their fear of being wrong or of impending intellectual humiliation. When we use jargon and bigger words, it immediately puts most people on the defensive without their even realizing it. Let your guard down, and your audiences can too. For example, one outcome that I promise to students at the beginning of an intervention appears on the slide as follows: "You will understand exactly what changes you need to implement to make an A in the course." But during a presentation, I might actually say, "You will understand the difference between what you *have* been doing and what you *need* to start doing." The meaning is the same, but the simpler language conveys the point more effectively.

I also make it a point to say "us" rather than "you" whenever possible. For example, when I am asking students whether they have been in "study mode" versus "learn mode," I might say, "How many of us, up to this point in the semester, have been in 'study mode' rather than 'learn mode'?" And then I raise my hand to not only model what the students should do but also include myself in the process of being converted from a superficial learner to a deep learner.

Secret Ingredient #6: Make the Sale

This point is important. You'll notice that during the intervention, after I have delivered important information, I do not leave it up to the students to do what they will with that information. I very explicitly tell them what they need to do and the results they can expect if they do it. For example, after explaining the homework strategy and the success that other students have had using that strategy, I do not leave it there. I explicitly tell the students, "So you should study your notes as if for a quiz or test, rework the examples without looking at the solutions, and then approach each homework problem by trying your very hardest to solve it before referring to your notes or the book." I go on to say, "If you do that, you will be much better prepared for the test, and you will do much better." Yes, it's a little bit of programming! We have to make the sale in order for our students to see results. During the intervention, we are not information-delivery systems. We are salespeople.

Feeding the Five Thousand—or Five Million!

I hope this chapter, along with the slide sets and supplemental video, serves as a valuable resource for those of you who would like to deliver these learning strategies to groups.

I have proven by working with large lecture classes at LSU that it is possible to efficiently deliver powerful learning strategies to hundreds of students at a time. Join with me, and let's increase those numbers together until students around the world are committed to deep, lasting learning.

12

TEACHING UNPREPARED
STUDENTS

"Without [this supplemental chemistry review/learning strategies class], I prob-
ably would have gotten a C. You showed us the first week a way to get an A in
[general chemistry], and I knew that was going to be my only way to achieve
that A. I was planning on just studying before the test. But when you stressed
how important it was to preview and review and study two hours a day or so, I
was in shock, but I followed the guideline and got myself an A."—Michael W.,
first-year LSU student in a learning strategies course required for students
unprepared to take general chemistry, personal communication, December
25, 2008

When I speak to faculty groups around the country, I hear many faculty say,
"If my students were better prepared for my class, they would be doing fine!"
They believe that lack of academic preparation is the primary reason that
students are not successful. I, too, used to lament, "If only these students had
learned basic problem solving skills in high school . . ." But I have seen with
my own eyes just how quickly unprepared students can gain lost ground. I
now know that it wasn't lack of preparation that was holding them back; I
wasn't teaching them the learning strategies that they needed.

In this chapter, I present six of the strategies discussed in Kathleen
Gabriel's (2008) excellent book *Teaching Unprepared Students*. The strategies
are appropriate for all students but are particularly effective with unprepared
students, who are more likely to feel overwhelmed and inadequate after
doing poorly on the first test or quiz. I have mentioned versions of many of
these strategies in previous chapters, but I offer them together in this chapter
because I have found that they work best in tandem. Whereas in previous
chapters I have suggested that you choose only one or two strategies to begin
with, I strongly recommend that if you teach unprepared students, you use
all six of the strategies presented here. All the strategies are summarized in

Figure 12.1. Remember that unprepared students are not lost causes. But they do need clear, specific guidance and direction.

Strategy #1: Establish High Expectations and Clearly Define *Student Success*

A version of this strategy has already been presented in chapter 8, where I suggest that you be exceedingly clear about your course structure and the specific behaviors that you expect from students. For example, your syllabus might include specific reading assignments from books or textbooks, weekly homework assignments that are pitched at an appropriate level, and frequent quizzes or tests. It is important to indicate what percentage of the students' grades will be determined by each assessment or assignment. If students know exactly how to approach each assignment and what kind of preparation they should undertake for each test, they will be more likely to succeed. For example, in some courses such as anatomy, students must spend a lot of time memorizing information, whereas other courses, like medical ethics, primarily emphasize high-level application of concepts. Unprepared students are less likely to know what they need to do to be successful in each of their classes, particularly because those requirements are likely to be different. Clear expectations are especially important for students whose previous academic experience may not have prepared them for your classroom or campus culture.

Let all students know exactly what you expect from them—using the same language for prepared and unprepared students alike. Aguilar et al. (2014) give several types of psychological interventions that can help unprepared students succeed. In the course of their discussion they describe the characteristics of a successful intervention: (a) it addresses specific student concerns, (b) it does not single out any student or group of students, (c) it asks the student to become the source of the intervention, generating thoughts and ideas rather than passively receiving them, and (d) it is not delivered as an intervention, nor is it delivered more than one time (Aguilar et al., 2014). For example, Aguilar et al. describe an introductory physics class asked to read a survey from a previous class that indicates how anxious and insecure all physics students feel at the beginning of the course. That survey also reassures students that, over time, they will grow in competence and confidence. Aguilar et al. (2014) also mention common mistakes that well-meaning instructors make: giving too much praise to students for average or subpar work or for merely participating in class; mentioning too many times that a *particular* student or a group of students can succeed; or becoming overexcited when a particular student makes an insightful comment or answers a question correctly.

If you can take the time to consider carefully how you communicate with your students, they will benefit tremendously and your job will be much more enjoyable.

Strategy #2: Interweave Assessment and Teaching

You've seen a version of this strategy in my advice in chapter 8 to test early and often. Unprepared students need a lot of feedback in order to find, by trial and error, which metacognitive strategies work for them. Rest assured that the students in your class who are well prepared will also benefit from frequent opportunities to test their understanding. As instructors, we also need feedback to gauge how our students are responding to our methods. If they are struggling, we can't just throw our hands up and dumb down the material; we can investigate how we might be able to adjust our methods, and strongly encourage the students to use the learning resources available to them, such as online study guides or tutorial services on campus, perhaps with the incentive of a few extra credit points.

Strategy #3: Meet Your Students Where They Are

We should be prepared to teach basic vocabulary, learning strategies, and time-management skills that we may not need to teach better prepared students. Or we can make it clear to our students where they can learn those skills, and we can regularly reiterate that information. We must not assume students aren't smart just because they lack foundational knowledge or basic skills. On the contrary, we should assume that every student can make an A in our classes if he or she undertakes the correct behaviors. And we must clearly and convincingly communicate our belief to our students.

Strategy #4: Present Metacognitive Strategies to Your Students

The 50-minute intervention discussed in chapter 11 (see also appendices D and H) can be presented to classes of prepared and unprepared students alike so that they will have the tools they need for success.

Strategy #5: Clarify Student Responsibility

After you have given your students everything they need in order to succeed, make sure they understand that they are responsible for the rest. Throughout the course, give constant, friendly reminders that you expect them to come to class prepared, having done the appropriate reading or finished the relevant assignments. If they bomb a particular quiz or test, make it clear that you expect better of them, and that you have high expectations because you are confident that they can meet them. We mustn't scold our students, because that will paralyze some of them. Instead we can challenge our students while communicating our faith that they can rise to the occasion. You'll probably be as pleasantly surprised as I was by how many students will successfully meet the challenge.

Strategy #6: Stay Connected

Encourage students to visit you during office hours. If your classes are small enough, get to know your students' names and use them. Try not to let your students be anonymous. A little bit of personal connection goes a long way.

If you have the time, consider staying in touch with your students via e-mail. You might try sending group e-mails to the entire class or personal e-mails to individual students, congratulating them on a job well done, or inviting them to office hours if they need a boost. If you do communicate with your students electronically, consider including an e-mail policy in your syllabus, explaining what is and isn't appropriate e-mail behavior. For example, tell them what should be in the subject line of their e-mails (e.g., name, course number), how you would like them to address you, and what types of e-mails you are willing to entertain (e.g., an alert about an unexpected absence, a request for an office hours visit). Also tell them what is not appropriate if there are particular things you do not want to see in an e-mail from a student (e.g., "Hey" as a salutation, requests for special favors not available to all their classmates).

Have Faith—This Stuff Works!

Why am I so confident that unprepared students can gain most of the ground they have lost in secondary school? I see living proof each and every semester. But don't take my word for it. Consider that many minority serving institutions (MSIs), including historically black colleges and universities (HBCUs), produce hundreds of students who go on to do very well at the nation's top graduate and professional schools. How does a student enter Xavier University of Louisiana with a 930 combined SAT score (writing score excluded) end up earning a PhD from an Ivy League institution? At Xavier, faculty meet students where they are and guide them to where they need to be.[1]

Let me tell you the story of an LSU student, Charles, from rural Louisiana. He had done very well in high school but was unprepared for the rigors of college. To make matters worse, his father contracted a serious illness in the middle of Charles's studies. But, after faltering twice, Charles prevailed with the help of these six strategies.

Charles's Story

We begin Charles's story at the low point of his academic career. As a math major, Charles had flunked out of LSU not once but twice. After he left school for the second time, Charles decided to volunteer as a football coaching assistant at a prestigious private middle school. An affluent businessman whose son played on the team noticed Charles's infectious optimism and unique brand of compassionate rigor. He also noticed Charles's uncommon rapport with the kids and how effectively he motivated them, so he hired Charles to tutor his son in math. As a result of Charles's tutoring, the businessman's son began to make As. When word got around that the coach's helper was an excellent math tutor, many more parents hired him to tutor their children. The children not only went from making Cs to As but also started to enjoy math.

The businessman thought to himself, "This guy's too smart not to have a degree." So he contacted a retired LSU administrator to see if he knew anyone who could get Charles readmitted to LSU. He promised that if LSU readmitted Charles, he would pay for everything—tuition, fees, books, meals, and housing. Keep in mind that LSU almost never readmits students who have been dismissed twice for academic reasons. This retired administrator called me and told me about the businessman's offer. He also told me that Charles had graduated from high school with a great GPA and had good standardized test scores but had bombed twice at LSU. I was intrigued and decided to meet with Charles.

During our meeting, I learned that Charles's father had been diagnosed with lung cancer during his fifth year in school. He had bounced from major to major during those five years and hadn't been doing well academically. After his father's diagnosis, he had spent every weekend driving eight hours round-trip to be with his father, who died during the second semester of that year. He was so devastated that he stopped attending classes and was dismissed for academic reasons. After sitting out for a year, he was readmitted. The second time around, Charles began taking more difficult math classes and attempted to do well in those courses on his own, without any assistance from anyone. Although he was encouraged to visit the learning center, he resisted because he thought that he should be able to excel in his courses without help. He told me that on one occasion, he even came to the learning center and stood in front of the door but couldn't make himself go in. Over the years I have learned that it is not uncommon at all for students to get to the door of the campus academic support center and then turn around before going in. But often those who do finally go in say, "I wish I had come sooner!" When I ask them why they didn't come sooner, a typical answer is, "I didn't know *this* is what you were gonna tell me. I thought you were just gonna tell me to study harder, or spend more time on my studies, or stop socializing so much." Students think we're going to tell them things they already know they should be doing, and they have no idea that they will leave the center with powerful learning strategies they can use for their entire academic experience. Tragically, so many students and faculty do not know the immediate and dramatic impact that learning strategies can have. For Charles, that ignorance resulted in his flunking out of school a second time.

After I found out that Charles was willing to learn and implement effective learning strategies, I called the director of admissions on his behalf. I told the director that if he admitted him on a provisional basis for the summer term, I would guarantee that Charles would earn a 4.0 GPA. I assured the director that I fully understood that if Charles didn't get a 4.0, he could be dismissed for good. After expressing surprise that I would guarantee a 4.0, the director agreed to grant Charles a conditional summer-only admission. Charles took nine credit hours of classes that summer and did achieve the 4.0 that earned him readmission to LSU. He graduated from LSU in August 2009 having earned a 3.4 GPA for all his coursework since that critical summer session. Charles is now living his dream of teaching mathematics to high school and middle school students. He also continues to coach football.

Charles was unprepared for the rigor of college, and he also suffered a major life crisis, as unprepared students often do. But with support and learning strategies, Charles fulfilled his intellectual and academic potential. Please do not give up on students who have not yet developed the skills they need to succeed. Help them acquire those skills, and you will be adding to our vibrant, productive citizenry.

Success Is Possible

It is daunting to face a classroom of students who have not been adequately prepared for the material we are responsible for teaching them. But the semester does not have to be one long, arduous, soul-destroying struggle. We must establish high and clear expectations, provide constant feedback,

Figure 12.1 Six Strategies for Teaching Unprepared Students

- Establish clear, high expectations.
- Interweave assessment and teaching.
- Meet your students where they are.
- Give a 50-minute presentation on metacognitive learning strategies (see online slide set).
- Clarify student responsibility.
- Stay connected.

Note. Figure lists six strategies for teaching students who are not prepared to learn the material you have been charged to teach them. Use all of them, and you and your students will have a much more successful, enjoyable semester.

give our students extra resources and learning strategies, keep their feet to the fire, and stay connected (see Figure 12.1). Most unprepared students will not only do much better in our courses but also learn how to succeed in all of their subsequent courses. The payoff will be enormous for them and for you.

Note

1. Xavier University is a small, private HBCU in New Orleans, Louisiana. Perenially, it has been the number-one supplier of African American students to medical schools (Cooper, 2012). The exceptional success of Xavier students can be traced to a program that was started in 1976 by four professors—representing biology, chemistry, physics, and mathematics—and Dr. Arthur Whimbey, thinking skills pioneer and author of the 1975 seminal text, *Intelligence Can Be Taught*. The motto of the group was "Take good students and make them super stars" (Lester W. Jones, personal communication, June 4, 2015). They felt that although Xavier enrolled good students, they could become academic superstars if given the right tools. The summer program, Stress on Analytical Reasoning (SOAR), taught students critical thinking, analytical reasoning, and problem solving skills. This impressive effort is discussed in an article that describes the components of the summer program and the statistically significant gains of the students on both the Preliminary Scholastic Aptitude Test (PSAT) and the Nelson-Denny Reading Test after only four weeks of what the authors termed *cognitive process instruction* (Whimbey, Carmichael, Jones, Hunter, & Vincent, 1980, p. 5). These students would definitely be candidates for anyone's miracle portfolio.

EPILOGUE

Experiment and Have Fun!

In the previous chapters, I have presented quite a few strategies, but I hope the underlying principles are clear:

- Students need to believe they can be successful.
- Students need to know exactly what is expected of them.
- Students need to have an arsenal of effective learning strategies.

Each of the strategies presented in this book fulfills one of those three aims.

In this chapter, we will look at how you can go about discovering which strategies work best for your students.

No Right or Wrong Approaches, Just Joyful Exploration

This book is not a collection of controlled, double-blind studies. I have presented observations, anecdotes, and some data. I have taken you on a highly personal journey, the one that I have traveled during my four decades of teaching. But your story is your own. You will discover new insights and strategies on your own journey. There is no right or wrong way to do it. Just experiment, and have loads of fun in the process!

Use the Scientific Method

Most of us probably learned the scientific method in middle or high school: Make observations and pose a question; create a hypothesis based on those observations; experiment to test your hypothesis; draw conclusions based on your results; revise the hypothesis according to your results; and design new experiments; continue the process until you have the answers you're looking for. That's exactly the process I went through to determine that the strategies provided in this book are effective with students.

Make a guess about which strategies will work best for your students based on what you have observed in past semesters or from your current classes. Experiment by introducing those strategies and encouraging your students to implement them. (Be sure to give them examples of students who have used the strategies and dramatically improved their performance.) Look at the results and determine which alternative or additional strategies might work. Keep at it until you are satisfied with your class's performance. Consider keeping a record of the strategies that turn student performance around so you can refer to it in future semesters or share it with colleagues.

For those of you who might be more ambitious, you can turn your results into publishable research, just as my colleagues Cook and Zhao have done (Cook et al., 2013; Zhao et al., 2014).

Different Strokes for Different Folks

Keep in mind that if a strategy does not work for one student or class, that doesn't necessarily mean it will not work for another. You will learn over time which strategies work best with which types of students or classes. For example, some students love flashcards and cannot wait to work their way through a hundred of them each day, whereas other students feel ill just looking at a single card. These students might do better with a large concept map and handwritten outlines.

A Simple Starter Kit

For those of you who may be wondering how on earth you're going to teach all of this in addition to the course content, rest assured that implementing only two or three of the suggestions in the book will make a huge difference for your students. Here's my suggested starter kit for beginners:

- Create a clear syllabus and course structure. If your syllabus and course structure have been finalized, consider adding just one additional assessment or clarification.
- Give or invite someone to give a 50-minute presentation to your students (chapter 11, appendices D and H). If you use the online slide set from chapter 11 as a template, your students will learn about Bloom's Taxonomy (chapter 4), the study cycle (chapter 4), and specific metacognitive strategies (chapter 5). They will also begin

to take responsibility for their learning by making the connection between behavior and performance (chapters 6–9).

- Remind students throughout the semester about the academic assistance resources available to them on campus (chapter 10).

And that's it! That's not so bad, right?

Exercise: Commit to Action

In the following space, please write down two to three strategies that you will commit to implementing in your classes as soon as possible. The sooner you start, the sooner your students will be on their way to becoming independent, self-directed learners who will succeed in not only your class but also in their lives!

The Final Frontier: Using Your Own Creativity to Transform Student Learning

After you've become comfortable with this starter kit, you can begin to introduce some of the other strategies I've suggested. Before long, you'll be developing your own strategies. Or maybe you've already had some great ideas as you've been reading. Go for it! In my view, a student's developing mind is the final frontier. I encourage you to boldly go where no educator has gone before. You'll have your students' galaxy-sized gratitude.

APPENDIX A: COMPILATION OF STRATEGIES FOR STUDENTS

The 39 strategies listed here are a combination of the metacognitive, learning, study, and testing strategies presented in this book.

1. Strive for higher levels of Bloom's Taxonomy. (Chapter 4)
2. Implement the study cycle and schedule three to four intense study sessions per day. (Chapter 4)
3. Actively prepare to read by previewing reading assignments. (Chapter 5)
4. Read actively by developing questions before you start to read. (Chapter 5)
5. Paraphrase information in each paragraph of a reading assignment. (Chapter 5)
6. Actively read and learn by using flashcards, concept maps, chapter maps, and other tools. (Chapter 5)
7. Read the textbook. (Chapter 5)
8. Always attend every class. (Chapter 5)
9. Take good class notes by hand. (Chapter 5)
10. Preview and review for every class. (Chapter 4)
11. Do homework assignments without using examples or textbook information. (Chapter 5)
12. Prepare as if you have to teach the information you are learning. (Chapter 5)
13. Study with a partner or study group, and go to each session prepared. (Chapter 5)
14. Create practice exams to evaluate your mastery of the material. (Chapter 5)
15. Start homework the day that it is assigned and do a little of it each day. (Chapter 10)
16. Memorize everything you're told to memorize. (Chapter 11)
17. Aim for 100% mastery of the material. (Chapter 11)
18. Adopt a growth mindset about intelligence. (Chapter 6)
19. Monitor your self-talk and stay positive. (Chapter 6)

20. Attribute results to actions, not ability. (Chapter 6)
21. Know and understand your MBTI personality type. (Chapter 9)
22. Know and understand your learning style preferences. (Chapter 9)
23. Get adequate rest, nutrition, and exercise. (Chapter 9)
24. Keep a semester calendar. (Chapter 10)
25. Keep a weekly calendar. (Chapter 10)
26. Commit to studying 20–25 hours per week. (Chapter 10)
27. Protect your free time. (Chapter 10)
28. Prioritize according to needs and wants. (Chapter 10)
29. Organize test information by preparing charts, outlines, or a study guide. (Chapter 10)
30. Determine the types of questions that upcoming tests will feature (essay, short answer, multiple choice, T/F, etc.). (Chapter 10)
31. Write down formulas or other information you may need before you begin an exam. (Chapter 10)
32. Read test directions *very* carefully; listen for additional directions; and ask for clarification. (Chapter 10)
33. Survey the exam before starting and budget your time. (Chapter 10)
34. Begin with the easiest test questions and work your way to the harder ones. (Chapter 10)
35. Expect memory blocks and recognize that the information will come back to you if you move on to other questions. (Chapter 10)
36. Perform deep breathing to relax, and use positive self-talk to reduce test anxiety. (Chapter 10)
37. Analyze all returned tests and quizzes, and develop a plan for improvement. (Chapter 10)
38. Use the campus learning center for group study, tutoring, and other helpful information. (Chapter 10)
39. Visit your professors' office hours on a regular basis. (Chapter 8)

APPENDIX B: BOOKS AND WEB LINKS RECOMMENDED FOR STUDENTS

Books

- David Ellis. (2014). *Becoming a Master Student.* Boston: Cengage Learning.
- John Medina. (2008). *Brain Rules.* Seattle, WA: Pear Press.
- Carol Dweck. (2006). *Mindset: The New Psychology of Success.* New York: Random House.
- Terry Doyle and Todd Zakrajsek. (2013). *The New Science of Learning: How to Learn in Harmony With Your Brain.* Sterling, VA: Stylus.
- Gary Demar. (2008). *Memory Mechanics: How to Memorize Anything.* Powder Springs, GA: American Vision Press.

Links

For information on how to start a study group:

students.lsu.edu/academicsuccess/studying/peer/groups

To assess your mindset:

www.mindsetonline.com

To discover your learning style preference:

www.vark-learn.com/english/page.asp?p=questionnaire

For study recommendations tailored to your learning preference:

www.vark-learn.com/english/page.asp?p=helpsheets

For time management tools:

    students.lsu.edu/academicsuccess/studying/strategies/time

For more test preparation strategies:

    www.howtostudy.org

For more learning, study, and testing strategies:

    www.cas.lsu.edu
    www.drearlbloch.com

For relaxation techniques and stress relief:

    www.ucdmc.ucdavis.edu/hr/hrdepts/asap/Documents/Relaxation_
      Techniques.pdf

APPENDIX C: COMPILATION OF STRATEGIES FOR INSTRUCTORS

The 33 strategies listed here are the strategies for instructors presented throughout this book.

1. Emphasize that students' actions, not their intelligence, will determine their success. (Chapter 6)
2. Create a supportive environment in the classroom by demonstrating your belief that all students can be successful and that you will help each one of them attain success. (Chapter 12)
3. Teach students about metacognition, Bloom's Taxonomy, and the study cycle. Teach Bloom's using the four-step process in Chapter 4. (Chapters 3 and 4)
4. Provide students with the information in appendices A and B.
5. Discuss attribution theory with students so they recognize if they are unrealistically attributing their successes and failures to causes outside of their control. (Chapter 8)
6. Give a 45–60-minute learning strategies presentation after students receive the results of their first test or quiz that executes the first five strategies. (Chapter 11; Appendices D and F)
7. Help students develop a growth mindset about intelligence by showing "before and after" exam scores of other students who went from Ds or Fs to As and Bs. Ask them to recall challenges they've already overcome, and share challenges from your own life. (Chapter 6)
8. Create a course syllabus that makes your expectations, course structure, requirements for success, and student responsibilities crystal clear. (Chapter 8)
9. Require the textbook. (Chapter 5)
10. Engage students in a metacognitive, get-acquainted activity on the first day of class. (Chapter 8)
11. Establish high expectations and show students how to meet those expectations on the first day of class. (Chapter 12)

12. Connect the course topics and learning activities to your students' interests. (Chapter 8)

13. Interweave assessment and teaching by testing early (within the first two weeks) and often. Doing so will encourage more students to keep pace with the course. (Chapters 8 and 12)

14. Provide early opportunities for success so that students can build confidence in their ability to excel in the course. (Chapter 8)

15. Help students achieve gradual, persistent growth by beginning with manageable homework and tests and incrementally increasing the level of difficulty. (Chapter 8)

16. Meet students where they are and teach them basic skills necessary for success. Students may not come fully prepared, but they can still do well if a little time is spent helping them review the basics. (Chapter 12)

17. Clearly articulate assignment expectations to students and provide rubrics and exemplars if possible. (Chapters 8 and 12)

18. Provide students targeted feedback, perhaps with a comment that you are providing the feedback because you have high standards and believe in their ability to meet or exceed them. (Chapter 8)

19. Make class sessions more engaging by introducing active learning strategies such as think-pair-shares, small group problem solving, and reflection questions. Do a 1–2-minute activity for every 15–20 minutes of class. (Chapter 8)

20. Give students a task to complete at the end of class as an "exit ticket." This one- or two-sentence summary of the day's important concepts will help students consolidate their comprehension. (Chapter 8)

21. Do a short weekly goal-setting exercise with students. (Chapter 8)

22. Allow students to choose paper, project, or discussion topics. (Chapter 8)

23. Assign students real-world tasks to help them develop a sense of belonging to the larger community. (Chapter 8)

24. Give students opportunities to work together in small groups by administering group quizzes, group problem-solving exercises, or group projects. (Chapter 8)

25. Provide guidelines for working effectively in groups. (Chapter 8)

26. Introduce "switch days" during which students will be called upon to teach some of the concepts. (Chapter 8)

27. Allow students to play learning games, like *Who Wants to Be a Millionaire* or *Jeopardy!*, to review course material. (Chapter 8)

28. Stay connected to each student so he or she does not feel invisible. (Chapter 12)

29. Partner with the campus learning center to provide learning strategies information. (Chapter 10)

30. Have students take a learning styles preference diagnostic test and write a reflection about the strategies they will use in class, while studying, and during exams to optimize their learning. (Chapter 9)

31. Discuss the importance of adequate rest, proper nutrition, and exercise for academic success. (Chapter 9)

32. Experiment with different ways to deliver learning strategies to students, and have faith that your students can and will improve their learning. Have fun during the process! (Epilogue)

33. Keep it simple and use the suggested starter kit on pages 164–165.

APPENDIX D: RESOURCES FOR PRESENTING LEARNING STRATEGIES TO GROUPS

At styluspub.presswarehouse.com/Titles/TeachStudentsHowtoLearn.aspx, you will find the following resources:

1. A slide set called *General Presentation*, a presentation about metacognitive learning strategies for a general student audience
2. A slide set called *Chemistry Presentation*, a presentation tailored specifically for first-semester general chemistry at LSU
3. A slide set called *Presentation Template*, which is identical to *Chemistry Presentation* except all of the course-specific material has been removed so that it can be replaced with whatever you choose
4. A video of my presentation of a learning strategies session to a group of students in general chemistry at LSU; the slides that appear during that video are similar to the slides that make up *Chemistry Presentation*, but be aware that there are differences

Ahead you will find a guide to introducing metacognition and learning strategies to students. Enjoy!

Introducing Metacognition and Learning Strategies to Students: A Step-by-Step Guide

Many faculty have asked me to explain just what happens in learning strategies sessions with students. The steps I usually take are listed ahead, but there is no right or wrong way to do it. (These steps can be used in individual sessions or with a class or other group.) If you believe that all students can succeed (as I do), and if you teach them about metacognition and learning strategies, help them develop a growth intelligence mindset, and motivate them to use the strategies, you will see positive results! Use these steps as a guide if you like, but please adapt them to your individual needs.

1. Wait until students have gotten the results of their first major test or quiz; they're more likely to listen.
2. Consider not revealing to the class that the session will present learning strategies; they're more likely to show up. (Or, you can indicate that the session will help them become more efficient learners.)
3. Ascertain career goals at the beginning of the session. (This will allow you to tether the strategies to goals the student ultimately wants to attain.)
4. Show dramatic before and after results from other students or classes.
5. Define *metacognition*.
6. Consider including the "Count the Vowels" exercise or another exercise that demonstrates the power of strategies.
7. Ask reflection questions, such as the ones here:
   a. What's the difference between *studying* and *learning*? Which have you been doing up to this point?
   b. For which task would you work harder: (a) to make an A on the next test, or (b) to teach the material that will be covered on the next test for a review session for the class? (The overwhelming majority of students say they would work harder if they have to teach the material.) Up to this point, when preparing for a test, have you been putting in the amount of effort commensurate with making an A or teaching the material?
8. Introduce Bloom's Taxonomy.
9. Introduce the study cycle and intense study sessions as a way of ascending Bloom's.
10. Discuss specific strategies, particularly emphasizing the following:
    a. Reading Comprehension: Preview material before reading, develop questions you expect the passage to answer, and read one paragraph at a time while stopping to paraphrase the information read.

b. Doing Homework Without Using Examples: Study the information before looking at the first homework problem, work the example problems without looking at the solutions, and treat the homework problems as if they were test questions. Work a few of them at a time before checking to see if you did them correctly.

11. Discuss reasons students may or may not have done well on the first exam or quiz. Highlight reasons that focus on the students' *behavior*, not on circumstances they can't control. Lead them to take responsibility for their results.

12. Ask students the following two questions "on a scale of 1 to 10" to bring it home: (a) How different are these strategies from what you were doing before? (b) How motivated are you to use them? (I'm very satisfied with answers of 8, 9, or 10; satisfied with 6 or 7; and concerned about answers of 5 or lower.)

13. Elicit a commitment by asking students to write down which strategy or strategies they will commit to using for the next few weeks.

14. Provide online resources and direct students to the campus learning center.

15. Express confidence that if students *use* the strategies they *will* be successful, no matter what their past performance has been.

APPENDIX E: LEARNING STRATEGIES INVENTORY

T his inventory lists behaviors that you should exhibit in order to excel in this course. Write "true" or "false" beside each of the following statements describing the way you study. The scoring scale at the end will predict your grade in the course.

1. I always preview the material that will be discussed before I go to class.
2. I go over my lecture notes as soon as possible after lecture to rework them and note problem areas.
3. I try to do my homework without using example problems as a guide or copying answers from my class notes or textbook.
4. I regularly go to office hours or tutoring to discuss problems or questions about the homework.
5. I rework all of the homework problems and questions before the test or quiz.
6. I spend some time studying for this class at least five days per week (outside of class).
7. I make mnemonics for myself to help me remember facts and equations.
8. I make diagrams or draw mental pictures of the concepts discussed in class.
9. I participate in a study group where we do homework and quiz ourselves on the material.
10. I rework all of the quiz and test items I have missed *before* the next class session.
11. I realize that I can still do well in this class even if I have done poorly on the quizzes and tests up to this point.

The predicted grade for your performance in this class is provided:

Number of True Responses	Predicted Grade
9 or more	A
6–8	B
4–5	C
2–3	D
less than 2	F

Note that you can change your predicted grade at any point by changing your behavior such that more of the statements are true.

APPENDIX F: DRAMATIC INDIVIDUAL STUDENT IMPROVEMENT

The following examples are of students whose performance increased dramatically after learning about metacognition, Bloom's Taxonomy, and the study cycle. The students were in classes at different institutions and from different disciplines. All are from semesters between fall 2005 and spring 2014. Underlined scores are from after the intervention. These are just a fraction of the success stories that have crossed my path.

Robert, freshman, general chemistry	42, <u>100, 100, 100</u>
Michael, senior, organic chemistry	30, 28, <u>80, 91</u>
Miriam, freshman, calculus	37.5, <u>83, 93</u>
Ifeanyi, sophomore, thermodynamics	67, 54, 68, <u>95</u>
Jazmin, freshman, history	44, <u>87, 86</u>
Kristy, freshman, general chemistry	60, <u>100, 99, 84</u>
Adam, senior, analytical chemistry	76, 61, 61, <u>107</u>
Blanche, freshman, general chemistry	63, <u>79, 87, 100</u>
Aaron, freshman, general biology	78, <u>92</u>
Maryan, freshman, art history	57, <u>87</u>
Jessie, freshman, general chemistry	60, <u>92, 83, 83</u>
Frederick, sophomore, analytical chemistry	77, 65, 68, <u>88</u>
Cathy, freshman, trigonometry	77, <u>99</u>
Natalie, freshman, general chemistry	63, <u>92, 79, 96</u>
Elizabeth, freshman, general chemistry	67, <u>84, 87, 87</u>
Stephanie, sophomore, analytical chemistry	83, 55, 65, <u>90</u>
Rachel, freshman, general chemistry	70, <u>92, 95, 84</u>
Morayo, sophomore, organic chemistry	61, 73, <u>99</u>

Cory, psychology	68, <u>83, 82, 86, 82</u>
Miranda, psychology	65, <u>84, 86, 88, 82</u>
M'Famara, sophomore, analytical chemistry	70, 46, 68, <u>88</u>
Matt, freshman, general chemistry	65, 55, <u>95</u>

APPENDIX G: SELECTED STUDENT FEEDBACK

I decided to include this somewhat arbitrary selection of student feedback so that readers might have a visceral experience of the relief and excitement some students feel when they are introduced to metacognition and learning strategies.

The content of student correspondence has been faithfully reproduced; spelling and grammar have been standardized.

From Matt J., Weber State University, Class of 2016

September 15, 2014

Dr. McGuire,

My name is Matt, I am a junior at Weber State. I was present on Thursday for your presentation on metacognition. Before I share the effect it is already having I would like to tell you about myself. I am a high school dropout, "class" of 06, I started college in 2011. I am 26, married with 2 kids ages 2, and 6 months. . . . With a truly incredible amount of things that need my attention every day, I really must make the most of my class time, and also my study time. Suffering toward the severe side of ADD, it is a task itself to stay focused, let alone deep focus. Honestly it can be so frustrating trying to learn or study and just not have the ability to focus my thoughts. I feel at times I am just not smart enough to keep up with college and should just quit. It is even a bit emotional as I think about the future for my family. I am not a quitter though. Now the exciting part! I have tried the suggestions you gave in your presentation, and it was like magic, seriously. When I was studying my chemistry this past week, even if I have to reference my outline multiple times to stay on track, organizing my information differently somehow has made what I was studying at the time stick so much better. I think probably because my brain knew where to put the information??? I hope to master these techniques and share them with everyone. My plan is to increase my GPA so I can get into grad school. I want to say thank you, because not only do I feel I am learning more efficiently and I feel like my self-esteem is going up. But it is also allowing me the much needed little bit of extra time to spend with my wife and kids because I am understanding concepts quicker and better. Thank you again so much. These methods are changing my life . . .

Best regards,
Matt J.

September 30, 2014

Dr. Mac,
I had my first test in principles of chemistry (II) this past weekend. Let's just say . . . I could not have dreamed of it going any better! My first two quizzes I failed, and my first lab report I did very poorly also. Luckily they are not worth many points. I definitely feel like I tripped straight out of the gate and fell flat on my face in this class. Now it is totally going up! My homework scores are progressively going up. I aced my last two quizzes and as far as my test I got an 85%! The reason I am so excited about that is, there were two questions that I knew I had not gone over enough to build the connections and reason my way through them, so I worked them the best I could. A third question I felt like I was 70% there with what I needed to know but at a crucial point just could not get past where I needed to and nearly ran out of time. What was so exciting was I was so confident in my answers because of the way I had organized the information in my head and how given the information I was to solve the problem. I knew almost instantly what formulas would apply, what exceptions needed to be taken into consideration, and so on. I really am starting to see things increase greatly in this class, and I know it will continue to get even better for me! I have realized also, now being in a position to help/explain concepts that, if I follow some of these metacognition methods it is so easy to clarify to other students. Then they go ("Oh!" well ok, that is simple enough). It's simple because they are looking at the problem now in a much more efficient way of understanding!

—Matt J.

From Sydnie L., LSU Class of 2017

January 20, 2014

Hi Dr. McGuire,
This is Sydnie L., the student you talked with after giving the CAS presentation to Dr. Cook's Honors Chem 1421 class. I just wanted to thank you for giving me the tools I needed to succeed in my classes. . . . For Chem 1421, I made sure to preview the textbook and note templates before class. I took detailed notes so that I wouldn't be confused by my gibberish later when studying. I tried to review my notes shortly after chemistry lecture, and to work homework problems while the information was still fresh. I studied hard before each exam. I would work as many practice problems as I could, and if I wasn't sure how to work a problem I would visit the tutors in the Tutorial Center. I made sure to work almost all of the recommended practice problems for the end of each chapter (I really think this was the most helpful change I made). I attended as many [supplemental instruction] sessions as time allowed. I also took advantage of every bonus assignment, not only for the points but also as a learning opportunity.

Sincerely,
Sydnie L.

May 7, 2014

Hey Dr. McGuire!
I'm so sorry that it has been so long since we have talked. This semester has been much more busy for me than last semester. I was much more active with LSU Ambassadors as well as my part-time job at a dermatology office. I also spent a great deal of time training to be an orientation leader for LSU this summer. You'll be pleased to hear that I expect to finish the semester with a 4.0 again! I made it my goal to work hard early in the semester, and maintain high averages in all of my courses. Toward the end of the semester things got crazy and I didn't study as hard, and my exams showed that. I didn't do well on Dr. Cook's final, but I earned the grade I received because I didn't study the way I should have. But because I worked hard early in the semester, I'll still pull a low A in Chem 1422. I'll be sure to use this exam as a reminder of why it's so important to stay dedicated to my study strategies all semester long, and will work much harder next semester. . . . All things considered, I'm still proud of myself and the grades that I have made this semester.

Sincerely,
Sydnie L.

From Morgan B., Nursing Major, Lynchburg College, VA, Class of 2017

February 3, 2014

I just wanted to thank you for coming to Lynchburg College and sharing your strategies with us. I have been practicing your studying recommendations and I just took a quiz in bio today and got a 100%! I find it extremely helpful and it should make nursing school easier on me. Thank you so much!
—Morgan B.

From Western Michigan University Program Director Anetra Grice: Feedback From Two Students

February 19, 2013

Hi Saundra!
. . . I wanted to pass along a few student comments we've received from recent meetings we've held as part of our early intervention project. These comments directly reference the benefits of sitting down with students and explaining the learning cycle. I thought you might enjoy hearing how your visit with us has directly impacted our students!

"My biggest problem last semester was sitting down and taking the time to study and evaluate the course material, for tests or homework, which hurt me the most! I spent maybe 3 hours or less a week on studying or doing homework. This semester I have made a MAJOR change in my study habits! Instead of hanging out with friends right after class, I now spend at least 30 minutes reviewing my class notes and digesting the lecture. I stopped going home on weekends, because I wasn't doing my homework or studying there. I now dedicate my Saturday and Sunday morning to studying and homework. While this is not an overnight fix I believe I'm taking a step in the right direction. The meeting with Bryan was helpful in the fact that it made me realize that I'm no longer in High School and that the study routine which worked for me there will NOT work here. I respect and VERY much appreciate the meeting. It's very nice knowing I go to a school where the faculty truly look out for your best interest and want you to succeed!! I very much look forward to follow up emails with you and any suggestion, ideas, or constructive criticism you have for me that will help me benefit in my studies here at WMU!"

"Yes I found the meeting to be extremely helpful. I have been following his advice on documenting my study times. I have not made it to 30 hours each week, but I am steadily increasing my study hours each week to reach the goal. Please give Dr. Tsang my thanks. What he showed me has been wonderful. On both of my exams so far this semester I passed them with flying colors and on one of the exams I got the highest grade in the class."

Thank you again for your help and I hope that you are well!

Anetra Grice
WMU-STEP Program Director
College of Engineering and Applied Sciences Western Michigan University

From Ben M., Mathematics Major, the University of Mississippi

September 4, 2012

My name is Ben. I am a math undergraduate at Ole Miss. We met over the summer at a mentor workshop during the SMILE program at LSU.

I just wanted to write and say thank you for the work that you have done. I have used a lot of the things that you presented to us during your workshop. And I only started this summer, but they are really helping me this semester.

I was the outstanding math student at Northwest Mississippi Community College when I graduated in 2008 and then I was out of school for 3 years. When I returned to school last fall I had a lot of trouble concentrating, procrastinating, and I did not do well at all. In the spring semester things were even worse. After two semesters my GPA went from a 3.97 to a 3.11. I thought I might not be able to finish a degree.

This semester I am armed with the resources and knowledge that you provided to us in your workshop, and without them I don't think I would have come back this fall, or been prepared when I did.

I know I have not finished the story here, but if you had to wait till the end to know you made a difference, well, that just wouldn't be any fun at all.

Thanks again,
Ben

From Student of Chemistry Instructor Catherine Situma, Louisiana State University

June 25, 2009

. . . I have always had a difficult time understanding Chemistry—even in high school. But I have always made good grades. Well, last fall I did not do well in Chemistry 1201 at all. I did not understand why I did so badly. Anyway I had to retake the class this semester and I failed the first test the second time around in Chem 1201! Thank you Dr. Situma for inviting the wonderful Dr. Saundra McGuire to teach us how to study general chemistry!! I had spoken with Dr. McGuire once before and she explained many of the situations to me like she did that day in class. Having met her and seeing her again that day made me realize I had been studying for Chem 1201 all wrong. Now I know that I cannot study for Chemistry the way I do in other classes. She made me understand that. I especially liked the idea of preview-review. That really helped me pass this class this semester—I got a B in Chem 1201 after flunking it last semester!!! I am very content with the B. Thanks again Dr. Situma.

From Student of History Instructor Carla Falkner, Northeast Mississippi Community College

February 8, 2007

Thanks. Metacognition made a BIG difference in my grade. I found out that I am an auditory learner recording the lectures works best for me. I realized that a lot of words are flying over my head while I am taking notes, key pieces that can help me to produce a clearer image. Some of my notes were taken so quickly that I couldn't make ANY sense out of them when I tried to read them, but now I have a tape to back them up so I can figure out what they were supposed to mean. I just thought you would like some positive feedback since you keep taking the time to inform us with metacognition. I cannot say the word hardly or spell it but without a doubt I know it WORKS!!!!

From Candace E., Southern University of New Orleans Chemistry Student

I wanted to say thank you for helping me improve my study skills in Chemistry. When I met you I was repeating General Chemistry for the second time, failed three tests, and I had an "F" average for midterms. I never understood how I could study for hours and still fail my chemistry tests. Then I went on LSU's Center for Academic Success website and realized that I was studying wrong. So with your help I'm no longer intimidated by

chemistry or any other subject for that matter. This semester my goal is to make As in General Chemistry 112 and 112 Lab. Today is the first day of school for Southern University at New Orleans and I went to my chemistry class ready to discuss Chapter 15. My Professor, Dr. Bopp asked ME to slow down. I told him you can't slow down when you're on a roll!!!!!!!!!!
—Candace E.

From Student of Chemistry Instructor Algernon Kelley, The College at Brockport SUNY

May 28, 2015

Dear Dr. Kelley,
First of all, I wanted to thank you very sincerely for taking the time early in the spring semester to come talk to our biochem 2 class. In addition, I cannot thank you enough for meeting with me to talk about how to adjust my own study strategies and improve my scholastic performance at the beginning of the semester.

When you came to our biochem class to talk about improving study habits, I hadn't done terribly on the first biochem exam—I just hadn't done as well as I would have liked. However, I was very worried about my present ineffective study strategies for physics 240 with Dr. Tahar. I also was hoping to improve my biochem 2 grade. You gave me some of the best advice I have received in my three years of undergrad. You told me to start (1) working out homework problems without the Internet on paper, (2) going to every class, (3) reviewing what would be taught in class, (4) get help from the professor as a last resort when I couldn't figure out a problem, rather than turning to the Internet, and finally (5) keeping my phone off as much as possible and not listening to music as I work. After hearing all this, I will be honest and say I really didn't think it would work for me. I thought that physics 235 with Dr. Tahar had been impossibly difficult and physics 240 would be equally, if not more so, difficult. I had been attending class before talking to you but had been texting and not paying attention during class thinking "there's no way I will understand anyway." However, after talking to you, I decided to try some of the strategies. I started working out 1–3 homework problems before class in a quiet room during my 1 hour break between classes. I also reviewed the chapter before going to class. I started keeping my phone off except for certain times, like lunch or when I had to meet up with someone. The results were surprisingly drastic. The next exam after talking to you I got over 20 points higher than the class average. I was so excited and couldn't wait to tell you. However, I decided to continue studying and in addition to the few things I had already tried that you advised me to do. I decided to also try to do as many odd-numbered end of chapter problems as possible to help prepare me for the next test. The last thing I wanted was to do worse on the next exam. Again, I improved from the last test.

For your future talks in front of freshman, sophomore, junior, or even senior audiences, my grades can be an example of how heeding your excellent suggestions can transform grades.

Biochem 2: spring, 2015—(there was a fourth exam but I never was able to see what I got on the take-home portion, which was 50% of the grade, so I left that grade out)
-> Exam 1: 84% (without your study strategies)
-> Exam 2: 87%
-> Exam 3: 90%
-> ACS Final Exam: 47/60 (this grade was in the 87th percentile nationally)
Final grade in class: A-

Physics 235 with Dr. Tahar: fall, 2014—(without your study strategies)
-> Exam 1: 66%
-> Exam 2: 52%
-> Exam 3: 36%
-> Exam 4: not sure what this grade was
Lab grade: 97%
Homework: 100% (thank-you Internet)
Rocket launch: extra 2% toward final grade
Final grade in class: C+

Physics 240 with Dr. Tahar: spring 2015—(with your study strategies for Exams 2–4)
-> Exam 1: 71% (without your study strategies)
-> Exam 2: 83%
-> Exam 3: 86%
-> Exam 4: 91%
Lab grade: 98%
Homework: 100% (doing problems out with the help of my book and professor when necessary for the most part)
Rocket launch: extra 2% toward final grade in class
Final grade in class: A

Thank you for giving me such great advice and for following up on me throughout the semester.

Thanks!
Sincerely,
Autumn

APPENDIX H: SLIDES FROM *CHEMISTRY PRESENTATION*

Figure H.1: Slide 1

Figure H.2: Slide 2

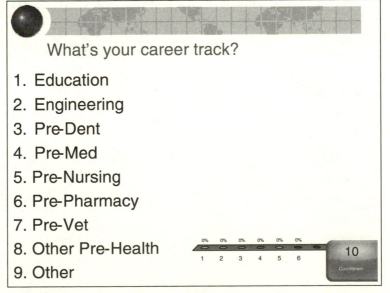

Figure H.3: Slide 3

Figure H.4: Slide 4

The Story of Four LSU Chem 1201Students

❖ Robert   Final Grade:
     42, <u>100, 100, 100</u>   A
❖ Kristy
     60, <u>100, 99, 84</u>   A
❖ Blanche
     63 <u>79, 87, 100</u>   A
❖ Joshua
     68, 50, (50), <u>87, 87, 97</u>   A

Figure H.5: Slide 5

Get the Most Out of Homework

- ◈ Start the problems early–the day they are assigned
- ◈ **Do not flip back to see example problems; work them yourself!**
- ◈ Don't give up too soon (<15 min.)
- ◈ Don't spend too much time (>30 min.)

Figure H.6: Slide 6

Performance in Gen Chem I in 2011 Based on One Learning Strategies Session

	Attended	Absent
Exam 1 Avg.:	71.65%	70.45%
Exam 2 Avg.:	77.18%	68.90%
Final course Avg*.:	81.60%	70.43%
Final Course Grade:	B	C

The one 50-min presentation on study and learning strategies again resulted in an improvement of one full letter grade!

Figure H.7: Slide 7

Performance in Gen Chem 1202 Sp 2013 Based on One Learning Strategies Session

	Attended	Absent
Exam 1 Avg.:	71.33%	69.27%
Homework Total	169.8	119.1
Final course Avg*.:	82.36%	67.71%
Final Course Grade:	B	D

The 50-min presentation on study and learning strategies resulted in an improvement of two letter grades!

Figure H.8: Slide 8

Desired outcomes

- You will analyze your current learning strategies for Chemistry 1421
- You will understand exactly what changes you need to implement to make an A in the course
- You will have concrete strategies to use during the remainder of the semester, and you will USE them in Chem 1421 and beyond!
- You will become a more efficient learner by studying *smarter*, not necessarily *harder*

Figure H.9: Slide 9

Reflection Questions

⊕ What's the difference, if any, between *studying* chemistry and *learning* chemistry?

⊕ For which task would you work harder:
   A. Make an A on the test
   B. Teach the material to the class?

Figure H.10: Slide 10

Which mode have you been in?

1. Study mode
2. Learn mode

Figure H.11: Slide 11

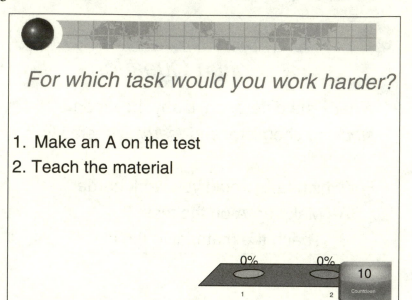

Figure H.12: Slide 12

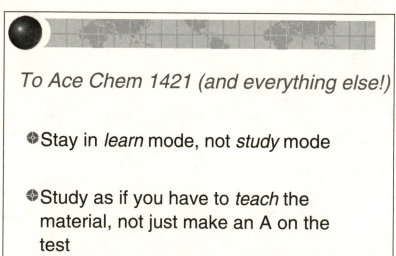

Figure H.13: Slide 13

Why is this so important?
Because 1421 is Harder Than HS Chem

- The course moves a lot faster
- The material is conceptually more difficult and cumulative
- The problems are more involved
- The tests are less straightforward and require you to **apply** several concepts at one time

Figure H.14: Slide 14

Example from Test 1:

Perform the indicated operations, expressing the answer to the proper number of sig figs and in scientific notation:

$$\frac{4.5600 \times 10^3 - 2.9 \times 10^1}{8}$$, where 8 is an exact number

A) 6×10^2
B) 5.7×10^2
C) 5.66×10^2
D) 5.664×10^2
E) 5.6638×10^2

Figure H.15: Slide 15

Example from Test 1 Correct Answer:

Perform the indicated operations, expressing the answer to the proper number of sig figs and in scientific notation:

$$\frac{4.5600 \times 10^3 - 2.9 \times 10^1}{8}$$, where 8 is an exact number

A) 6×10^2 39%
B) 5.7×10^2 44%
C) 5.66×10^2 4%
D) 5.664×10^2 7%   Correct answer
E) 5.6638×10^2 6%

Figure H.16: Slide 16

Second Example from Test 1:

Which of the reaction equations correctly describes this reaction?

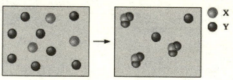

A) $3\,X + 8\,Y \rightarrow 3\,XY_2 + 2\,Y$
B) $3\,X + 6\,Y \rightarrow X_3Y_6$
C) $3\,X + 8\,Y \rightarrow X_3Y_8$
D) $X + 2\,Y \rightarrow XY_2$
E) $X + Y_2 \rightarrow XY_2$

Figure H.17: Slide 17

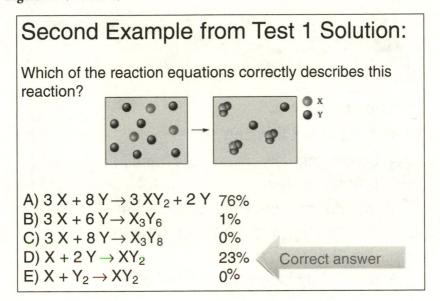

Second Example from Test 1 Solution:

Which of the reaction equations correctly describes this reaction?

○ X
● Y

A) $3 X + 8 Y \rightarrow 3 XY_2 + 2 Y$ 76%
B) $3 X + 6 Y \rightarrow X_3Y_6$ 1%
C) $3 X + 8 Y \rightarrow X_3Y_8$ 0%
D) $X + 2 Y \rightarrow XY_2$ 23%   ◁ Correct answer
E) $X + Y_2 \rightarrow XY_2$ 0%

Figure H.18: Slide 18

Using Metacognition to Become an Expert Learner in Chemistry

Figure H.19: Slide 19

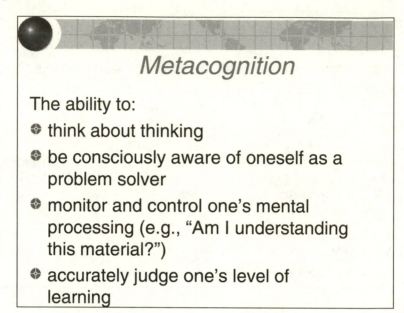

Figure H.20: Slide 20

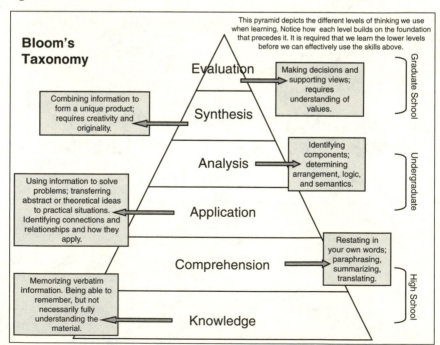

Figure H.21: Slide 21

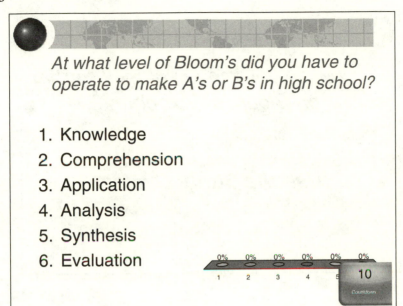

Figure H.22: Slide 22

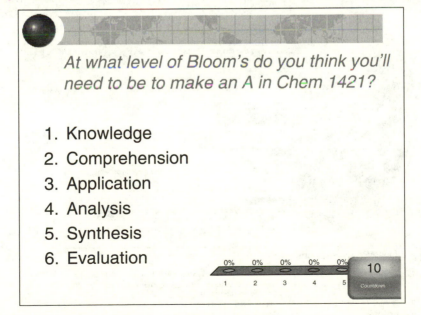

Figure H.23: Slide 23

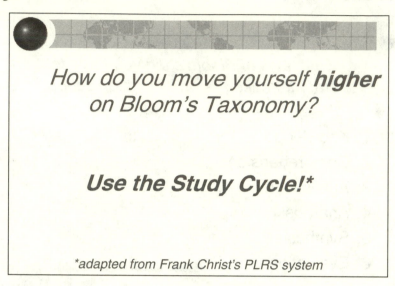

Figure H.24: Slide 24

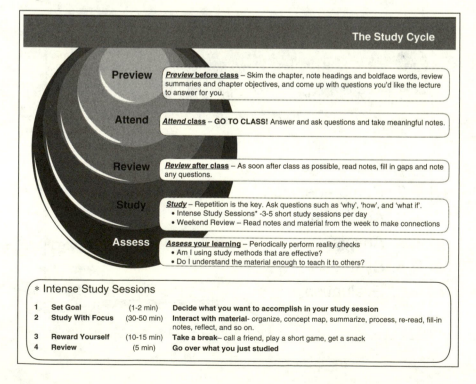

Figure H.25: Slide 25

Effective Metacognitive Strategies

- Always solve problems without looking at an example or the solution
- Memorize everything you're told to memorize (e.g., polyatomic ions)
- Always ask why, how, and what if questions
- Test understanding by giving "mini lectures" on concepts
- Spend time on chemistry every day
- Use the Study Cycle with Intense Study Sessions
- Attend SI sessions on a regular basis
- Aim for 100% mastery, not 90%!

Figure H.26: Slide 26

Concept maps facilitate development of higher order thinking skills

Figure H.27: Slide 27

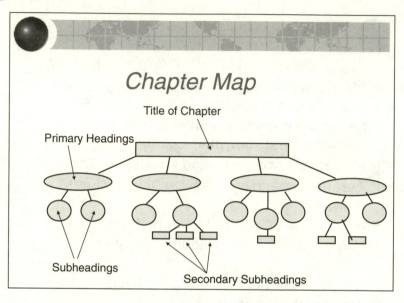

Figure H.28: Slide 28

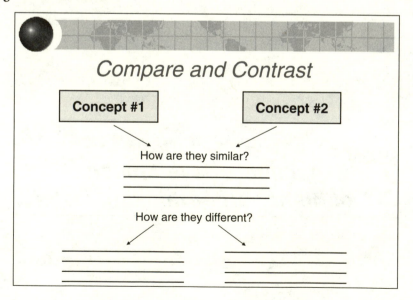

Figure H.29: Slide 29

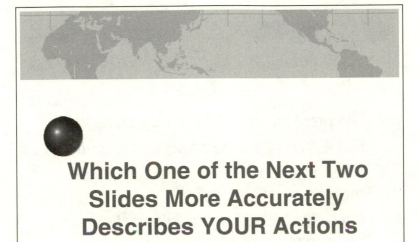

Which One of the Next Two Slides More Accurately Describes YOUR Actions Before Test 1?

Figure H.30: Slide 30

Top 5 Reasons Folks Did Not Do Well on Test 1 in Gen Chemistry in Fall 2009:

❖ 1. Didn't spend enough time on the material
❖ 2. Started the homework too late
❖ 3. Didn't memorize the information I needed to
❖ 4. Did not use the book
❖ 5. Assumed I understood information that I had read and re-read, but had not applied

Figure H.31: Slide 31

Top 5 Reasons Folks Made an A on Test 1:

1. Did preview-review for every class
2. Did a little of the homework at a time
3. Used the book and did the suggested problems
4. Made flashcards of the information to be memorized
5. Practiced explaining the information to others

Figure H.32: Slide 32

Which group did you most resemble?

1. Group that did not do well
2. Group that made an A

0%   0%

10
Countdown

1   2

Figure H.33: Slide 33

 Email from Joshua, Chem 1201 student

"...Personally, I am not so good at chemistry and unfortunately, at this point my grade for that class is reflecting exactly that. I am emailing you inquiring about a possibility of you tutoring me."

April 6, 2011

"I made a 68, 50, (50), 87, 87, and a 97 on my final. **I ended up earning a 90 (A) in the course, but I started with a 60 (D)**. I think what I did different was make sidenotes in each chapter and as I progressed onto the next chapter I was able to refer to these notes. I would say that in chemistry everything builds from the previous topic.

May 13, 2011 Semester GPA: 3.8

Figure H.34: Slide 34

Get the Most Out of Homework Reprise

- Start the problems early – the day they are assigned
- Do not flip back to see example problems; work them yourself!
- Don't give up too soon (<15 min.)
- Don't spend too much time (>30 min.)

Figure H.35: Slide 35

Get the Most from SI Sessions, Tutorial Centers, Office Hours, and Study Groups

◆Try to understand the concept or work the problem by yourself first

◆Come prepared to ask questions

◆Explain the material to the tutor or instructor

Figure H.36: Slide 36

CAS Resources

Figure H.37: Slide 37

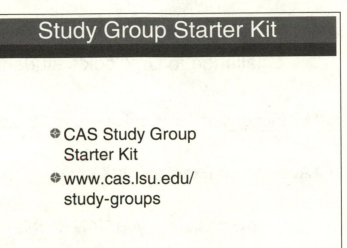

Figure H.38: Slide 38

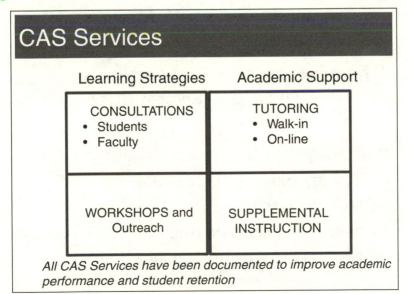

Figure H.39: Slide 39

Challenge to Dr. Cook's students

◆ Metacognition Discussion – Sep 23, 2013

◆ Average on Exam 2: 120 (80%)

How do I know you CAN do this?

Because students at the
LSU Dental School did it!

Figure H.40: Slide 40

The 2004 LSU Dental School First Year Class:
An Amazing Success Story!

◆ Metacognition Discussion – August 13, 2004
◆ Histology Exam – August 23, 2004
◆ Previous class averages: 74 – 78
◆ Challenge to class on August 13: 84 average
◆ Reported average on August 24: 85!

Figure H.41: Slide 41

Writing Exercise

What strategy will you use

for the next three weeks?

Figure H.42: Slide 42

Which one strategy are you most likely to implement for the next test?

1. Do preview review
2. Do homework differently
3. Use the textbook more
4. Do more problems
5. Practice teaching the material
6. None of the above

Figure H.43: Slide 43

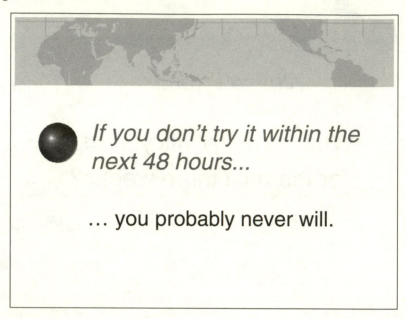

Figure H.44: Slide 44

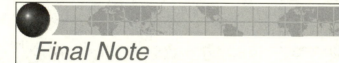

APPENDIX I: AN ADVANCED PLACEMENT PHYSICS CLASS

I met Lorenzo Foster, now a high school chemistry and physics teacher, about ten years ago when he was an undergraduate at LSU. He was an invaluable tutor for the CAS, and we have kept in touch over the years. This year, Foster taught Advanced Placement physics for the first time at a school in rural Louisiana. A few weeks into the term, he sensed that his students were in trouble, so he asked me to present a learning strategies session before their first exam. I told him that he was more than capable of giving the session and that he should do it *after* the first exam so that they would not dismiss the strategies (see chapter 11). I e-mailed him the PowerPoint presentation in appendix H, and he adapted it for his physics students. After they began using the strategies, their performance radically improved. Here are their exam scores.

Student	Exam 1	Exam 2	Exam 3
1	73	95	100
2	90	86	100
3	50	90	67
4	83	100	100
5	57	98	93
6	80	85	100
7	50	95	100
8	37	89	100
9	89	100	100
10	47	79	100
11	95	98	100
12	67	74	78
13	39	87	84
14	43	64	95

Student	Exam 1	Exam 2	Exam 3
15	40	90	100
16	85	100	100
17	90	75	100
18	84	94	100
19	67	94	93
20	90	97	93.5
21	100	85	88
22	42	100	100
23	22	86	98
24	99	100	100
25	53	69	100
Avg	66.9	86.8	95.6

Foster kept me apprised of the class's performance throughout the term and e-mailed me their results after each exam. When I opened his e-mail containing the scores on exam 3 and saw all of the perfect scores, I assumed that he had made the test easier or given lots of bonus questions. But when I asked him whether exam 3 was a softball, he said, "Nope. This test was just as hard as the others, but they said they're just studying differently." Moreover, the data show that some students performed worse on exam 3 than on the other exams, further suggesting that there was not a huge difference in difficulty across exams.

Because of their outstanding effort, I visited the class at the end of the school year and gave them a pizza party. During the party I asked the class to tell me exactly what they started doing differently after the first exam. Their responses made it clear that high school students are mature enough to change their study habits when given effective tools.

REFERENCES

Aguilar, L., Walton, G., & Wieman C. (2014). Psychological insights for improved physics teaching. *Physics Today, 67,* 43–49.

Ambrose, S. A., Bridges, M. W., DiPietro M., Lovett, M. C., & Norman, M. K. (2010). *How learning works: Seven research-based principles for smart teaching.* San Francisco, CA: Jossey-Bass.

Anderson, L. W., Krathwohl, D. R., Airasian, P. W., Cruikshank, K. A., Mayer, R. E., Pintrich, P. R., . . . Wittrock M. C. (2001). *A taxonomy of learning teaching and assessing: A revision of Bloom's taxonomy of educational objectives.* New York, NY: Longman.

Angelo, T. A., & Cross, K. P. (1993). *Classroom assessment techniques: A handbook for college teachers* (2nd ed.). San Francisco, CA: Jossey-Bass.

Barr, R. B., & Tagg, J. (1995). From teaching to learning: A new paradigm for undergraduate education. *Change, 27*(6), 12–25.

Bloom, B. S., Englehart, M. B., Furst, E. J., Hill, W. H., & Krathwohl, D. R. (1956). *Taxonomy of educational objectives: The classification of educational goals* (Vol. 1). New York, NY: McKay.

Bransford, J. (1979). *Human cognition: Learning, understanding, and remembering.* Belmont, CA: Wadsworth.

Bransford, J. D., Brown, A. L., & Cocking, R. R. (Eds.). (2000). *How people learn: Brain, mind, experience, and school.* Washington, DC: National Academy Press.

Bringle, R. G., & Hatcher, J. A. (1995). A service-learning curriculum for faculty. *Michigan Journal of Community Service-Learning, 2,* 112.

Bruce, L. L., & Neary T. J. (1995). The limbic system of tetrapods: A comparative analysis of cortical and amygdalar populations. *Brain, Behavior and Evolution, 46*(4–5), 224–234.

Bruner, J. (1985). Vygotsky: An historical and conceptual perspective. In J. V. Wertsch (Ed.), *Culture, communication, and cognition: Vygotskian perspectives* (pp. 21–34). London, UK: Cambridge University Press.

Carey, B. (2010, September 6). Forget what you know about good study habits. *The New York Times.* Retrieved from http://www.nytimes.com/2010/09/07/health/views/07mind.html

Carey, B. (2014, November 22). Studying for the test by taking it. *The New York Times.* Retrieved from http://www.nytimes.com/2014/11/23/sunday-review/studying-for-the-test-by-taking-it.html

Christ, F. L. (1997). *Seven steps to better management of your study time.* Clearwater, FL: H & H.

Cook, E., Kennedy, E., and McGuire, S. Y. (2013). Effect of teaching metacognitive learning strategies on performance in general chemistry courses. *Journal of Chemical Education, 90*, 961–967.

Cooper, K. J. (2012). Besting the Ivies. *Diverse: Issues in Higher Education, 29*(9), 13–14.

Dawood, M. (2014). Unpublished results. Department of Engineering, New Mexico State University, Las Cruces, NM.

Doyle, T. (2008). *Helping students learn in a learner-centered environment: A guide to facilitating learning in higher education.* Sterling, VA: Stylus.

Dweck, C. S. (2006). *Mindset: The new psychology of success.* New York, NY: Random House.

Eagan, K., Lozano, J. B., Hurtado, S., & Case, M. H. (2013). *The American freshman: National norms fall 2013.* Los Angeles, CA: Higher Education Research Institute, UCLA.

Felder, R. M. (2010). Are learning styles invalid? (Hint: no!) *On-Course Newsletter.* Retrieved from www.ncsu.edu/felder-public/Papers/LS_Validity(On-Course).pdf

Flavell, J. H. (1976). Metacognitive aspects of problem solving. In L. B. Resnick (Ed.), *The nature of intelligence* (pp. 231–236). Hillsdale, NJ: Erlbaum.

Fleming, N. D., & Mills, C. (1992). Not another inventory, rather a catalyst for reflection. *To Improve the Academy: A Journal of Educational Development, 11*, 137–155.

Frodl, T., & O'Keane, V. (2013). How does the brain deal with cumulative stress? A review with focus on developmental stress, HPA axis function and hippocampal structure in humans. *Neurobiology of Disease, 52*, 24–37.

Gabriel, K. F. (2008). *Teaching unprepared students.* Sterling, VA: Stylus.

Grant, H., & Dweck, C. S. (2003). Clarifying achievement goals and their impact. *Journal of Personality and Social Psychology, 85*(3), 541–553.

Gregorc, A. F., & Butler, K. A. (1984). Learning is a matter of style. *Vocational Education Journal, 59*(3), 27–29.

Gregory, G., & Parry, T. (2006). *Designing brain-compatible learning.* Thousand Oaks, CA: Corwin Press.

Hirsch, G. (2001). *Helping college students succeed: A model for effective intervention.* Philadelphia, PA: Brunner-Routledge.

Hobson, E. (2001). *Motivating students to learn in large classes.* Unpublished manuscript, Albany College of Pharmacy, Albany, NY.

Hoffmann, R., & McGuire, S. Y. (2009). Teaching and learning strategies that work. *Science, 325*(4), 1203–1204.

Hoffman, R., & McGuire, S. Y. (2010). Learning and teaching strategies. *American Scientist, 98*, 378–382.

Hopper, C. H. (2013). *Practicing college learning strategies* (6th ed.) Boston, MA: Wadsworth.

Howard, P. J. (2006). *The owner's manual for the brain* (3rd ed.). Austin, TX: Bard Press.

Jung, C. (1921). *Psychological types.* Zurich, Switzerland: Rascher Verlag.

Kandel, E. R., Schwartz J. H., Jessell, T. M., Siegelbaum, S. A., & Hudspeth, A. J. (2013). *Principles of neural science* (5th ed.). New York, NY: McGraw-Hill.

Karns, C. M., Dow, M. W., & Neville, H. J. (2012). Altered cross-modal processing in the primary auditory cortex of congenitally deaf adults: A visual-somatosensory fMRI study with a double-flash illusion. *Journal of Neuroscience, 32*(28), 9626–9638.

Kim, J. J., Lee, H. J., Han, J. S., & Packard, M. G. (2001). Amygdala is critical for stress-induced modulation of hippocampal long-term potentiation and learning. *Journal of Neuroscience, 21*(14), 5222–5228.

Klingner, J., & Vaughn, S. (1999). Promoting reading comprehension, content learning, and English acquisition through collaborative strategic reading (CSR). *Reading Teacher, 52*(7), 738–747.

Kolb, D. A. (1984). *Experiential learning: Experience as the source of learning and development.* Englewood Cliffs, NJ: Prentice Hall.

Lanuza, E., Belekhova, M., Martinez-Marcos, A., Font, C., & Martinez-Garcia, F. (1998). Identification of the reptilian basolateral amygdala: An anatomical investigation of the afferents to the posterior dorsal ventricular ridge of the lizard *Podarcis hispanica. European Journal of Neuroscience, 10*(11), 3517–3534.

Learning Support Centers in Higher Education. (2014). *A learning center chronology.* Retrieved from http://www.lsche.net/?page_id=1206

Longman, D. G., & Atkinson, R. H. (1996). *College learning and study skills* (4th ed.). St. Paul, MN: West.

Lovett, M. C. (2013). Make exams worth more than the grade. In M. Kaplan, N. Silver, D. Lavaque-Manty, & D. Meizlish (Eds.), *Using reflection and metacognition to improve student learning: Across the disciplines, across the academy* (pp. 18–52). Sterling, VA: Stylus.

MacLean, P. D. (1990). *The triune brain in evolution: Role in paleocerebral functions.* New York, NY: Plenum Press.

McGuire, S. N. (2003). *Some aspects of the auditory processing of sinusoidally rippled spectra in humans* (Unpublished doctoral dissertation). University of Oxford, UK.

Medina, J. (2008). *Brain rules.* Seattle, WA: Pear Press.

Mueller, P. A., & Oppenheimer, D. M. (2014). The pen is mightier than the keyboard: Advantages of longhand over laptop note taking. *Psychological Science, 25*(6), 1159–1168.

Myers, I. B. (1962). *Manual: The Myers-Briggs type indicator.* Princeton, NJ: Educational Testing Services.

Nilson, L. (2004). *Teaching at its best: A research-based resource for college instructors.* Bolton, MA: Anker.

Nilson, L. (2013). *Creating self-regulated learners.* Sterling, VA: Stylus.

Nixon, C. L. (2007, November 2). Learned helplessness [Video file]. Retrieved from https://www.youtube.com/watch?v=gFmFOmprTt0

Novak, J. D., & Gowin, D. B. (1984). *Learning how to learn*. Cambridge, UK: Cambridge University Press.

Oakley, B., Felder, R. M., Brent, R., & Elhajj, I. (2004). Turning student groups into effective teams. *Journal of Student Centered Learning, 2*(1), 9–34.

Overbaugh, R. (n.d.). Image of revised versions of Bloom's Taxonomy featuring definitions. Old Dominion University. Retrieved from http://ww2.odu.edu/educ/roverbau/Bloom/blooms_taxonomy.htm

Overbaugh, R., & Schultz, L. (n.d.). Bloom's Taxonomy. Old Dominion University. Retrieved from http://ww2.odu.edu/educ/roverbau/Bloom/blooms_taxonomy.htm

Pashler, H., McDaniel, M., Rohrer, D., & Bjork, R. (2008). Learning styles: Concepts and evidence. *Psychological Science in the Public Interest, 9*(3), 105–119.

Peirce, W. (2003). Metacognition: Study strategies, monitoring, and motivation. Retrieved from http://academic.pg.cc.md.us/~wpeirce/MCCCTR/metacognition.htm

Pennebaker J. W., Gosling S. D., & Ferrell J. D. (2013). Daily online testing in large classes: Boosting college performance while reducing achievement gaps. *PLoS ONE, 8*(11). doi:10.1371/journal.pone.

Phelps, E. A. (2004). Human emotion and memory: Interactions of the amygdala and hippocampal complex. *Current Opinion in Neurobiology, 14*, 198–202.

Raffini, J. P. (1995). *150 ways to increase intrinsic motivation in the classroom*. New York, NY: Allyn and Bacon.

Roediger, H. L., III, & Karpicke, J. D. (2006). Test-enhanced learning. *Psychological Science, 17*(3), 249–255.

Seligman, M. E. P., & Maier, S. F. (1967). Failure to escape traumatic shock. *Journal of Experimental Psychology, 74*, 1–9.

Sellers, D., Dochen, C. W., & Hodges, R. (2005). *Academic transformation: The road to college success*. Upper Saddle River, NJ: Pearson Education.

Shenk, D. (2010). *The genius in all of us: Why everything you've been told about genetics, talent, and IQ is wrong*. New York, NY: Doubleday.

Simpson, M. (2012). Program evaluation studies: Strategic learning delivery model suggestions. In R. Hodges, M. L. Simpson, & N. A. Stahl (Eds.), *Teaching study strategies in developmental education* (pp. 391–408). New York, NY: Bedford/St. Martin's Press.

Stevens, D., & Levi, A. (2012). *Introduction to rubrics: An assessment tool to save grading time, convey effective feedback, and promote student learning*. Sterling, VA: Stylus.

Stevenson, H. W., & Stigler J. W. (1992). *The learning gap: Why our schools are failing and what we can learn from Japanese and Chinese education*. New York, NY: Summit Books.

Suskie, L. (2009). *Assessing student learning: A common sense guide* (2nd ed.). San Francisco, CA: Jossey-Bass.

Ullman, M. T. (2004). Contributions of memory circuits to language: The declarative/procedural model. *Cognition, 92*, 231–270.

Uttal, D. H. (1997). Beliefs about genetic influences on mathematics achievement: A cross-cultural comparison. *Genetica, 99,* 165–172.

Vygotsky, L. (1978). *Mind in society: The development of higher psychological processes.* Cambridge, MA: Harvard University Press.

Weimer, M. (2002). *Learner-centered teaching: Five key changes to practice.* San Francisco, CA: Jossey-Bass.

Whimbey, A. (1975). *Intelligence can be taught.* New York, NY: Dutton.

Whimbey, A., Carmichael, J. W., Jones, L. W., Hunter, J. T, & Vincent, H. A. (1980). Teaching critical reading and analytical reasoning in Project SOAR. *Journal of Reading 24*(1), 5–10.

Yeager, D. S., Garcia, J., Brzustoski, P., Hessert, W. T., Purdie-Vaughns V., Apfel, N., . . . Cohen, G. L. (2013). Breaking the cycle of mistrust: Wise interventions to provide critical feedback across the racial divide. *Journal of Experimental Psychology: General, 143*(2), 804–824.

Zhao, N., Wardeska, J. G., McGuire, S. Y., & Cook, E. (2014). Metacognition: An effective tool to promote success in college science learning. *Journal of College Science Teaching, 43*(4), 48–54.

Zull, J. E. (2002). *The art of changing the brain.* Sterling, VA: Stylus.

Zull, J. E. (2011). *From brain to mind: Using neuroscience to guide change in education.* Sterling, VA: Stylus.

ABOUT THE AUTHORS

Saundra Yancy McGuire

Saundra Yancy McGuire is the director emerita of the nationally acclaimed Center for Academic Success and a retired assistant vice chancellor and professor of chemistry at Louisiana State University. She has received many awards for her work with students and faculty, the most recent of which is the 2015 American Association for the Advancement of Science (AAAS) Lifetime Mentor Award. She has also received the Presidential Award for Excellence in Science, Mathematics, and Engineering Mentoring in a White House Oval Office Ceremony, and she is an elected fellow of the American Association for the Advancement of Science, the American Chemical Society, and the Council of Learning Assistance and Developmental Education Associations. Additionally, she has achieved Level Four Lifetime Leadership Certification through the National College Learning Center Association. Prior to joining Louisiana State University in August 1999, she spent 11 years at Cornell University, where she was acting director of the Center for Learning and Teaching and recipient of the coveted Clark Distinguished Teaching Award.

Dr. McGuire has been teaching and mentoring students for more than 40 years and conducting faculty development workshops for three decades. She has delivered keynote addresses or presented student and faculty development workshops at more than 200 institutions in 40 states and six countries. Her work has been published in *Science, The Journal of Chemical Education, American Scientist, The Learning Assistance Review, To Improve the Academy,* and *New Directions for Teaching and Learning*.

Dr. McGuire received her bachelor's degree *magna cum laude* from Southern University in Baton Rouge, LA, her master's degree from Cornell University, and her doctoral degree from the University of Tennessee at Knoxville, where she received the Chancellor's Citation for Exceptional Professional Promise. She is married to Dr. Stephen C. McGuire, a professor of physics at Southern University. They are the parents of Dr. Carla McGuire Davis and Dr. Stephanie McGuire and the doting grandparents of Joshua, Ruth, Daniel, and Joseph Davis.

Stephanie McGuire

Stephanie McGuire holds a bachelor's degree in biology from Massachusetts Institute of Technology, master's and doctoral degrees in neuroscience from the University of Oxford, and a master's degree in opera performance from the Longy Conservatory. She attended Oxford on a Marshall scholarship and recieved a graduate fellowship from the National Science Foundation. Her doctoral dissertation (McGuire, 2003) explored how the human ear and brain process broadband, 20-microsecond clicks. At the Longy Conservatory, she received the Victor Rosenbaum medal, given yearly to the most outstanding graduate of the conservatory.

Partly as a result of long and stimulating conversations with her mother about pedagogy and learning strategies, Stephanie became a highly sought-after private academic tutor in the New York City area. By coauthoring this book, she is delighted to contribute to Dr. Saundra McGuire's admirable and revolutionary mission to make all students expert learners.

Since graduating from conservatory, Stephanie has enjoyed forging a successful career as a classical mezzo-soprano. She has performed with the New York City Opera at Lincoln Center, with the Boston POPS Orchestra in Symphony Hall, and several times at Carnegie Hall. She now lives in Berlin. Please visit www.mcguiremezzo.com to discover more and learn about Stephanie's upcoming performances.

This book provides professors and their graduate teaching assistants—those at the front line of interactions with students—with techniques and approaches they can use in class to help at-risk students raise their skills so that they can successfully complete their studies.

The author shares proven practices that will not only engage all students in a class, but also create the conditions—while maintaining high standards and high expectations—to enable at-risk and underprepared students to develop academically and graduate with good grades. The author also explains how to work effectively with academic support units on campus.

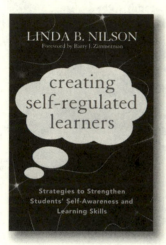

Creating Self-Regulated Learners

Strategies to Strengthen Students' Self-Awareness and Learning Skills

Linda B. Nilson
Foreword by Barry J. Zimmerman

"Linda Nilson's book is a timely contribution to the faculty development literature. Its focus on empowering professors with instructional strategies that, in turn, empower students to become strategic learners is critical to promoting the success of the rising wave of first-generation college students, to meeting the current demand for workers who have 'learned how to learn,' and to realizing a long-standing goal of a college education: developing self-reliant, lifelong learners."—*Joseph B. Cuseo, Professor Emeritus, Psychology; and Educational Consultant, AVID*

"A clear introduction to self-regulated learning and metacognition, followed by a thorough compendium of techniques that faculty can use to help their students better understand and foster their own deep learning. Highly recommended."—*James M. Lang, Associate Professor of English, Assumption College and author of* On Course: A Week-by-Week Guide to Your First Semester of College Teaching

22883 Quicksilver Drive
Sterling, VA 20166-2102

Subscribe to our e-mail alerts: www.Styluspub.com

Also available from Stylus

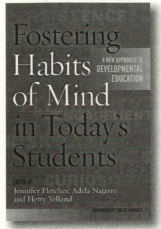

Fostering Habits of Mind in Today's Students

A New Approach to Developmental Education

Edited by Jennifer Fletcher, Adela Najarro, and Hetty Yelland

Foreword by Emily Lardner

"Innovative, engaging, and cheerful, this highly readable book invokes the spirit of Mina Shaughnessy in its positive regard for developmental writers. The authors make a powerful case against a 'deficit-based' view of developmental instruction in favor of a long view that values each learner's unique gifts, intellectual capacity, and potential for growth. The theoretically grounded and effectively scaffolded chapters are loaded with class-tested assignments for teaching the 'habits of mind' needed for college and job success. A collaborative effort of 15 veteran teachers of developmental English and math, this must-read book will help any teacher create a transformative classroom that promotes engagement, curiosity, motivation, risk-taking, self-efficacy, and persistence."
—**John C. Bean**, *Professor of English (Emeritus), Seattle University*

Students need more than just academic skills for success in college and career, and the lack of an explicit instructional focus on the "soft skills" critical to postsecondary success poses a challenge for many students who enter college, especially the underprepared.

This contributed volume, written with full-time and adjunct faculty in mind, provides the rationale for this pedagogical approach and presents the sequential instructional cycle that begins by identifying students' assets and progressively focusing on specific habits to develop their capacity to transfer their learning to new tasks and situations.

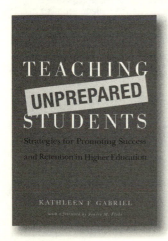

Teaching Unprepared Students

Strategies for Promoting Success and Retention in Higher Education

Kathleen F. Gabriel

Foreword by Sandra M. Flake

"Concrete examples and detailed instructions of what, when, and how to carry them out make this book a valuable resource for faculty and graduate assistants new to the classroom as well as experienced faculty who increasingly find themselves dealing with unprepared students. If a department, college, or university is truly serious about improving student learning, presenting a copy of this book to all incoming faculty and graduate assistants and perhaps arranging for informal discussion groups throughout the year would send a powerful signal."
—**Mimi Wolverton**, *Retired Professor of Higher Education*

(*Continues on preceding page*)

MEMBERSHIP HAS ITS PRIVILEGES!

NISOD is a membership organization committed to promoting and celebrating excellence in teaching, learning, and leadership at community and technical colleges.

INNOVATION ABSTRACTS

This weekly publication features best ideas from community and technical college practitioners about programs, projects, and strategies that improve students' higher education experiences.

EXCELLENCE AWARDS

The NISOD Excellence Awards, the most coveted award among community and technical college educators, have honored more than 25,000 recipients since their inception.

MONTHLY WEBINARS

Monthly webinars are led by community and technical college leaders and other experts in the field. This benefit provides action-oriented, measurable, and learning-focused objectives to help faculty members improve their teaching techniques.

ANNUAL CONFERENCE

NISOD's International Conference on Teaching and Leadership Excellence is the definitive gathering of faculty, administrators, and staff exploring best and promising practices designed to improve student achievement.

SCOTT WRIGHT STUDENT ESSAY CONTEST

Three winning students and three faculty members, staff members, or administrators receive a $1,000 check. In addition, the winning colleges receive a complimentary NISOD membership.

DIVERSITY AWARDS

The Promising Places to Work in Community Colleges Award identifies and recognizes exceptional commitment to diversity at NISOD member colleges. This benefit can be used by recipient colleges to promote their commitment to providing campuses where all individuals and groups feel welcomed, respected, and valued.

STUDENT ART CONTEST

Students at NISOD member colleges are invited to design the official Conference Program cover for NISOD's International Conference on Teaching and Leadership Excellence. The artist of the winning design receives $1,000 as well as other benefits. The student's college receives a complimentary NISOD membership.

For a complete list of benefits, go to www.nisod.org.